THE HISTORY OF
HUMAN
MIGRATION

General Editor
Russell King

NEW
HOLLAND

Published in 2007 by New Holland Publishers (UK) Ltd.
London • Cape Town • Sydney • Auckland

www.newhollandpublishers.com

Garfield House, 86-88 Edgware Road, London W2 2EA, UK
80 McKenzie Street, Cape Town 8001, South Africa
Unit 1, 66 Gibbes Street, Chatswood, NSW 2067, Australia
218 Lake Road, Northcote, Auckland, New Zealand

Conceived, edited and designed in the United Kingdom by
Marshall Editions
The Old Brewery
6 Blundell Street
London N7 9BH
www.marshalleditions.com

ISBN 978-1-84537-796-0

A CIP catalogue for this book is available from the British Library

10 9 8 7 6 5 4 3 2 1

For Marshall Editions:
Publisher: Richard Green
Commissioning Editor: Claudia Martin
Art Director: Ivo Marloh
Editor: Johanna Geary
Picture Manager: Veneta Bullen
Layout: 3RD-I
Indexer: Hilary Bird
Production: Anna Pauletti

Originated in Hong Kong by Modern Age
Printed in China by Midas Printing International Limited

Opposite page: An immigrant family looks out at the New York skyline while arriving in the United States aboard the S.S. *Nieuw Amsterdam*, c. 1930s.

CONTENTS

INTRODUCTION

The standard dictionary definition of human migration, which usually runs along the lines of "the movement of people from one place or country to settle in another", suggests little of the depth of meaning or the scale of the phenomenon, both in the contemporary world and throughout history. The current preoccupation with controlling immigration in the so-called developed world tends to overlook the fundamental benefits that migration has brought to many places through the ages, contributing to both the economic development and the special character of many cities and even entire countries. This book tells this epic story of civilisations and their movement – of ideas and cultures that travel, and of people leaving home in search of a different and better way of life. Like all good books that seek to inform and educate, it brilliantly illuminates the "grand narrative" – of the constant thread of migration running through the weave of human history – using the fascinating detail of local case studies carefully selected from around the world.

Left: Some of the steerage arrivals on the steamship *Conte Russo* get their first look at New York in July 1922. In order to be included in the restricted quota for immigrants, thousands of travellers by ship had to wait outside New York Harbour for some days before racing up the harbour to Ellis Island on July 1st.

The message of this book is so important that it bears repeating here at the outset: migration *is* the history of the world. Humans are born migrants: human evolution is linked to the very act of moving from one habitat to another and then adapting to that new environment. This statement is paraphrased from the first section of the book, where it was written in the context of the early movement of protohumans out of the forests onto the plains of East Africa, but it holds true across eons of time to the present day. The Africans who now risk their lives in flimsy boats crossing the Mediterranean to Italy and Spain are repeating million-year-old journeys that their *Homo erectus* forebears took, traversing the Mediterranean from the North African coast, then walking north into Europe.

While my focus in this introduction will mainly be on the contemporary global scene, everywhere we look we find historical echoes, often ignored by those who claim that migration is somehow a "new" challenge facing the world, and who often overlook the lessons of the past. On the other hand, current migratory phenomena do differ from those of the past. In today's supercharged, globalised world, the spread of information via satellite and Internet communication is virtually instantaneous. Transport, too, is quicker and cheaper than in the past, facilitating faster and more frequent mobility. Yet, despite these advances, the continuing rise of nation-states and economic power blocs increasingly turn migration – rightly or wrongly – into a tool of economic, political and cultural policies. The "freedom to migrate" remains, for many, an illusion.

Below: A woman pledges allegiance after being sworn in as a citizen of the United States in a 4th of July naturalisation ceremony.

Double Standards for Migrants

Despite its continuity throughout history, migration has undoubtedly accelerated and diversified in recent decades, causing migration scholars to call the last 20 years the "age of migration". But several paradoxes underlie this new migration epoch. One has just been mentioned: despite technological advances, people overall are less free to migrate now than they were a hundred years ago. A second paradox is linked to this, namely that the freedom of capital, goods and Western cultural images to circulate internationally in today's globalised world is not matched by unfettered human mobility. A third is that freedom to migrate is highly selective today. Some people – mainly the residents of the rich countries of the world – are allowed, even encouraged, to move. Others – the nationals of poor countries – are not. This exposes the stark social inequalities that result from globalisation and migration control policies.

A final paradox is that, despite increasingly stringent controls over international migration from poor countries, more and more people find ways to circumvent these barriers. They migrate as "illegals", crossing borders clandestinely, often with the help of paid people-smugglers; or they arrive legally, on tourist or visitor visas, and then overstay. Governments eager to exploit the benefits of cheap migrant labour play a double game here. On the one hand, they assert the need for strong migration controls, aiming to placate those portions of the domestic population who are afraid of too many people arriving with different cultures. On the other hand, they turn a blind eye to the realities of clandestine entry because migrants' low-wage labour increases the competitiveness of the industries and farms where they work.

Voluntary or Involuntary Migration?

Contemporary migrations around the world are extraordinarily diverse. Three common divisions are made: between internal and international migration; between forced and voluntary moves; and permanent versus temporary migration. These are useful classifications for creating a conceptual map of human mobility, but each of these dichotomies is easily blurred. To begin with, some people are both internal and international migrants. They may migrate internally (from village to town, for example) and subsequently migrate internationally to once again become internal migrants within their chosen destination country. In Europe, the creation and expansion of the EU as an integrated "European space" has blurred the definition of international migration by differentiating between

internal (intra-EU) migration and the immigration of non-EU citizens, who are known as "third-country nationals". The dismemberment of the Soviet Union, on the other hand, has turned what was once internal migration into international movement, so that those who were once perceived as internal migrants may now be seen as "foreigners".

The distinction between forced and voluntary migration is also an uneasy one in practice. The terrible tragedy of the slave trade is an obvious example of long-distance forced transmigration of labour, and remains migration history's darkest hour. In contrast, wealthy US and Canadian citizens who move on retirement to the "sunshine states" of Florida and California are clearly exercising a voluntary option. Between these two extremes are many other situations. When economic collapse or environmental disaster threatens a people's livelihood, are the ensuing migrations forced or voluntary? Migration for survival remains a coping strategy for poor and hungry people, but such people, who today may be called economic migrants or environmental refugees, do not satisfy the definition of a refugee inscribed in the 1951 Geneva Convention. What about the young Filipino woman who is instructed by her father that she must migrate to work as a domestic servant in the Gulf or Singapore in order to ensure the survival and improvement of the family at home? An element of coercion exists here, but the global migration of Filipino (and other) women to work as maids in the rich West is not classed as forced migration.

Thirdly, the time span of migration is often a flexible continuum rather than a fixed period. One scholar has written that there is nothing so permanent as temporary migration – meaning that many migrants start off intending to remain abroad for a short time but end up staying. But the reverse happens too. The 19th- and early 20th-century migrations to the United States and Australia were framed as migrations of permanent settlers, of people who would dedicate the rest of their days to building a new life and a new country. In fact, surprisingly high percentages of these migrants returned to their home countries.

A Foreigner at Home and Abroad

Why did they go back? Return is the great unwritten chapter in the history of migration. From the available evidence, decisions to return-migrate are more complex and ambivalent than the often economically driven motives for emigration. Some returns take place because it was always the migrant's intention to do so; it is the natural corollary of temporary migration. Others are triggered by nostalgia or family responsibilities, such as the need to care for aged parents or the wish to educate young children in the language and culture of the home country. Yet other returns are economically motivated, when a migrant comes home to invest foreign-earned income and savings in a new business or some other project. Finally, return migration can be driven by negative factors operating within the host country: racism, unemployment or poor health.

The return, however, is not always a happy homecoming. Many returnees feel they have been doubly marginalised: first when they go abroad and have to face discrimination, low-grade work and a new language and culture; and again when they return. Having absorbed something of foreign values, they find it hard to readapt to a home environment that has undergone its own changes during their absence. Failing to make this second readjustment, and hindered further perhaps by difficulties of finding work, some returnees become disillusioned and re-emigrate.

Unfortunately, reliable statistics on return migration are rarely available for most places.

Opposite page:

The freighter *Cliff's Victory* steams into industrial Chicago in 1950, carrying migrants seeking work from the south and from rural areas, during the period of huge industrial expansion in the United States.

The validity of statistics on any form of migration is restricted by country-specific methods of data collection and complicated by definitions of migration. Generally speaking, in order for migration to be recorded, a statistical boundary must be crossed and some threshold of time spent in the destination place must be exceeded. For international migration, migrants are recorded at an entry point, picked up in a census or registered in the local administrative unit, such as the town where they are living. Often, one year is the threshold time for migration to be said to have taken place, thereby screening out tourists, short-stay visitors and business travellers. It is easy to see how this process overlooks many people who have migrated, such as undocumented migrants whose exact enumeration is by definition impossible, and seasonal migrants who take short-term jobs in tourism, construction and farming.

Similar criteria apply to internal migration: a geostatistical boundary, such as a province or municipality, must be crossed if the "move" is to be registered. This procedure produces anomalies: in the United States, for example, interstate migration statistics will record an 8-kilometre (5-mile) move that crosses a state line but will not record a 320-kilometre (200-mile) relocation from one end of the state to the other.

Migration to the Industrial Cities

Internal migrations, like international migration in the modern era, are largely driven by economic considerations. They are closely related to the staged evolution of a country's development and way of life. In the United States, for example, massive migrations from rural to urban areas and from south to north accompanied the great era of industrial expansion during the first two-thirds of the 20th century. The main targets for these migrations were New York and its satellite cities, together with the powerhouses of heavy industry: Chicago, Detroit, Buffalo and Philadelphia. Subsequently, a new economic cycle of development based on aerospace, high-tech production, information technology and leisure industries saw the migration currents reoriented towards California and other western and southwestern states, Florida and Colorado.

While rural-urban has so far been the historically dominant type of internal migration in the developing world, in more developed countries new mechanisms of population redistribution became evident in the decades following the 1960s. Rural-urban migration was replaced by urban-rural. Cities suddenly stopped growing as some of their inhabitants decided to move out to rural areas and small towns. The many causes of this "counterurbanisation"

trend include a search for a better quality of life, high urban property prices, increasing employment opportunities away from metropolitan areas, increasing flexibility of working practices and the computer revolution.

Not all categories of people were equally affected by this flight from urban dwelling. Students and young professionals have continued to congregate in cities for study and for work. Wealthy professionals – singles, couples and young families – have spearheaded another urban migration in recent decades. This gentrification trend involves the upgrading of inner-city areas that have become run-down and the restoration of attractive properties that offer desirable homes relatively close to the city centre. Partly as a result of this, some major cities in Europe and North America entered a new phase of regrowth during the 1990s.

The World's Largest Urban Society

All this is a world away from ongoing processes of internal migration in the developing world. Here, rural-urban migration continues to run ahead of the ability of the population to gain sustainable employment and secure homes in the cities, leading to the growth of sprawling shantytowns and informal economies geared to mere survival and the hope of getting a toehold in the city. Where a large, poor country does achieve rapid economic growth over a lengthy period of time, as China has in recent decades, consistently posting annual growth rates of about 10 per cent, enormous internal migration flows are generated. In China's case, long-range, interior-to-coast, rural-to-industrial migrations have brought between 100 million and 200 million people to the country's burgeoning coastal provinces during the last 20 years. This is currently the world's biggest ongoing migration, and it will continue, adding a further 300 million to 500 million rural-urban migrants by 2050 according to estimations. Rural-urban migration both reflects and drives fundamental changes in the Chinese economy and society. The average city dweller earns more than three times as much as a rural dweller, and by 2020 China will be a predominantly urban society, with 60 per cent of its vast population living in urban areas.

These figures on internal migration in one country – admittedly the world's largest in population terms – help to contextualise the scale of international migration. The global data on international migration are revealing, since they show many common misconceptions to be false. According to the United Nations, there were 191 million international migrants in 2005 – people officially recorded as residing in a country other than that of their birth.

This figure represents only 3 per cent of the world's population, a proportion that has changed little in recent decades (it was 2.3 per cent in 1965). In other words, international migration is increasing only fractionally faster than global population growth. In addition, half of these migrants are female (95 million versus 96 million males), proving the common conception of migration as a mainly male practice – with females staying behind or following on later – to be false.

Of the total "stock" of international migrants, 21 per cent are in the European Union and 20 per cent are in the United States. These proportions have been increasing in recent years. On the other hand, much migration still goes on between poorer countries and between richer ones. Taking the broad categories of the global North and the global South, and based again on the stock of migrants in 2005, 33 per cent are South-North migrants, 32 per cent are South-South, 28 per cent are North-North and 7 per cent are North-South. Therefore, only one in three global migrants moves from the poorer South to the richer North.

Who Benefits: Individual or State?

Is migration a good thing? Like many "big questions", this has a complex answer that leads to other questions and qualifications. First, it depends on the type of migration. Second, for whom is it good? Let us consider one migration archetype of the last 150 years – that of poor people from less-developed countries to find jobs and a better way of life in richer countries. In this migration system, the receiving countries are the immediate beneficiaries. They receive "ready-made" workers, for whose upbringing and education they have not had to pay, and who arrive to take jobs in factories and on farms and building sites that the native workforce is unwilling to do. They therefore boost economic growth and the national income.

For the sending countries, the benefits are more debatable. They benefit from the "export" of some of their otherwise unemployed workers and from the money that flows back into the country. In countries such as Mexico, Morocco and the Philippines, such monies total billions of dollars annually and constitute a major element in sustaining the economy. Such earnings are potentially a stimulus for economic development, if they are invested wisely, but the general trend is for them to be spent on consumer goods and new housing. Migrant-sending countries may also suffer from "brain drain" – the loss of their most talented and highly educated young adults to more lucrative jobs in wealthy countries. "Brain waste" occurs when well-

educated people migrate to high-wage economies where their qualifications go unrecognised, sometimes because they are undocumented workers. Following the model of the "taxi driver with a PhD", they work in menial jobs because the wages they receive are far superior to what they could earn at home, even as teachers or engineers.

As for the migrants themselves, the benefits and costs may be experienced in a variety of ways and combinations. For millions of people worldwide, both now and in the past, migration has been an escape route from poverty, ensuring the survival, and even prosperity, of individuals and their families. Such rewards are rarely instantaneous. Years of sacrifice, demeaning work and separation may yield results only much later, when the migrant is able to return home to build a future with savings accrued from foreign labour, or when the family reunites in the country of destination to create a new life there. For many, the deferred gratification is embodied in their children – the so-called second generation, whose education and upward mobility in the new country are a source of satisfaction for their migrant parents. The second generation do not always live up to their parents' dreams, however; often they underachieve, drop out of school, remain unemployed, suffer high rates of alienation and become confused as to their identities.

Winners and Losers

In the best scenario, migration is a "triple-win" situation that benefits both the sending and receiving countries and the migrants themselves. This triple-win is achievable, provided that the migration process is well managed and safeguards are in place to guarantee the dignity, human rights and welfare of the migrants. Too often, however, there are negative outcomes and the contemporary world remains a far from benign place for migrants. Many suffer deskilling, humiliation, racism and ruination of their health; thousands die in the very act of migration, in the fierce heat of trackless deserts, or in pathetically inadequate boats on stormy seas. The global division of labour is driven by capitalist forces, which foster inequality and deny the possibility of a decent life for all, including many migrants.

Migration and exile remain dominant themes of our times, as people continue to be forcibly displaced by war or ethnic cleansing and to migrate more or less of their own free will. In a world still dominated by nation-states and global corporations, migration creates mobile and hybrid identities. Trauma, nostalgia and social exclusion are counterbalanced by pluralism, cosmopolitanism and a celebration of other cultures. The story of migration will never end as long as the human race continues.

Above: Beijing Road, a busy shopping street in Guangzhou, China, will become even more crowded in future decades as internal migration continues to grow in response to China's economic growth. An estimated 100 million to 200 million people have moved from rural to industrialised coastal areas during the last 20 years, and many more millions are expected to follow them in the coming decades.

THE DAWN OF MANKIND

T he history of human migration reaches back to the very birth of humanity, when the first apelike humans emerged from the African forests and began to colonise the East African savanna about seven million years ago. These protohumans lived on the temperate East African grasslands for five million years before *Homo erectus* emerged, the first hominid to venture further afield. *Homo erectus* spread through Africa and embarked on the first exploration of the Earth before succumbing to extinction. Much later, *Homo sapiens* evolved in the same East African cradle as *Homo erectus*. About 125,000 years ago, they too made the journey out of Africa, into Asia and beyond. For better or worse, these hairless apes were set to dominate the planet.

Left: This footprint, made by an early hominid strolling through wet ash, was discovered in Laetoli, Tanzania, in 1978. It proves that mankind was walking upright as long as 3.6 million years ago.

THE NOMADIC APE

Below: This early hominid skull, *Australopithecus boisei*, is about two million years old. It was found at Olduvai Gorge, Tanzania, in East Africa, the birthplace of humanity.

It is generally accepted that the first hominids, or protohumans, emerged in Africa over four million years ago. For millions of years, Africa was our ancestors' only home. It was not until the development about two million years ago of a new hominid, *Homo erectus*, that humanity began its first migration.

Human history began approximately seven million years ago when our ancient apelike ancestors began to leave their home in the African forests. As food and shelter became scarce, possibly because of overpopulation or environmental changes, these protohumans found that they could no longer survive in their traditional habitat. They were forced to emerge from the comforting green shadows of their homeland and venture out onto the flat, sun-drenched grasslands of the East African plain. Over the course of many thousands of years, the world's first migrants adapted to their new environment. They shed their thick coat of hair, and they began to stand upright and walk on two legs. These physical changes separated them from their forest-dwelling cousins and placed them closer to the early bipedal hominid species from which humans descend. In a sense, humans are born migrants: our evolution is fundamentally linked to the act of migration, to moving from one place to another and adapting to that new environment.

The Spread of *Homo erectus*

Although the people known as *Homo erectus* were very different from modern humans, they nevertheless share some similarities with our own species. They were almost as tall as modern humans, but had a more muscular build. They made hand axes and cleavers out of stone, and they could communicate with each other – though they did not have anything that we would recognise as language. Their facial features were markedly different from those of modern humans: their noses were flat; their nostrils were upturned, like a gorilla's; and a thick, prominent ridge of bone protruded above their eyes, lending their faces a furrowed, rather troubled expression.

But *Homo erectus* did not need to worry. The species emerged in Africa about two million years ago, a mere 100,000 years or so before a propitious moment in the climatic history of the planet: one of the Earth's periodic ice ages came to an end. Much of the water that had been locked in the ice caps melted, and the world became a warmer, damper place. In Africa, this caused the

THE SPREAD OF *HOMO ERECTUS*

3.5 million B.C.E.
Australopithecus afarensis, a bipedal ape, is alive in Africa.

2.1 million B.C.E.
Homo habilis, 'tool-making man', is alive in Africa. These apelike humans are probably ancestors of modern humans.

B.C.E.	4,000,000	3,900,000	3,800,000	3,700,000	3,600,000	3,500,000	3,400,000	3,300,000	3,200,000	3,100,000	3,000,000	2,900,000	2,800,000	2,700,000	2,600,000	2,500,000	2,400,000	2,300,000	2,200,000	2,100,000

2.5 million B.C.E.
Various species of intelligent apes populate the African grasslands.

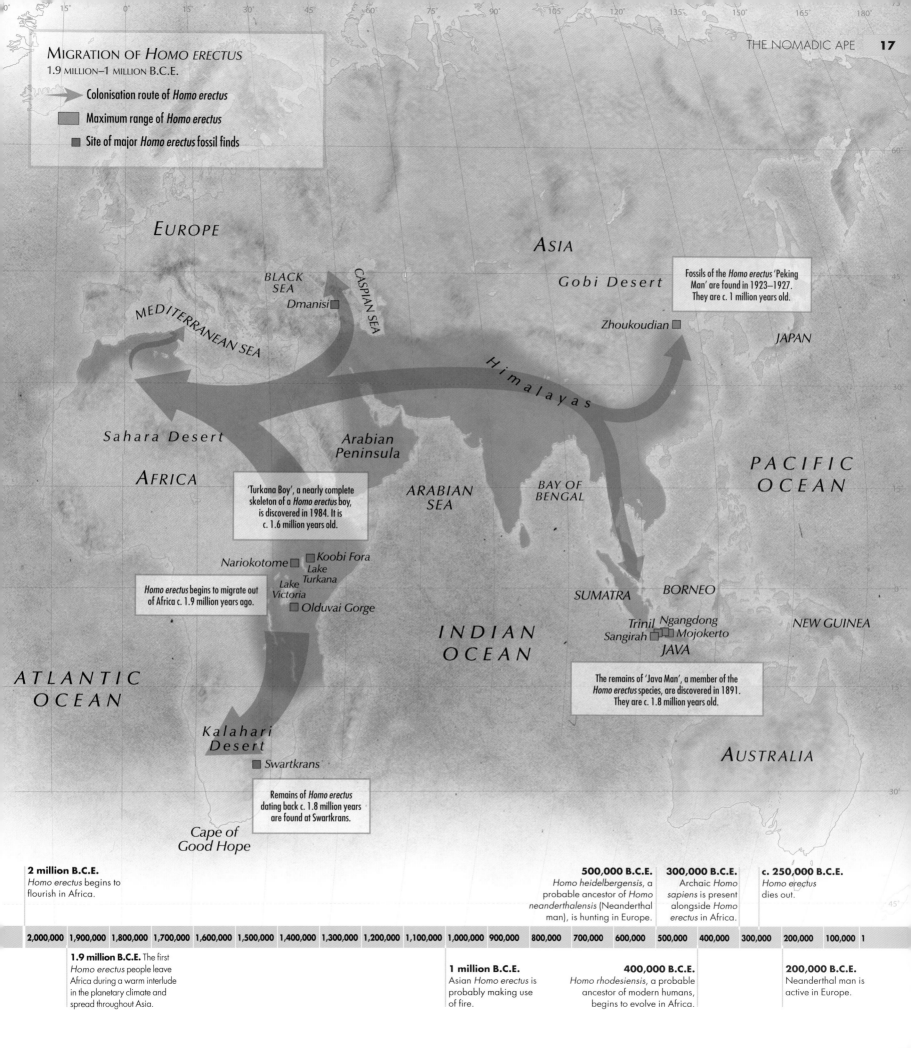

MIGRATION OF *HOMO ERECTUS*
1.9 MILLION–1 MILLION B.C.E.

➤ Colonisation route of *Homo erectus*

■ Maximum range of *Homo erectus*

■ Site of major *Homo erectus* fossil finds

EUROPE

ASIA

BLACK SEA

CASPIAN SEA

Dmanisi ■

Gobi Desert

Fossils of the *Homo erectus* 'Peking Man' are found in 1923–1927. They are c. 1 million years old.

Zhoukoudian ■

JAPAN

MEDITERRANEAN SEA

H i m a l a y a s

Sahara Desert

Arabian Peninsula

AFRICA

'Turkana Boy', a nearly complete skeleton of a *Homo erectus* boy, is discovered in 1984. It is c. 1.6 million years old.

ARABIAN SEA

BAY OF BENGAL

PACIFIC OCEAN

Nariokotome ■ ■ *Koobi Fora*
Lake Turkana

Homo erectus begins to migrate out of Africa c. 1.9 million years ago.

Lake Victoria

■ *Olduvai Gorge*

INDIAN OCEAN

SUMATRA

BORNEO

Trinil *Ngangdong*
Sangirah ■■■ *Mojokerto*
JAVA

NEW GUINEA

ATLANTIC OCEAN

The remains of 'Java Man', a member of the *Homo erectus* species, are discovered in 1891. They are c. 1.8 million years old.

Kalahari Desert

AUSTRALIA

■ *Swartkrans*

Remains of *Homo erectus* dating back c. 1.8 million years are found at Swartkrans.

Cape of Good Hope

2 million B.C.E.
Homo erectus begins to flourish in Africa.

500,000 B.C.E.
Homo heidelbergensis, a probable ancestor of *Homo neanderthalensis* (Neanderthal man), is hunting in Europe.

300,000 B.C.E.
Archaic *Homo sapiens* is present alongside *Homo erectus* in Africa.

c. 250,000 B.C.E.
Homo erectus dies out.

2,000,000	1,900,000	1,800,000	1,700,000	1,600,000	1,500,000	1,400,000	1,300,000	1,200,000	1,100,000	1,000,000	900,000	800,000	700,000	600,000	500,000	400,000	300,000	200,000	100,000	1

1.9 million B.C.E. The first *Homo erectus* people leave Africa during a warm interlude in the planetary climate and spread throughout Asia.

1 million B.C.E.
Asian *Homo erectus* is probably making use of fire.

400,000 B.C.E.
Homo rhodesiensis, a probable ancestor of modern humans, begins to evolve in Africa.

200,000 B.C.E.
Neanderthal man is active in Europe.

deserts to bloom, and the Sahara became a lush grassland populated by grazing animals and the carnivores that fed on them. This brought about a significant change in the *Homo erectus* people's way of life. Food sources became more widely available, which meant that *Homo erectus* were no longer dependent on a local supply. They were free to explore as individuals, or to migrate in groups, safe in the knowledge that they could source food wherever they found themselves.

As a result, the *Homo erectus* species migrated very quickly, moving in groups and travelling south. Within generations, they had reached the cul-de-sac located at the southern end of the African continent – *Homo erectus* fossils have been found at Swartkrans, about 32 kilometres (20 miles) from Johannesburg. Other groups struck north towards the Horn of Africa, and then journeyed across the land bridge of Sinai. *Homo erectus* were on the move; and their travels took them ever farther east, and perhaps west into southern Europe.

The speed with which *Homo erectus* travelled, spreading quickly across the Russian steppe and into Asia, is remarkable. One of the most famous human fossils ever discovered, 'Java Man', is unequivocally a member of the *Homo erectus* species. His bones were found on Java, an island of Indonesia, in the 19th century, but his antiquity was established only recently. Java Man is 1.8 million years old. This means that a mere 400 generations separate him from his African ancestors – a mere blink of the eye in the timescale of prehistory. *Homo erectus* bones have also been found in China. 'Peking Man', the name sometimes given to the group of fossils found at Zhoukoudian, near Beijing, is a younger representative of the *Homo erectus* species. He dates back to one million years ago, when an entire community of *Homo erectus* people lived in caves at Zhoukoudian, competing with hyenas for food and shelter, and possibly using fire to scare off animals and cook their meat. *Homo erectus* were the first intercontinental travellers, and the first Asians to walk the Earth.

Fossil evidence also tells us that the *Homo erectus* species travelled to the eastern shores of the Black Sea. While some *Homo erectus* people were following a path out of Africa towards the rising sun, others turned north and made their way over the mountains towards Europe. An almost complete skeleton of a *Homo erectus* human was found in the 1990s in Georgia, north of the Caucasus range.

Further fossils have also been found at Gran Dolina, a cave in the Atapuerca hills of Spain. Five or six hominids were discovered at the site that date back between 850,000 and 780,000 years ago. Although it is still debated whether these species belong to the *Homo erectus* species, it is possible that *Homo erectus* reached as far as southern Europe.

Identifying the African 'Eve'

For many years, archaeologists and paleontologists speculated about how the widespread *Homo erectus* people were related to modern humans. To some experts, it seemed logical to infer that after colonising so much of the planet (the Americas and Australia remained beyond the reach of *Homo erectus*), their future evolutionary success was assured. It was believed that they adapted to their different environments peacefully over the course of many millennia and eventually evolved into modern humans. Asians, it was asserted, were the descendants of Asian *Homo erectus* people, such as Java Man and Peking Man; Africans were the descendants of those *Homo erectus* people who had remained in their native land; and Europeans evolved from *Homo erectus* people who travelled north out of Africa. It was thought that these separate *Homo erectus* heritages, influenced by the physical environment, explained the racial differences between modern peoples.

This explanation of human origin was called the multiregionalist or 'Candelabra' theory because it envisaged groups of isolated *Homo erectus* peoples evolving in parallel, like the candlesticks on the stem of a menorah. But there was another competing theory, known popularly as 'Out of Africa'. This hypothesis states that the *Homo erectus* people are not our direct ancestors. They cannot be, it was argued, because it does not make sense in

Darwinian terms to suppose that diverse populations, living in varied environments that should have influenced their development differently, evolved separately into the same species. The only explanation for the uniformity of the modern human population is that humans evolved in one place and then spread around the world – in the same way that *Homo erectus* had done in its time. There must have been, in other words, another more recent migration out of Africa. It was this later odyssey, and not the travels of the *Homo erectus* people, that carried modern humankind around the globe.

The only evidence that could be used to support either theory was the fossil record, and for decades paleontologists argued over bones in an attempt to make a case for one view or the other. Neither opinion was provable until the entirely new technique of DNA testing was developed in the 1980s. Using this new tool, geneticists found that by comparing certain genetic differences in various modern populations they could accurately calculate the date at which those populations split off from each other. In effect, they could construct a biological family tree for the human race and establish the time when the common ancestor of all living humans walked the Earth. The astonishing truth, when it was revealed, was that the mother of all modern people walked the Earth a very recent 200,000 years ago. That is not to say that she was the only woman alive at the time, only that a scrap of her DNA has survived to this day in every living person: she is the 10,000th grandmother of every human on the planet. Since all traces of the *Homo erectus* people disappeared long before the lifetime of that African Eve, they cannot have contributed to our blood heritage. The discussion on whether archaic hominids, including Neanderthals and possibly East Asian *Homo erectus* descendants, may have contributed to the gene pool of modern humans continues, and there is some DNA and anthropological evidence to support this. Most experts, however, would agree that such contributions were minor at most.

DNA evidence can only lead experts to conclude that the *Homo erectus* people eventually died out. It is not known how or why this happened, but the fact remains that, for all their skill and mobility, and even though they flourished for so long, *Homo erectus* ceased to walk the Earth some time within the past 500,000 years. The account of humankind and their colonisation of the globe is not a story about *Homo erectus*: it is about *Homo sapiens* – 'knowing man' – the species to which all humans belong.

HOMO SAPIENS ON THE MARCH

Some time between 400,000 and 130,000 years ago the first genetically identifiable humans, *Homo sapiens*, evolved in the same African home that had given rise to *Homo erectus*. These early people, with their large brains and sophisticated stone tools, would eventually spread around the world.

Like *Homo erectus*, *Homo sapiens* was for a long time confined to its ancestral homeland. The Sahara had become a desert once again. Its dry, barren expanse was uncrossable, and for tens of thousands of years it locked humankind within the southern half of the African continent. Then, about 125,000 years ago, the desert became green once more, and it remained so for several thousand years. Following in the footsteps of the *Homo erectus* people almost two million years earlier, bands of *Homo sapiens* began to move north.

Homo sapiens followed the River Nile, possibly to the Egyptian coast, and then moved east, passing out of Africa and into modern-day Israel and Lebanon at the eastern end of the Mediterranean. Once they had left the continent, the path that had led them out of Africa once again disappeared. The Sahara reverted to desert, and the Mediterranean coast slowly dried out, too. This process took tens of thousands of years, and during this time life gradually became harder for the humans who had left Africa, with food and shelter becoming increasingly scarce. They were trapped in a dying landscape, and it is possible that these *Homo sapiens* died out themselves.

About 30,000 or 40,000 years passed before another opportunity presented itself for *Homo sapiens* to move out of Africa. Somewhere between 90,000 and 85,000 years ago, a new group of migrants left its home continent.

Evidence suggests that this time they crossed into Arabia from the northern edge of the Horn of Africa. This group's existence was no less precarious than that of their wandering ancestors, but science tells us that these people survived, and even flourished. Experts have been able to trace the DNA of modern-day humans back to these individuals: they are the group of *Homo sapiens* from which all of humanity descends.

Homo sapiens cross the Bering land bridge c. 20,000 B.C.E.

NORTH AMERICA

Rocky Mountains

Clovis: evidence of big-game hunting in North America c. 10,000 years ago

PACIFIC OCEAN

THE SPREAD OF *HOMO SAPIENS*

170,000 B.C.E.
Homo sapiens, modern humans, are living in East Africa.

B.C.E.	200,000	190,000	180,000	170,000	160,000	150,000	140,000	130,000	120,000	110,000

160,000 B.C.E.
Bands of *Homo sapiens* spread into southern and western Africa.

125,000 B.C.E.
The first modern humans leave Africa and arrive on the eastern Mediterranean shore.

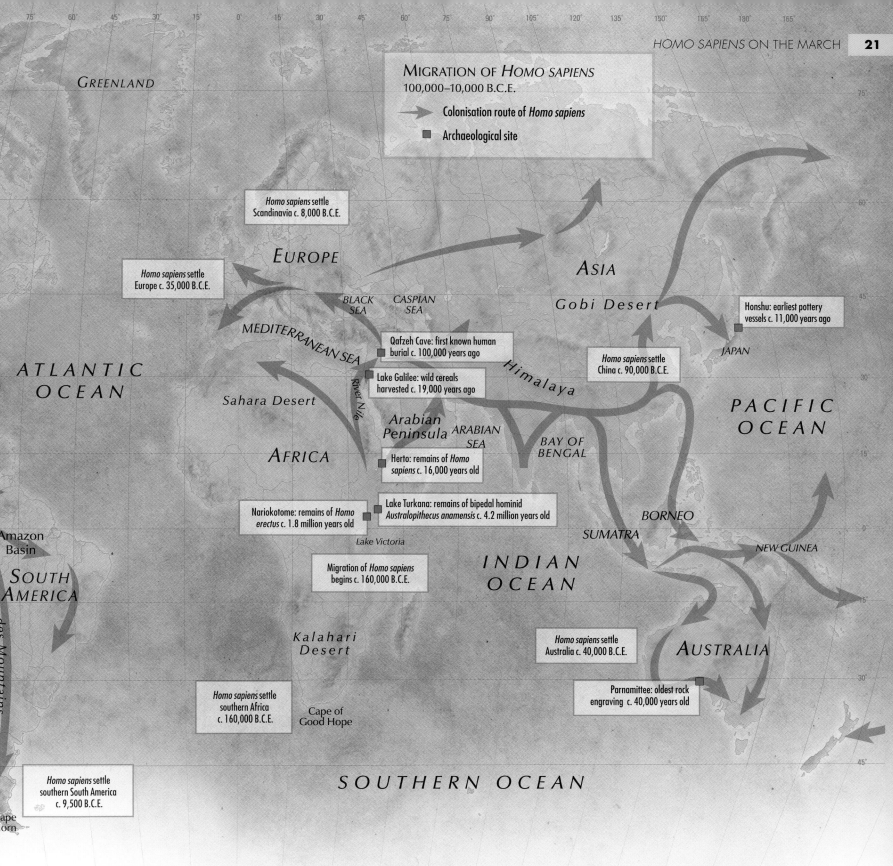

MIGRATION OF *HOMO* SAPIENS
100,000–10,000 B.C.E.

→ Colonisation route of *Homo sapiens*

■ Archaeological site

GREENLAND

Homo sapiens settle
Scandinavia c. 8,000 B.C.E.

EUROPE

ASIA

Homo sapiens settle
Europe c. 35,000 B.C.E.

BLACK
SEA

CASPIAN
SEA

Gobi Desert

Honshu: earliest pottery
vessels c. 11,000 years ago

MEDITERRANEAN SEA

Qafzeh Cave: first known human
burial c. 100,000 years ago

Homo sapiens settle
China c. 90,000 B.C.E.

JAPAN

ATLANTIC
OCEAN

Sahara Desert

Lake Galilee: wild cereals
harvested c. 19,000 years ago

Himalaya

PACIFIC
OCEAN

River Nile

Arabian
Peninsula

ARABIAN
SEA

AFRICA

Herto: remains of *Homo
sapiens* c. 16,000 years old

BAY OF
BENGAL

Amazon
Basin

Nariokotome: remains of *Homo
erectus* c. 1.8 million years old

Lake Turkana: remains of bipedal hominid
Australopithecus anamensis c. 4.2 million years old

BORNEO

SOUTH
AMERICA

Lake Victoria

SUMATRA

NEW GUINEA

Migration of *Homo sapiens*
begins c. 160,000 B.C.E.

INDIAN
OCEAN

Andes Mountains

Kalahari
Desert

Homo sapiens settle
Australia c. 40,000 B.C.E.

AUSTRALIA

Homo sapiens settle
southern Africa
c. 160,000 B.C.E.

Cape of
Good Hope

Parnamittee: oldest rock
engraving c. 40,000 years old

Homo sapiens settle
southern South America
c. 9,500 B.C.E.

SOUTHERN OCEAN

Cape
Horn

90,000 B.C.E. *Homo sapiens* dies out in the eastern Mediterranean.	**50,000 B.C.E.** Cro-Magnon people, the earliest known European examples of *Homo sapiens*, are living in Europe.	**25,000 B.C.E.** *Homo sapiens* in Europe are producing highly skilled cave paintings.	**18,000 B.C.E.** The peak of the last Ice Age.	**15,000 B.C.E.** *Homo sapiens* may have penetrated South America by boat.

100,000	90,000	80,000	70,000	60,000	50,000	40,000	30,000	20,000	10,000	1

85,000 B.C.E.
Homo sapiens embark on a new coast-hugging migration out of Africa and reach Java within 10,000 years.

71,000 B.C.E.
Mount Toba erupts.

65,000 B.C.E.
Humans migrate from the Middle East northwards towards Europe.

40,000 B.C.E.
Ancestors of Australian aborigines arrive on the Australian continent.

20,000 B.C.E.
The first humans may have found their way into North America.

10,000 B.C.E.
Northern Europe is colonised as the climate continues to improve. Humans begin to cultivate plants for food: agriculture is born.

Above: Flint hand axes such as these were humankind's only effective tool for thousands of years. They were used for chopping trees, scraping hides and butchering meat.

The Last of Its Kind

The migrant humans found that they could best survive by hugging the coastline, where clams, crabs and oysters were plentiful. They used tools fashioned from stone to open the oyster shells wherever they found them, and moved along the beach as soon as these easy sources of food ran out. In this way, over the course of many centuries, *Homo sapiens* crept up the southern edge of the Arabian peninsula, farther and farther away from Africa. Eventually, they crossed the Strait of Hormuz, which at that time was a land bridge, into Asia. They travelled south along the western edge of India, north along the eastern coast, and then south again through the coastal areas of Burma and Thailand to a point somewhere near Java, which had been the farthest-flung outpost of *Homo erectus* more than 1.5 million years before. It is estimated that this overland journey took our forebears 10,000 years to complete – twice as long as all recorded history.

It is remarkable to consider that every time a band of *Homo sapiens* rounded a headland or walked the fringes of a new beach, they were walking into territory where no modern human had ever set foot. They were pioneers, exploring new worlds with every generation. This does not mean, however, that *Homo sapiens* were alone in this new land. Their early migrations probably brought them into contact with dwindling groups of *Homo erectus* people. In later migrations, they would certainly have encountered groups of their stockier northern cousins, *Homo neanderthalensis* (Neanderthals), who had evolved from *Homo erectus* outside Africa at roughly the same time as *Homo sapiens*. It is impossible to know what the first modern humans made of these creatures who looked so much like themselves. Did they wage war on them, or interbreed with them? Did they seek them out to trade, or avoid them altogether? All that is known is that wherever *Homo sapiens* appeared, other *Homo* species gradually disappeared. This process, whatever the cause, has left humankind in the sad and unusual biological position whereby *Homo sapiens* are the only surviving representatives of its genus. At present there are two kinds of elephant in the world, many varieties of cats, and thousands of different beetles, but there is only one solitary type of human now living on the planet. All our relatives are dead and gone.

Surviving Global Disaster

The survival of *Homo sapiens* was by no means assured. Around 71,000 B.C.E., there occurred a natural disaster of such magnitude that the human race was almost wiped out. The volcano of Toba, on the island of Sumatra, exploded with unimaginable force. The eruption lasted for about six weeks, during which time almost 3,000 cubic kilometres (700 cubic miles) of ash and rock were spewed into the air. (By way of comparison, the violent eruption of Mount St. Helens, the largest of its kind in living memory, produced about 1 cubic kilometre or 0.25 cubic miles, of ash.) The ash drifted westwards across Asia, blotting out the sun completely. Plants and animals died within days, and much of India was covered in a blanket of searing-hot ash that measured 6 metres (20 feet) deep. It was a global disaster on a scale far more destructive than even a nuclear holocaust. The world was plunged into six years of volcanic winter, followed by at least 1,000 years of global cooling that was as bitter as any ice age.

The effect on humanity was catastrophic. It is possible that the worldwide *Homo sapiens* population dwindled to less than 10,000 individuals, and for many generations humans were a highly endangered species. But in the millennia following the eruption of Toba, *Homo sapiens* managed to repopulate the devastated quarters of the world. They also found their way to places that had never before borne the mark of a human footprint. During glacial periods, when the sea level around the world was much lower, the Southeast Asian archipelago made up of Sumatra, Java and Borneo was part of the Asian landmass: it was possible for *Homo sapiens* to walk from Korea to the tip of Java without getting their feet wet. Humans also made their way to the Australian landmass, which at the time was a much larger island that incorporated New Guinea and Tasmania, and is known to paleogeographers as Sahul. Exactly when humans got to Sahul is unclear – they may have travelled by boat when the global tide was out and the distances by sea relatively short. However they arrived, archaeological evidence tells us that the ancestors of the Australian aborigines were in Sahul by 40,000 years ago.

Colonising New Worlds

Shortly before *Homo sapiens* reached Sahul, about 50,000 years ago, a group of humans moved northwest from the area of south-central Asia, through another temperate corridor that had been created by a long spell of warm weather. This particular grassy highway was to become known in later human history as the Fertile Crescent, and it led through the Near East to the narrow isthmus of the Bosporus – a gateway to Europe. The travelling band of *Homo sapiens* crossed over to the other side of the water and joined the Neanderthals, who had long had all of Europe to themselves.

The Neanderthals' other vast bailiwick was Central Asia. But in the 20,000 years after the first *Homo sapiens* arrived in Europe, others of their species made inroads in Asia, too. Soon there were modern humans living throughout the Asian continent. They spread north from the coastal fringes, skirted around the Himalayas, and then moved along the inland river systems of Eurasia. Some ventured as far north as the Arctic Circle, and ever farther east into the coldest parts of modern Siberia. Across this inhospitable land, at the far eastern extremity of the Eurasian landmass, lay another of nature's doorways, and this one led to the Americas.

The earliest known human artefacts found in North America date back around 10,000 years, but some authorities believe that the first North Americans arrived 11,000– 12,000 years earlier – before the onset of the last Ice Age, which was as its height 18,000 years ago. It is thought that they crossed a broad land bridge that joined Eurasia to North America, where the Bering Strait now divides them. During the Ice Age, groups of people might well have become isolated in the more temperate zones of southern Europe and modern-day Ukraine. There may have also been a few groups of *Homo sapiens* living in the far north of Europe, after the traditional fashion of modern Inuit. What is certain is that once the ice receded, people poured into North America through a gap between the receding ice sheets and quickly fanned out across the continent. Eventually, they also found the causeway that leads through Mexico to South America.

Left: The so-called *Venus of Willendorf* was carved perhaps 24,000 years ago. Its meaning and its purpose are a mystery, though it seems likely that it was intended by its makers to function as a charm or a fertility symbol.

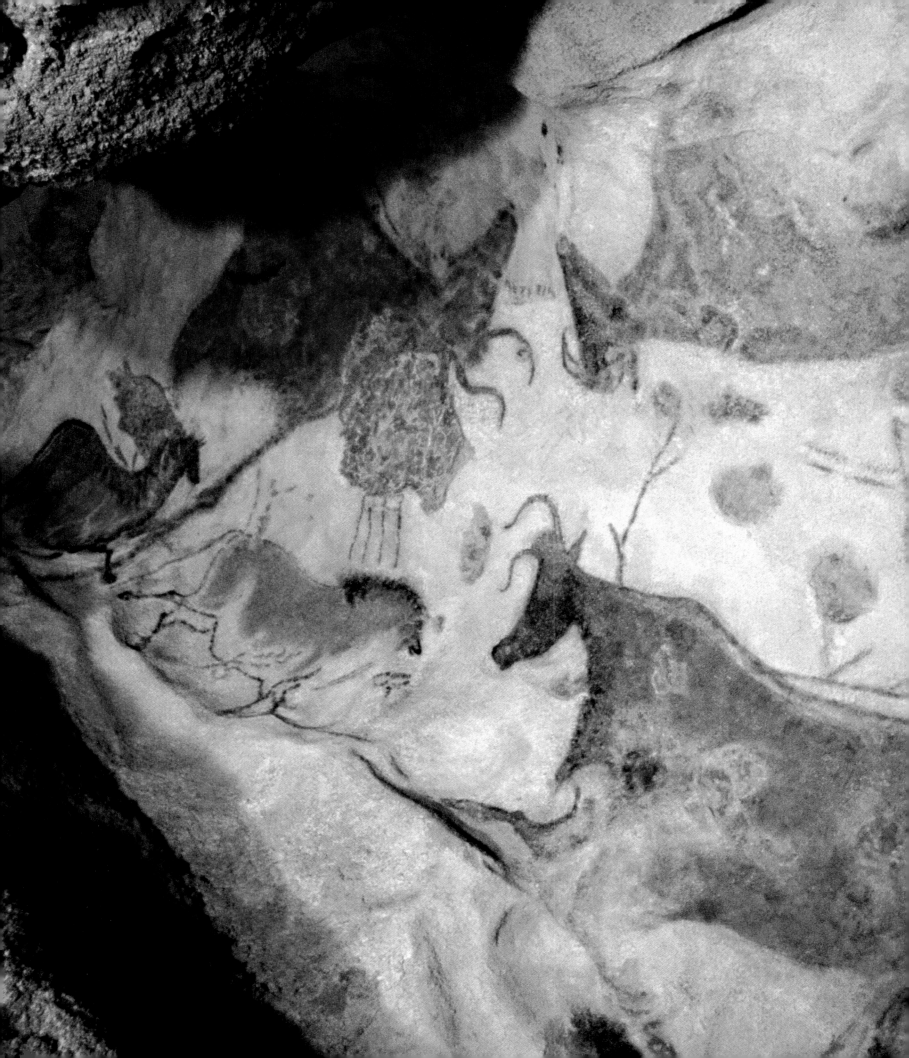

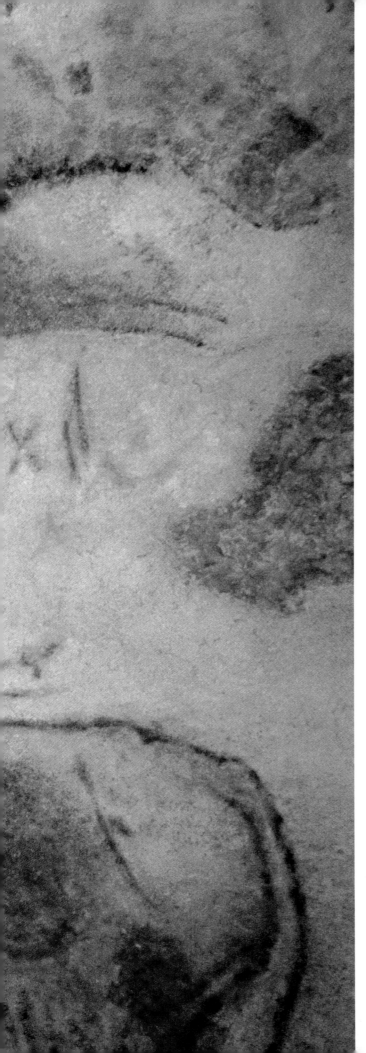

Strangely, there is a site at Monte Verde in Chile that seems to be at least a couple of thousand years older than the oldest signs of habitation in North America. Various theories have been put forward to explain this archaeological anomaly. One enticing but entirely unproven scenario suggests that an ancient seafaring people from modern Japan could have sailed north along the coast, around the shores of Beringia (the landmass then connecting Siberia to Alaska) and then south along the west coast of North and South America. By this method they could have reached Monte Verde centuries before the northern ice had melted to the extent that the journey from Asia to North America could be made on foot. It is an intriguing but unlikely theory.

The global warming that took place at the end of the last Ice Age opened up one final area for colonisation by *Homo sapiens*: Scandinavia. Around 9,000–10,000 years ago, as the glaciers retreated, humans advanced into these green lands, which had been irrigated by meltwater and populated by a variety of wildlife. By now, they had Europe to themselves: the last of the Neanderthals died out 35,000 years ago. The end of the Ice Age, like all climatic turning points, brought about vast geographical changes around the world. The seas rose and Australia was cut off from the rest of the world, forcing the *Homo sapiens* living there to forge their own culture in isolation. Britain and Japan became islands, and the land bridge connecting Siberia and Alaska disappeared. Many places on which human feet once marched were swallowed by the sea – particularly the coastal routes that had allowed early men and women to travel from one continent to the next.

Once the climate stabilised, the continents and the oceans acquired their familiar modern shape. The people who had spread around the globe in the course of some 100,000 years began to find ways to work the land or otherwise use the environment for their own benefit. Over time they began to develop manifestations of the social and creative human sensibility, including art, religion, writing, domesticity and community. But humankind never quite lost the urge to migrate. The epic story of civilisation, which was about to begin on a global scale, is one of ideas and cultures that travel, and of people leaving home – often forever – in search of a different way of life.

Left: The paintings of bulls and other animals in the Lascaux Caves, France, bear witness to the extraordinary sophistication of early human society. The person who made these images 19,000 years ago was a fine artist by any standard.

THE ANCIENT
WORLD

The act of migration did not cease once humankind had spread around the globe. Peoples continued to uproot themselves from time to time and move to other lands, but there are many gaps in our knowledge of these ancient peregrinations. By examining the commonalities in many of the world's languages, linguists have determined that there must have once been an "Indo-European" people, but exactly who they were remains a mystery. It is known, however, that the Indo-Europeans eventually colonised Europe and northern India, where their speech developed into the distinct languages known today. At roughly the same time, skilled sailors on the eastern seaboard of Asia were navigating the Pacific – but again experts have little idea as to what prompted their journey. The Old Testament provides a written account of the ancient migration of the Israelites, but it is difficult to say where history ends and biblical mythology begins. Although archaeological evidence provides many clues about the expansion of the Greek and Roman Empires, there still remain huge gaps in the history of their citizens' movements. Experts must use what they can to piece together the migrations of the world's ancient civilisations.

Left: The Roman army can be seen at work on the 2nd-century C.E. Trajan's column. Soldiers move out across a pontoon bridge to new conquests, while a garrison is built, the base from which they will subdue new territories.

THE COMMON TONGUE

The world's languages can be grouped into families that are believed to have common ancestors. Although language today has evolved into a multitude of colourful and diverse tongues, linguists are able to identify key words and phrases that are common to many. From this evidence, it is possible to garner some idea about the movements of our migrating ancestors.

All our knowledge about the movements of peoples in the distant prehistoric era is derived from archaeology. The presence of human bones tells us, at the very least, that people were in a particular place at a particular time. The objects associated with human remains – the arrowheads and other trinkets that are sometimes found in graves, trash sites and the remains of buildings – provide clues about what kind of people the bones once belonged to, how those people lived, what they knew, and what was important to them. These remains are all the tools archaeologists have to build a picture of the past. There is no recorded history – that is, no written text – that goes back more than 5,000 years, which is a mere blink of the eye in the timescale of human existence. To find out anything about the migrations of our ancestors before that point, archaeologists are dependent on evidence that is dug out of the ground. Almost – but not entirely. Every human being possesses a valuable artifact that is passed down from our prehistoric ancestors, one that reveals volumes about their extinct world: language.

The Family Tree of Language

Language can be thought of as a kind of cultural DNA, as it can be traced back through generations to establish family links. For example, the English language is recognised as being related to German because the English word "uncle" looks so much like the German *Onkel*, and the word "swim" is clearly linked to the German *schwimmen*. In this instance, the connections

THE SPREAD OF THE
INDO-EUROPEAN LANGUAGE
4500–2000 B.C.E.

▪ Possible homelands of the Indo-Europeans

▪ Area possibly settled by c. 2500 B.C.E.

▪ Area possibly settled by c. 1000 B.C.E.

→ Possible migration routes of the Indo-Europeans

THE EVOLUTION OF LANGUAGE

c. 4000 B.C.E. Speakers of Proto-Indo-European are living somewhere in the Black Sea region.

c. 2000 B.C.E. A separate Indo-European group moves south through Persia and into the Indian subcontinent.

c. 1400 B.C.E. Proto-Greek speakers are living on the island of Crete.

c. 600 B.C.E. Gaulish inscriptions are being written in Celtic languages.

B.C.E. 5000	4500	4000	3500	3000	2500	2000	1500	1000	500	1

c. 3000 B.C.E. The westward migration of the Indo-European people begins.

c. 1500 B.C.E. The *Rigveda*, the first known text in Sanskrit, is written.

c. 700 B.C.E. An early form of Latin is being spoken on the Italian peninsula.

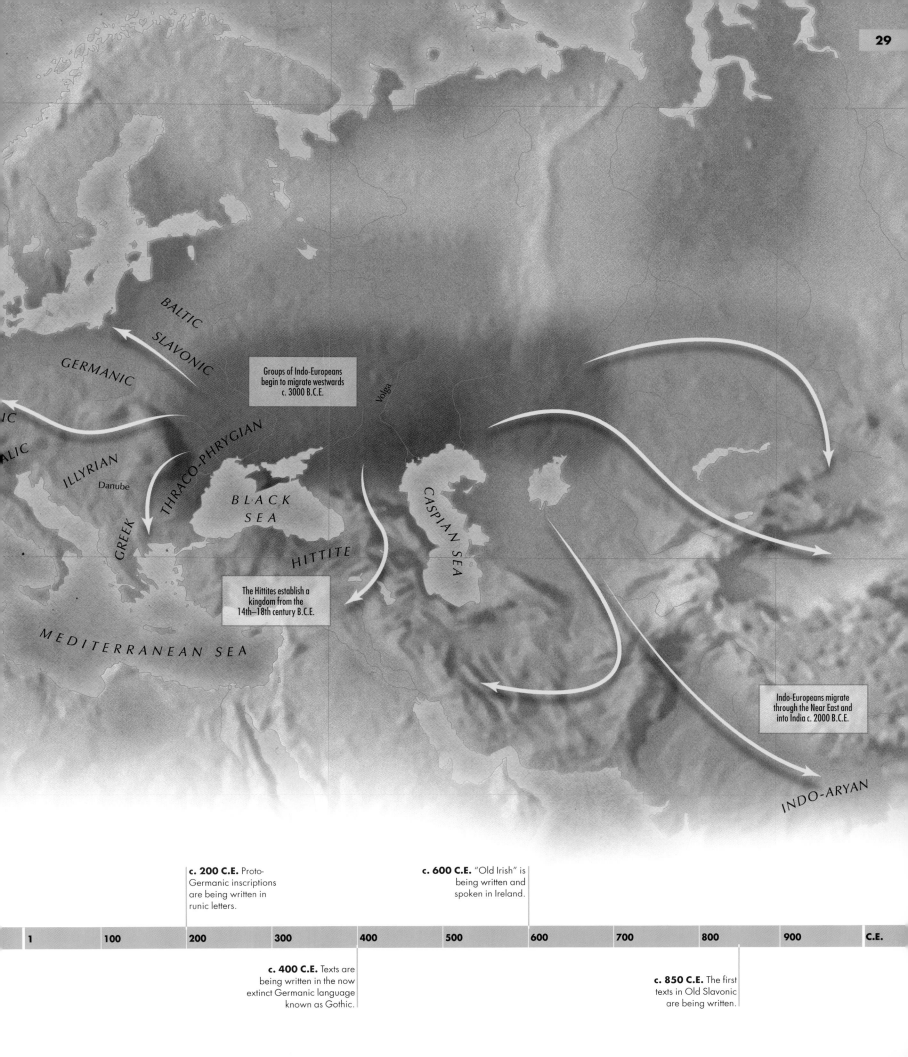

BALTIC

SLAVONIC

GERMANIC

Groups of Indo-Europeans
begin to migrate westwards
c. 3000 B.C.E.

Volga

IC

ALIC

ILLYRIAN

Danube

THRACO-PHRYGIAN

GREEK

BLACK
SEA

CASPIAN SEA

HITTITE

The Hittites establish a
kingdom from the
14th–18th century B.C.E.

MEDITERRANEAN SEA

Indo-Europeans migrate
through the Near East and
into India c. 2000 B.C.E.

INDO-ARYAN

c. 200 C.E. Proto-
Germanic inscriptions
are being written in
runic letters.

c. 600 C.E. "Old Irish" is
being written and
spoken in Ireland.

| 1 | 100 | 200 | 300 | 400 | 500 | 600 | 700 | 800 | 900 | C.E. |

c. 400 C.E. Texts are
being written in the now
extinct Germanic language
known as Gothic.

c. 850 C.E. The first
texts in Old Slavonic
are being written.

(Sanskrit manuscript image — Rigveda page in Devanagari script)

Right: The *Rigveda* is a Hindu book of hymns composed about 3,500 years ago. It is written in Sanskrit and is one of the oldest texts in an Indo-European language. As such it is an invaluable source for linguists engaged in reconstructing the speech of our wandering ancestors.

between the two languages fall well within the written record of history, and are thoroughly backed up by archaeological evidence: Germanic tribes invaded England in the early Middle Ages, and in time their speech evolved into a form that was different from the Germanic tongue spoken by those living on the continent. Eventually the various Germanic dialects became separate but related languages. English and German (and also Dutch) are cousins on the same branch of a linguistic family tree.

The family tree of language, however, goes back much further than the early Middle Ages. An examination of the words for the most fundamental ideas and concepts in different languages reveals that some are related across a wide range of European tongues. The English word "night", for example, is clearly cognate with the German *Nacht*, but also with the Lithuanian *naktis*, the Welsh *nos*, the Polish *noc*, the Latin *nox* and the ancient Greek *nux*. What is more, the cognate *nak* appears in texts written in Sanskrit, the ancient liturgical language of India. Such similarities across many languages in hundreds of words naturally leads to the conclusion that many of the languages of Europe and some of the languages of India are derived from a common source. However, Indo-European is only one of many major linguistic families in the world – within Europe non-Indo-European languages include Hungarian and Basque. There also must once have been a mother tongue that is the ancestor of languages as diverse as Urdu and Serbo-Croatian, Welsh and Italian.

There are no written records of such a language, but linguists have designated it Proto-Indo-European, or PIE for short. Like paleontologists who reconstruct entire dinosaur skeletons from a fossilised tooth, paleolinguists have developed techniques that allow them to re-create entire grammars and dictionaries of the Indo-European tongue. For example, the Indo-European word from which nearly all languages take their name for the hours of darkness was something like *nokti*. Linguists can be certain of this, even though the word appears in no existing text, and even though PIE was extinct long before any word was ever written down.

If there was an Indo-European language, it follows that there must have been a people – Indo-Europeans – who spoke this language. Members of this group may not have all been ethnically or culturally homogenous, and theirs was not the only language spoken at the time. But at some point, all Indo-Europeans spoke the same language, and at

some later point various groups must have spread across Europe in one of the great undocumented migrations of prehistory. This explains how forms of the Indo-European language came to be spoken in places as far apart as the Atlantic coast of Ireland and the Gulf of Bengal.

Locating the Indo-European Homeland
Who were the Indo-Europeans, and where exactly did they come from? This is one of the great mysteries of migratory history, and one of the most hotly contested debates among historical linguistics. Many Indo-European homelands have been proposed, ranging from northern Germany to western Turkey. There has even been the extraordinary suggestion that the Indo-Europeans came from the North Pole or from Egypt. During the time of the Nazis, in mid-20th-century Germany, the concept of an Indo-European root language was used to support the totally unscientific and unhistoric idea that there must once have been an original tribe of fair-haired, muscular Europeans – the racially unadulterated descendants of whom were deemed by the Nazis to be the only true Germans.

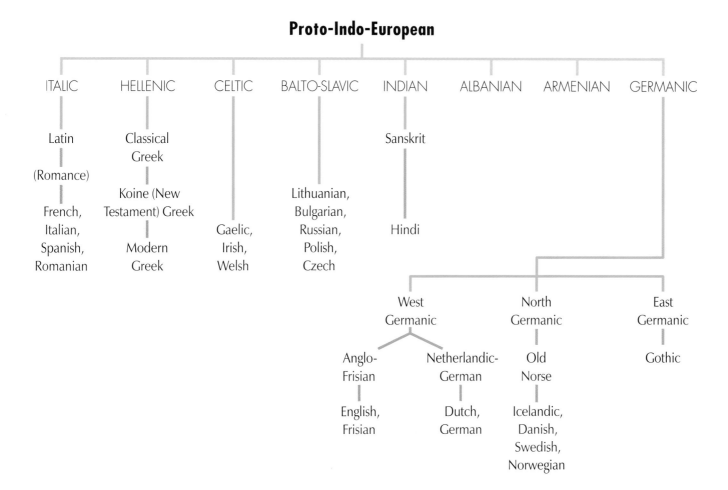

Left: The languages of Europe and northern India can be arranged in a kind of family tree that goes back to a single Proto-Indo-European predecessor. English is a close cousin of Dutch, but both are more distantly related to the Scandinavian languages. Armenian and Albanian have no close relatives among modern tongues.

The clues that help to solve the mystery of the Indo-European identity lie like fossils in the Indo-European languages. Almost as soon as it was realised that most of the languages of India and Europe are related, linguists began to scour dictionaries in search of words that are so similar across a range of languages that they can only have come from the common PIE source. Some of these words, it was thought, were bound to contain a cultural or geographical

believe that their homeland must be in northern Europe, where salmon are native (there are also words for "otter", "bear" and many other cold-weather animals). Later it transpired that the word *laksi* might just as easily denote the salmon trout, which is found in rivers throughout Eurasia.

Words such as "snow" and "salmon/trout" do not help to pin down the Indo-European homeland exactly, but they do at least rule out an origin on the Indian subcontinent. This means that the speakers of the languages that evolved into Urdu, Hindi and Gujarati must have settled in India after migrating from somewhere else. But where did they come from? A different line of enquiry used to deduce the Indo-European homeland involves using linguistic methods to gain some idea of the religious and social life of the Indo-Europeans, and then trying to match that picture to a culture that is known from the archaeological record.

Linguists estimate that about 6,000 years ago, the Indo-Europeans were still a coherent group – they had not yet begun to migrate. This means that they belong to the Neolithic Age. They had a word for "god," and they venerated the horse – there is a word for "horse-sacrifice" and a word meaning "horse-drunk", which seems to be something to do with a religious rite involving fermented mares' milk. They had a complicated system of kinship in which male relationships – uncle, nephew and father – were paramount. They had a word, *bhergh*, that denoted a fortified settlement, which is the root of the English "borough", and the German *Burg* (city) and also *Berg* (mountain – since settlements tended to be in high places). They had priestly kings who bore the title *reg* – whence the Latin *rex*, the Indian word *raj* and the English verb "reign". They had a warrior class that fought with spears and daggers, and they were acquainted with wheeled transport.

Is there in the archaeological record a Neolithic culture that was located in a region where it was cold enough to snow, which appeared to be patriarchal and practised some form of horse-worship, and that had stockaded towns and made use of domesticated animals? There is – in fact, there are many. Recent scholarship has identified the Indo-Europeans with several different sets of archaeological remains, of which the most likely candidates are the so-called "Kurgan culture", on the northern shore of the

Above: The beautiful Gundestrup cauldron is most likely the work of a Celtic people living on the lower Danube in around 200 B.C.E. The images appear to come from a variety of cultures and mythologies, including Greek, Indian and Iranian. It seems that speakers of various Indo-European tongues were in touch with each other.

hint as to where the Indo-Europeans were living before they split into their separate groups. The word "snow", for example, is cognate with the Russian *snyeg* and the Latin *nix* (the initial "s" having dropped off long before the classical language of the Romans evolved). The Indo-European root of all these cognate words has been shown to be *snoigho*. So then, if the speakers of Indo-European had a word for "snow", they must have lived somewhere that had cold winters.

Much more can be deduced from the lists of reconstructed Indo-European words. Linguists have discovered, for example, that Indo-Europeans had words for "cow", "sheep", "dog" and "pig", and also for "stall" or "stable"; so they must have been herders and keepers of livestock rather than nomads. They also had a word for "salmon" – *laksi* – which for a while led some scholars to

Left: Hittite ruins in Anatolia, modern Turkey. The Hittites spoke an Indo-European tongue, but they disappeared from the record some time after the Old Testament era. They left their mark on the Turkish landscape – and on the Turkish tongue: place names such as Sinop and Adana are of Hittite origin.

Black Sea and west of the Caspian Sea, and the "Linear Ware culture" that once flourished in the Balkans and Central Europe.

The Descendants of the Indo-Europeans

The fact is, it is still not known exactly where the Indo-Europeans originated from, but archaeologists are fairly certain about where they went. About 5,000 years ago some of the Indo-European-speaking people began to drift westwards from their homeland. Most of these migrants passed along the northern shore of the Black Sea, but one small group rounded the sea to the south, and in time became the warlike Hittite people, who make a brief appearance in history and in the Old Testament before disappearing completely. The larger group began to splinter while still rounding the coast of the Black Sea. Some struck north along the broad and navigable Volga River; they became the speakers of the Baltic languages (Lithuanian and Latvian) and of the Slavonic languages (Russian and its relatives). To the west of them, a Germanic group plunged into the forests of northern Europe, emerged on the North Sea coast, and eventually colonised modern Denmark and Scandinavia.

Another group rounded the Black Sea and headed south: Indo-European speakers arrived in Greece, where they displaced the non-Indo-Europeans who already occupied the jagged coastline. Alongside these future Greek speakers travelled a group who became the speakers of Illyrian. They settled in the Balkans and eventually became extinct, but the Albanian language is a descendant of their tongue. An Italic group moved into the boot-shaped peninsula that bears their name,

leaving a Celtic group to move along the course of the River Danube and eventually into Western Europe, the Iberian Peninsula and the British Isles. Celtic survived only on the farthest-flung edge of Europe, in Ireland, Scotland, Wales and Cornwall. From Cornwall the Celtic tongue was reexported to mainland Europe by migrating Britons. They gave their name to the land they colonised, which became known as Brittany.

While this was happening in Europe, a different group of Indo-Europeans were embarking on an entirely separate migration. Around 4,000 years ago, migrants from the Indo-European homeland travelled south through the Near East and into India. As had happened with their European relatives, their speech, over decades and centuries, split and evolved into new languages and new groups of languages. The branch of the PIE family tree that resulted is usually termed "Indo-Aryan", to distinguish it from the European branch. In the Near East, Indo-Aryans were ancestors of speakers of Iranian languages: Farsi, Kurdish and Baluchi. When they arrived in India, the Indo-Aryans displaced the Dravidian civilisation that they encountered and replaced it with a culture and a suite of languages that includes Hindi, Bengali, Assamese, Punjabi, Gujarati, Marathi, Rajasthani and Sinhalese.

However unlikely it seems, English and Czech, as well as many other languages, are distant relatives of the same tongue: both peoples share a common ancestor in the Proto-Indo-European people. Even more incredible, the staggering linguistic variety that exists in the world today, all essentially corruptions of an original language, was largely influenced by the consequences of early migration.

LET MY PEOPLE GO

The history of the Jews is punctuated with episodes of exile and migration. From the Exodus to Babylonian captivity and Diaspora, Jewish populations have undergone repeated journeys to and from their homeland. The will to prevail over the hardships surrounding these travels, described in both the Old Testament and the annals of history, has inspired similar migrations throughout the generations.

Below: An inscription from Nebuchadnezzar's Babylon, the place of exile of the defeated Jews of Jerusalem. Many remained there when the time of exile ended, and made Babylon one of the great centres of Jewish culture and scholarship.

THE JEWISH DIASPORA, c. 1300 B.C.E.–300 C.E.

- Extent of the Roman Empire, c. 300 C.E.
- Extent of Kingdom of David, 10th century B.C.E.
- Kingdom of Israel, 931–722 B.C.E.
- Kingdom of Judah, 931–587 B.C.E.
- Probable route of the Exodus, 13th century B.C.E.
- Route of Babylonian exile, 587 B.C.E.
- Jewish dispersion routes, c. 70 B.C.E.–c. 300 C.E.

THE JEWISH DIASPORA

1279–1213 B.C.E Ramses II rules in Egypt – the traditional date of the Exodus.

970 B.C.E. King Solomon begins his reign in Jerusalem. The First Temple is built.

B.C.E.	1500	1400	1350	1300	1250	1200	1150	1100	1050	1000	950	900	850	800	750

c. 1500 B.C.E. A volcano erupts on Thera, providing the evidence for one possible date of the Exodus.

1010 B.C.E. King David begins his reign in Jerusalem.

931 B.C.E. The state is divided into the Kingdom of Israel in the north and the Kingdom of Judah in the south.

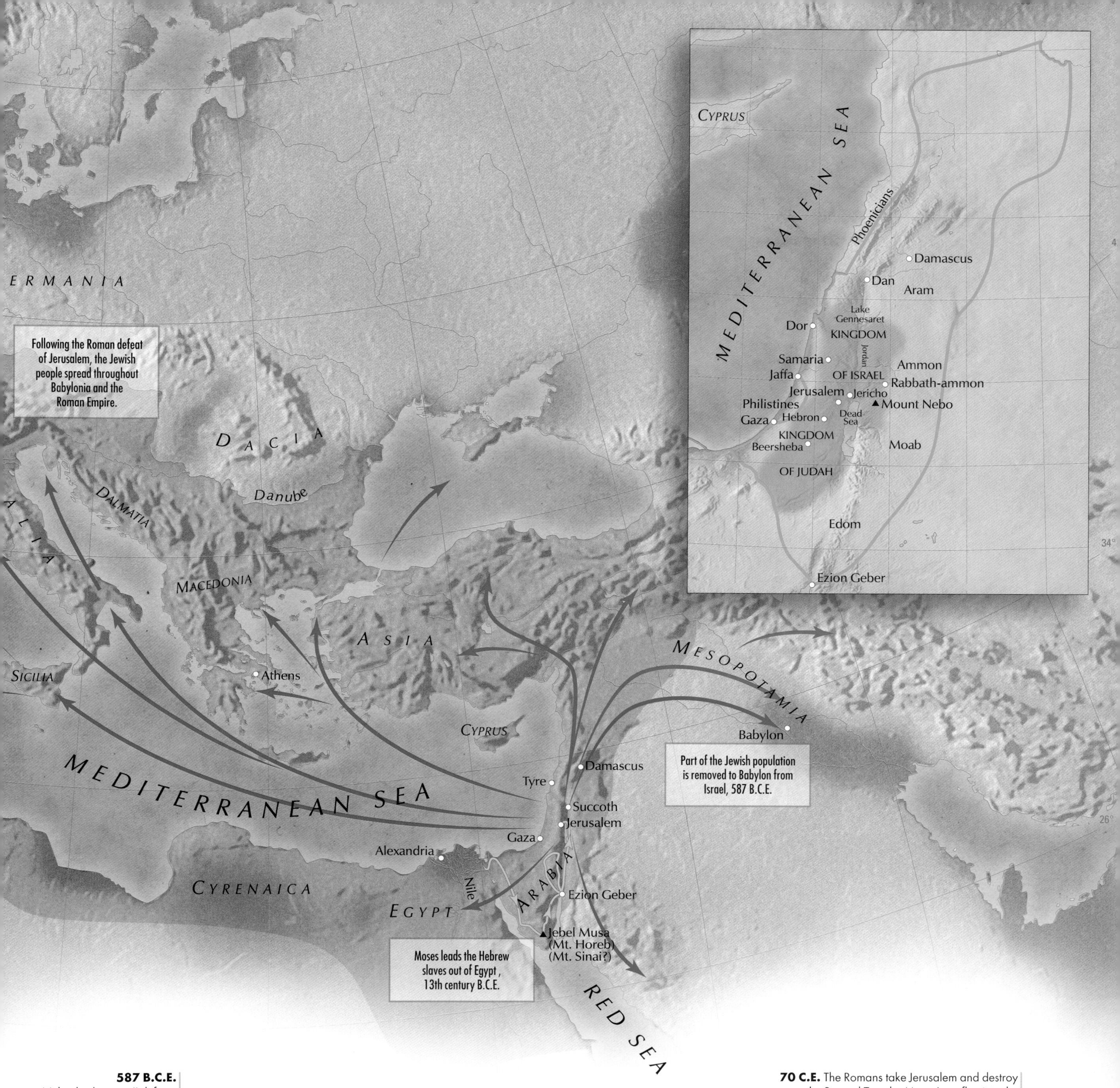

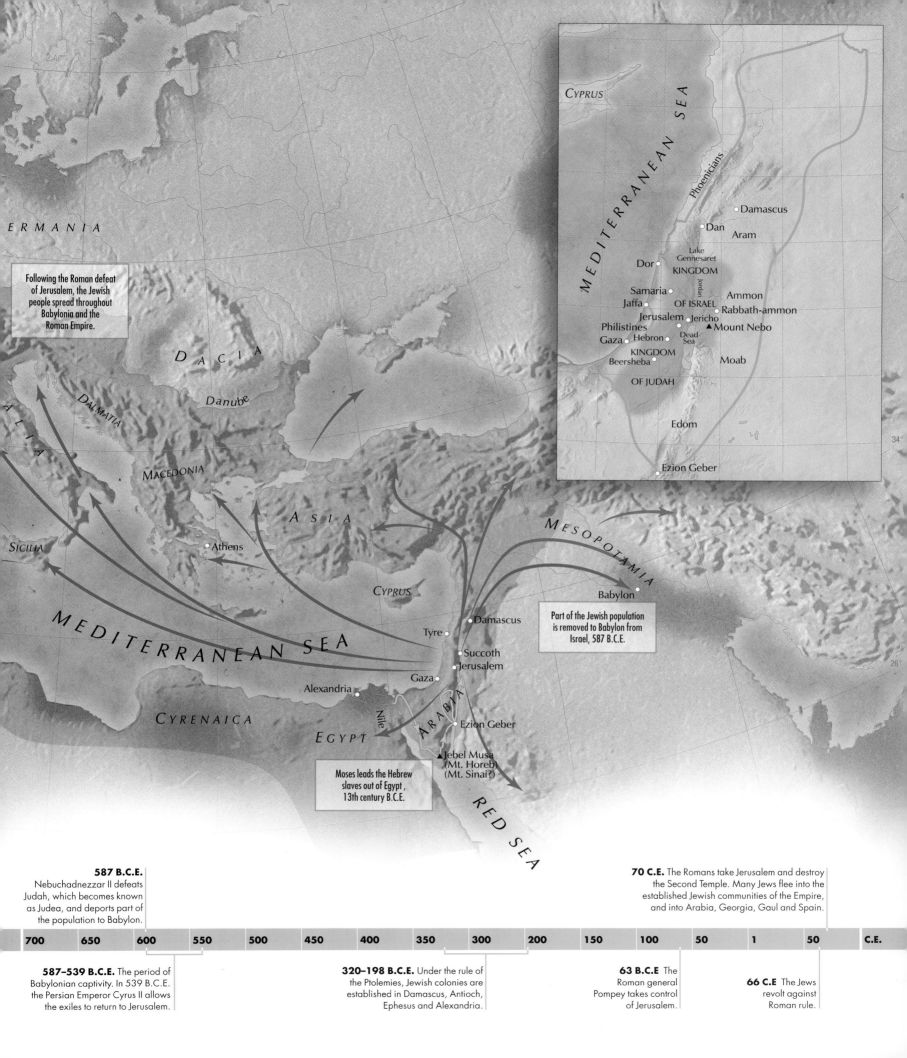

Following the Roman defeat of Jerusalem, the Jewish people spread throughout Babylonia and the Roman Empire.
Part of the Jewish population is removed to Babylon from Israel, 587 B.C.E.
Moses leads the Hebrew slaves out of Egypt, 13th century B.C.E.
ERMANIA
DACIA
Danube
DALMATIA
MACEDONIA
ALIA
SICILIA
Athens
ASIA
MESOPOTAMIA
Babylon
CYPRUS
MEDITERRANEAN SEA
Tyre
Damascus
Succoth
Jerusalem
Gaza
Alexandria
Nile
ARABIA
Ezion Geber
CYRENAICA
EGYPT
Jebel Musa
(Mt. Horeb)
(Mt. Sinai?)
RED SEA
CYPRUS
MEDITERRANEAN SEA
Phoenicians
Damascus
Dan
Aram
Lake Gennesaret
Dor
KINGDOM
Jordan
Samaria
Ammon
Jaffa
OF ISRAEL
Rabbath-ammon
Jerusalem
Jericho
Philistines
Mount Nebo
Gaza
Hebron
Dead Sea
KINGDOM
Beersheba
Moab
OF JUDAH
Edom
Ezion Geber

587 B.C.E. Nebuchadnezzar II defeats Judah, which becomes known as Judea, and deports part of the population to Babylon.

70 C.E. The Romans take Jerusalem and destroy the Second Temple. Many Jews flee into the established Jewish communities of the Empire, and into Arabia, Georgia, Gaul and Spain.

700 | 650 | 600 | 550 | 500 | 450 | 400 | 350 | 300 | 200 | 150 | 100 | 50 | 1 | 50 | C.E.

587–539 B.C.E. The period of Babylonian captivity. In 539 B.C.E. the Persian Emperor Cyrus II allows the exiles to return to Jerusalem.

320–198 B.C.E. Under the rule of the Ptolemies, Jewish colonies are established in Damascus, Antioch, Ephesus and Alexandria.

63 B.C.E The Roman general Pompey takes control of Jerusalem.

66 C.E The Jews revolt against Roman rule.

According to the Old Testament books of Genesis and Exodus, Abraham, the founding patriarch of the Israelites and Arabic people, migrated from Babylonia (part of modern Iraq) to the land commensurate with present-day Israel, the West Bank and Gaza: Canaan, "a land flowing with milk and honey". When famine drove Abraham's descendants from Canaan, they took refuge in Egypt, where Joseph, their kinsman who had become an advisor to the pharoah, welcomed them. Over the years, the Hebrew people in Egypt grew in numbers but declined in status until, under a new pharoah, "who knew not Joseph", they were reduced to a nation of slaves. They were forced to work as labourers until the Hebrew leader Moses, commanded by God to deliver the Hebrews from slavery, took charge of his people and led them through great tribulation back to the Promised Land of Canaan.

Below: The Dome of the Rock, on Temple Mount in Jerusalem, was the site of the Second Temple, which according to the Bible was built by the Jews who returned from exile in Babylon.

Babylonian Captivity and Roman Rule

The subsequent history of the Hebrew nation is contained in the Book of Joshua and in the further books of the Old Testament. The Book of Joshua states that the people of Moses occupied the Promised Land (after subjugating the peoples who already lived there) and created a nation of Israelites. They established a monarchy and built a capital city at Jerusalem under the kings David (r. c. 1011–971 B.C.E.) and Solomon (r. c. 971–928 B.C.E.). Later, this kingdom split into two to form the kingdoms of Israel and Judah. No longer a unified nation, the Israelites were weakened, and in 586 B.C.E. both kingdoms were conquered by Nebuchadnezzar II (r. c. 605–562 B.C.E.) of the Babylonian Empire. In 587 B.C.E., the Babylonians destroyed the Temple in Jerusalem – considered in Judaism to be the primary resting place of God's presence in the physical world – and carried off

part of the Jewish population to Babylon in the east. One of the most poignant and best-known verses of the Book of Psalms describes the sorrow brought on by this exile: "By the rivers of Babylon, there we sat down; yea, we wept, when we remembered Zion. We hanged our harps upon the willows in the midst thereof. For there they that carried us away captive required of us a song … How shall we sing the Lord's song in a strange land?"

The Babylonian exile was relatively short-lived. In 539 B.C.E., Cyrus II (r. 539–529 B.C.E.), founder of the Persian Empire, took control of Babylon and issued a decree to free the Israelites. Some Jews returned to Zion, and by 515 B.C.E. the Temple had been rebuilt. Many of the deportees, however, remained in Babylon. Among them were many scholars, and Babylon was for generations to come one of the world centres of Jewish learning.

Judea, as the land of Israel became known, continued to be subject to invasion by various peoples. The Macedonians invaded in 332 B.C.E. under Alexander the Great (r. 336–323), and in the 1st century B.C.E. the land came under Roman control. The Romans usually respected the unfamiliar religious practices of their subject peoples, and as Judea was initially a client kingdom of Rome, largely independent but ruled by Roman prefects who were responsible for keeping the peace and collecting taxes, the conquered Jews managed to preserve the essentials of their faith. Over time, however, the semi-independence allowed to Judea was steadily eroded. The rule became less and less Jewish, until Judea came under the direct control of Roman administration. In 66 C.E., Judeans rose up in rebellion against Rome, but the revolt was crushed by Roman troops, and the Second Temple was destroyed. Judea was reduced to a Roman province and its population dispersed around the Roman world. This was a continuation of the so-called Diaspora, the diffusion of the Jewish people that had begun several centuries earlier when the Assyrian and Babylonian conquests resulted in the creation of Jewish communities in Mesopotamia. The Diaspora was prophesied hundreds of years previously in the Book of Deuteronomy: "If thou wilt not observe to do all the words of this law … the Lord shall scatter thee among all people, from one end of the Earth even unto the other … And among these nations shalt thou find no ease, neither shall the sole of thy foot have rest."

Tracing the Events of the Exodus

The Babylonian captivity of the Jews and the events of the Roman period are well attested to in historical records. The early epic of the Hebrew escape from Egyptian tyranny is,

however, much harder to pinpoint. As described in the Book of Exodus, Moses, a Hebrew adopted by the Egyptian royal family, is summoned by God to lead his people out of captivity. He goes to the pharaoh and tells him that God demands that he "let my people go." When the pharaoh refuses, God visits a series of plagues upon Egypt: he sends hordes of frogs and locusts, and pestilence, and converts the Nile to blood. When none of these calamities succeeds in persuading the pharaoh to free the Hebrews, God decrees that all Egyptian first-born sons will be slain. At this point, the pharaoh allows the Hebrews to leave, but afterwards changes his mind and sends an army in pursuit of them. As the Egyptian troops approach the procession by the shore of the Red Sea, the waters part to allow the Hebrews to escape, before engulfing and drowning the pursuing Egyptians. The Hebrews proceed to Mount Sinai, where Moses spends 40 days communing with God and receiving the Ten Commandments. While he is away, the people make a golden calf that they worship as an idol. To punish them for their idolatry, God condemns the Hebrews to wander in the wilderness for 40 years.

Above: A medieval Christian depiction of the crossing of the Red Sea, as described in the Book of Exodus. Much ingenuity and scholarship has since been brought to bear to explain how the sea parted to allow the people of Moses to pass and so escape the pursuing Egyptians.

Although there is no proof outside of the Bible of the existence of Moses as a historical figure, scholars can be sure about the existence of his people. There is plenty of evidence outside the Old Testament for a nomadic people that the Egyptians called "Hapiru", a word that may be derived from the same root as "Hebrew." According to Egyptian accounts, the Hapiru were "sand-dwellers" and "wretched Asiatics." This derogatory language suggests that they may have been subject to Egyptian oppression from time to time – perhaps forced to work on the construction of the "treasure cities" of Pithom and Ra'amses spoken of in the Book of Exodus, in the eastern delta of the Nile. Any charismatic leader who headed a rebellion against Egyptian domination and led some of the slaves away would very likely have become fixed in the folk memory.

Many scholars place the events of the Exodus in the 19th Egyptian dynasty, during the reign of Ramses II (r. 1279–1213 B.C.E.). This would mean that Moses and his people left Egypt in the late 1200s B.C.E. One theory puts the date of the Exodus 200 years earlier and connects it with the massive eruption of a volcano on the island of Thera in the Aegean Sea, 800 kilometres (500 miles) away from the Nile Delta. This natural disaster might well have caused the destruction of the Minoan civilisation on Crete, and it has been theorised that it could have had a profound effect on Egypt, too. For historians, the strength of the Thera hypothesis is that it provides tentative scientific explanations for many of the miraculous events surrounding the Exodus in the Bible story. For example, the parting of the Red Sea can be explained as the effects of a tsunami that may have resulted from the eruption. The biblical Red Sea is not the body of water known by that name today – it was a "Reed Sea", so most likely a coastal marshland. As a consequence of the tsunami, the Mediterranean waters may have retreated for a time, allowing the Hebrews to pass before a devastating wall of water washed over the pursuing Egyptians.

The eruption on Thera also provides explanations for many of the plagues visited upon Egypt. The unusual swarming of insects often precedes or accompanies seismic disturbances, and the volcanic ash produced by the eruption could be the source of the "hail, and fire mingled with the hail" described as another of the plagues. The ash's toxic effect can also explain the death of livestock ("all the cattle of Egypt died") and even the plagues of boils and sores,

since volcanic dust is known to be a skin irritant ("small dust in all the land of Egypt … shall be a boil breaking forth with blains upon man, and upon beast"). The distinctive red-coloured pumice thrown out by the Thera volcano could also have polluted rivers in countries as far away as Egypt ("all the waters that were in the river were turned to blood, and the fish that were in the river died, and the river stank"). The great plume of smoke from Thera would for a time have blotted out the sun throughout the Mediterranean region ("there was a thick darkness in all the land of Egypt for three days"). Later, the plume from the burning volcano would even have risen so high into the atmosphere that it would have been visible to the Hebrews as they trekked through the Sinai Peninsula ("the Lord went before them by day in a pillar of cloud … and by night in a pillar of fire").

According to the Bible, 600,000 men "besides women and children" followed Moses into the Sinai Peninsula. This figure implies that more than two million people in total took part in the Exodus, but this is far more than the arid land of Sinai could have sustained. The language used to describe the size of the procession is probably symbolic of a large number and not intended to be taken literally. The

Bible also states that the Hebrew people remained in the wilderness for 40 years – but this too can be interpreted as a symbolic number implying a long time. The itinerary of the migrating Hebrews is spelled out in some detail in the Bible, but few of the places mentioned can now be identified. Even the location of Mount Sinai, where Moses received the Ten Commandments, is disputed among scholars. An early Christian tradition identifies it with Jebel Musa ("Moses' Mount") in the south of the Sinai Peninsula. The assumption is that the Hebrews marched southeast down one edge of the peninsula, and then northwest up the other side.

The migration of the Hebrews to the Promised Land is one of the great narratives of biblical history and of world mythology. It is a journey's end, a covenant fulfilled and a universal parable of the search for a better life. Throughout the centuries, the Exodus story has inspired migrants as diverse as the Mormons, the Pilgrim Fathers and the remnants of European Jewry who found refuge in the new-fledged Israel. These travellers were all able to undergo the hardships and tribulations of their "wilderness years" by holding on to the belief that a Promised Land waited for them in the end.

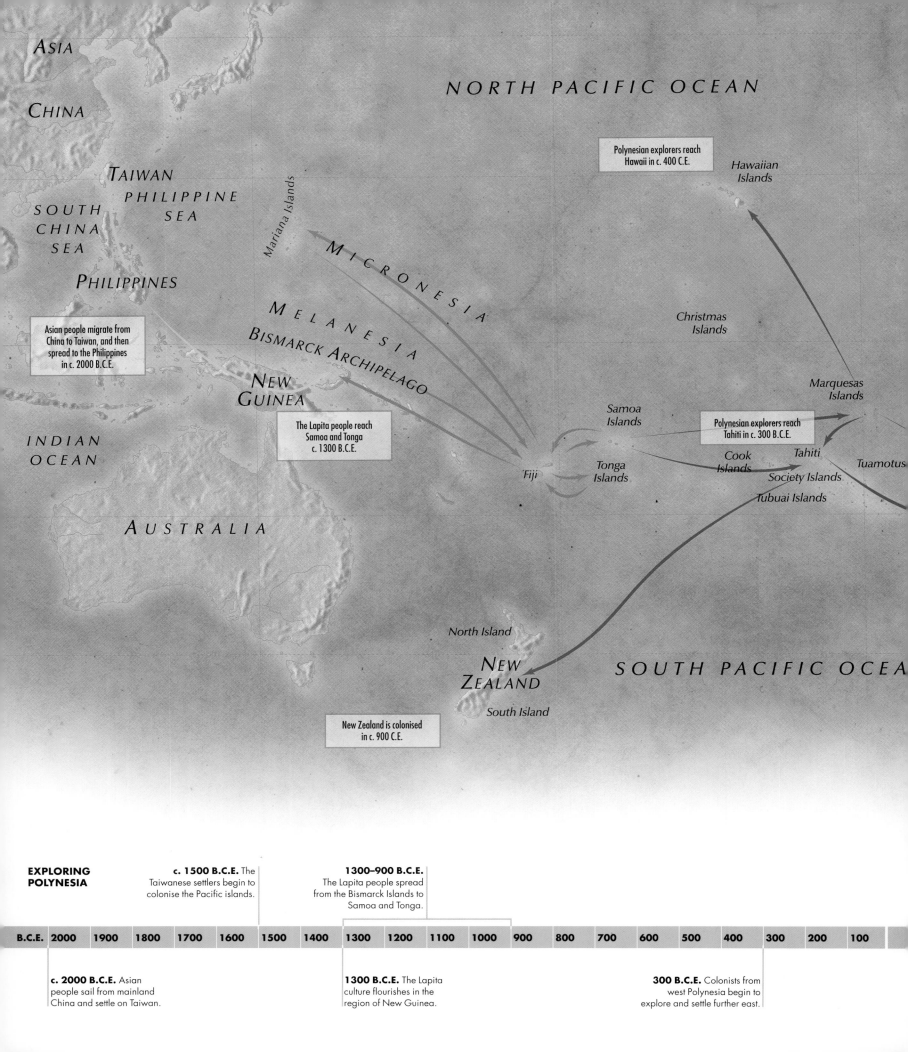

ASIA

CHINA

NORTH PACIFIC OCEAN

TAIWAN

PHILIPPINE SEA

SOUTH CHINA SEA

PHILIPPINES

Mariana Islands

MICRONESIA

Polynesian explorers reach
Hawaii in c. 400 C.E.

Hawaiian
Islands

MELANESIA

BISMARCK ARCHIPELAGO

Asian people migrate from
China to Taiwan, and then
spread to the Philippines
in c. 2000 B.C.E.

NEW
GUINEA

The Lapita people reach
Samoa and Tonga
c. 1300 B.C.E.

INDIAN
OCEAN

Christmas
Islands

Samoa
Islands

Marquesas
Islands

Polynesian explorers reach
Tahiti in c. 300 B.C.E.

Fiji

Tonga
Islands

Cook
Islands

Tahiti

Tuamotus

Society Islands

Tubuai Islands

AUSTRALIA

North Island

NEW
ZEALAND

SOUTH PACIFIC OCEA

South Island

New Zealand is colonised
in c. 900 C.E.

EXPLORING
POLYNESIA

c. 1500 B.C.E. The
Taiwanese settlers begin to
colonise the Pacific islands.

1300–900 B.C.E.
The Lapita people spread
from the Bismarck Islands to
Samoa and Tonga.

B.C.E.	2000	1900	1800	1700	1600	1500	1400	1300	1200	1100	1000	900	800	700	600	500	400	300	200	100

c. 2000 B.C.E. Asian
people sail from mainland
China and settle on Taiwan.

1300 B.C.E. The Lapita
culture flourishes in the
region of New Guinea.

300 B.C.E. Colonists from
west Polynesia begin to
explore and settle further east.

Above: The hundreds of mournful statues on Easter Island are all that is left of a remarkable civilisation. The people of Easter Island eventually destroyed their own habitat and with it their culture.

Easter Island

Polynesian explorers reach Easter Island in c. 400 C.E.

MIGRATION TO POLYNESIA
c. 2000 B.C.E. – 1000 C.E.

Migration routes of Polynesian ancestors, c. 2000–1500 B.C.E.

→ Migration routes of the Lapita people, c. 1300–900 B.C.E.

→ Migration routes throughout the Polynesian Triangle, 300–1000 C.E.

THE PEOPLE OF MANY ISLANDS

Three thousand years before Columbus ventured across the Atlantic, the ancestors of the Polynesian people were exploring the vast expanse of the Pacific Ocean. Over the course of hundreds of years, these resourceful people discovered and successfully colonised the 1,000 or more islands that fall within the "Polynesian Triangle", made up of Hawaii in the north, Easter Island in the east, and the southernmost tip of New Zealand in the west.

Captain James Cook (1728–1779), who explored the islands of Polynesia in the 18th century, was the first European to note the similarities between the cultures of the various Polynesian peoples. When Cook arrived in New Zealand in 1769, he was astonished to find that a Tahitian priest whom he had brought with him could converse freely with the local Maori people, even though their homelands were separated by 3,200 kilometres (2,000 miles) of ocean. The Maoris and the Tahitians were clearly related culturally as well as linguistically: they had the same gods and myths and they shared many customs, such as the practice of tattooing. Such traditions were also common to the other island peoples of the Polynesian Triangle: the Samoans and Tongans, and the peoples of the Cook and the Marquesas Islands. When did the ancestors of these people come to inhabit these tiny oases of land in the flat emptiness of the Pacific? And where did they hail from originally?

400 C.E. Eastern Polynesian explorers reach Easter Island and Hawaii.

800–1000 New Zealand is colonised, probably by migrants from Tahiti.

1700s European sailors explore Polynesia and Australasia.

| 1 | 100 | 200 | 300 | 400 | 500 | 600 | 700 | 800 | 900 | 1000 | 1100 | 1200 | 1300 | 1400 | 1500 | 1600 | 1700 | 1800 | 1900 | C.E. |

1500 The last statues are erected on Easter Island.

These questions baffled Cook, and they have intrigued ethnographers up to the present day. One of the most ingenious and influential theories put forward to explain the origins of the Polynesian people was suggested by the Norwegian anthropologist Thor Heyerdahl in the 1940s. He proposed that the Polynesians had sailed to the islands of the Pacific from South America, making use of the prevailing winds from the west. He tested the feasibility of this theory by making the journey himself on a balsawood raft in 1947. His voyage was one of the great ethnographic adventures of the 20th century, and Heyerdahl proved that his theory at least belonged in the realm of possibility. Evidence later emerged, however, that proved Heyerdahl's theory wrong. DNA testing, along with a better understanding of archaeological evidence, have proved beyond doubt that the Polynesians came from the east. The starting point of the Polynesian navigators was the mainland of Asia.

The Lapita People

Around 4,000 years ago, a people speaking a language now termed Proto-Oceanic sailed from the southern rim of China to settle in Taiwan. What prompted their eastward migration is unknown, but their talent for sailing has led some scholars to describe these ancestors of the Polynesians as "the Vikings of the rising sun". Keeping the sun to the left of them, colonists from Taiwan spread into the Philippines, and then proceeded southeast to the large island of New Guinea. Here the colonisers must have encountered settled people who were the distant cousins of the Australian Aborigines. The newcomers skirted the northern coast and set sail again, founding communities in the Bismarck Archipelago, a long loop of islands that curves away from the eastern end of New Guinea like a cat's tail. They settled on the islands of Melanesia for some time, and developed a culture – now known as "Lapita" – that is recognised by its pottery. Lapita earthenware is often decorated with geometric designs that are stamped into the wet clay before it is fired.

Perhaps 700 years after leaving the mainland and settling in the islands of Melanesia, the Lapita people were seized by another bout of wanderlust. Over the course of 300 years, they made their way to the Mariana Islands in the north, and travelled as far east as Samoa and Tonga, all the while honing their boatbuilding and navigational skills. They travelled in double-hulled canoes, taking their skills for embossed pottery with them, along with other useful items for colonisation: plants and seeds, livestock such as chickens, and tools. These crossings were not one-way journeys. Archaeological evidence shows that the Lapita style of pottery remained uniform across the zone of colonisation rather than evolving into different styles on different islands. This suggests that the Lapita culture was bound by a network of trade routes that connected the islands to each other.

Settling the Islands of the South Pacific

Some time around 1000 B.C.E., the age of Lapita exploration came to a halt, and the Lapita culture began to fragment. A distinctively Polynesian culture emerged on the islands of Tonga and Samoa. The island people developed seafarer myths, such as the origin myth of the hero Maui who fished up their islands from the depths of the ocean using a magic fishhook. These tales were later transported to newly discovered islands, where they were locally embellished, drawing the territory into the Polynesian cultural orbit.

But the discovery of New Zealand by the Polynesians still lay in the distant future. After another sedentary period of about 700 years, explorers set off from Samoa and Tonga to investigate the islands even further to the east. The navigational expertise required for the expedition was either handed down or was rediscovered by a new generation of sailors – but either way the colonisation of the Cook Islands, Tahiti and the Tuamotus required incredible seafaring skills. The Polynesians had no compasses or navigational instruments. What they did have was an understanding of the complex workings of the ocean, won through years of seagoing experience. Polynesian sailors could examine the swells and eddies of the ocean and know that they were the result of currents swirling around islands out of sight. They were aware that a hidden landmass can have an effect on the shape of the clouds; they could read the stars; and they knew how to follow the migration routes of seabirds from one landfall to another. Like the biblical Noah, the Polynesians also released land birds while at sea and waited to see if they returned to the boat: if they did not come back, they knew that an island must be nearby.

Using these techniques, colonists voyaged as far as Easter Island, the easternmost outpost of the Polynesian Triangle. They must have gone even further still, since at some point the South American sweet potato was introduced to Polynesia. (As it turns out, Heyerdahl was correct in thinking that Polynesian boats could make the journey between the islands of the South Pacific and South America; only South America was their destination rather than their point of embarkation.)

As Polynesian colonists moved further and further east, their way of life began to develop differently from that of

were living on the verge of starvation, and most of them had died out by the end of the century. The same burst of migration that carried some colonists to Easter Island took others north to Hawaii. Here, the ancient Polynesian skill for reading the ocean waves was transformed into the sacred art of *he'henalu* – surfing.

Some time between 800 and 1000 C.E., a final wave of South Sea migration carried the Polynesians to New Zealand. They called the country *aoteoroa*, "the land of the long white cloud" – a name that suggests they had registered New Zealand's meteorological effect long before they ever

> " Both sexes paint their Bodys, Tattow, as it is called in their Language ... The colour they use is lamp black, prepar'd from the Smoak of a Kind of Oily nut, used by them instead of Candles. The instrument for pricking it under the Skin is made of very thin flat pieces of bone or Shell. One end is cut into sharp teeth, and the other fastened to a handle. The teeth are dipped into black Liquor, and then drove, by quick, sharp blows struck upon the handle with a Stick for that purpose, into the skin so deep that every stroke is followed with a small quantity of Blood. The part so marked remains sore for some days before it heals. As this is a painful operation, especially the Tattowing of their Buttocks, it is perform'd but once in their Life times; it is never done until they are 12 or 14 years of Age. "

James Cook on the Polynesian method of tattooing, 1770

their cousins to the west. The peoples of eastern Polynesia lost the art of making pottery, but developed distinctive woodcutting tools and fishhooks. A unique culture took root on Easter Island, the population of which, it seems, was never bolstered by new colonists after the island was initially discovered and settled in around 400 C.E. The isolated Easter Islanders instituted a cult of ancestor worship that led them to build hundreds of sentinel statues. These sinister figures still line the coast of the island today, all of them staring unblinkingly. The statues were, unhappily, the death of the Easter Islanders themselves. During the years that they were erected, all the trees on the island were cut down to make the rollers on which the statues were transported to the coast. The deforestation had a disastrous effect on the ecology of the island. Birds and other animals that needed the trees for food and shelter became extinct, and there was such a lack of wood that the islanders could not make canoes to go sea fishing. When Cook visited the island in 1774, its inhabitants

came in sight of dry land. It is not known exactly where the ancestors of the first New Zealanders came from, but the culture they developed seems to be most closely related to Tahitian traditions. Although Fiji, Samoa and Tonga are closer to New Zealand, the winds and currents in that part of the ocean are such that it may have been easier to get to New Zealand from Tahiti.

Whatever the precise origin of New Zealand's settlers, it is certain that the country was one of the last places on Earth to be peopled. The cool weather, boundless forests, snow-capped mountains, unusual plants and trees, and easily hunted animals – and the sheer immensity of the landmass – would have astonished the Polynesian men and women who were used to life on a tiny subtropical island. In time, however, the newcomers adapted to the climate, as colonisers everywhere had done before them. In time they came to see their changed lives as so normal that they called themselves *maori* – which in the Polynesian dialect of New Zealand means "ordinary".

THE GREEK PHENOMENON

Evolving from numerous competing poleis (self-governing cities), over the course of hundreds of years, many aspects of the Panhellenic culture of the ancient Greeks were taken up by the Romans, who in turn spread them throughout their empire. Ancient Greek culture has also had a strong influence on Western language, philosophy, science, arts and politics.

Below: Silver coins bearing the owl of Athens, like this tetradrachm, were for centuries a symbol of Athenian ascendancy within the Greek world.

Near the beginning of the second millennium B.C.E., speakers of a form of Proto-Greek migrated to the Macedonian peninsula. They found that the region had been populated by various ethnic groups, including migrants from Asia and Asia Minor, who had already given names to settlements and many features of the region. In fact, some of the place names we most associate with Greece are actually "foreign" in origin – they do not have their roots in the Greek language and so indicate that there must have been people living in Macedonia before the Greeks arrived. These names comprise all those that end in "-ssos" and "-inth" (for example, Knossos, Parnassos and Corinth), and also include names such as Olympus, which simply means "high mountain".

The Minoan Civilisation

The first important Greek civilisation arose not on the mainland, but on the large island of Crete. The inhabitants of the island were not Greek but Minoan, a peaceful mercantile people who had also settled on other islands in the Aegean Sea, including Rhodes and Thera (the largest of the small volcanic group of islands called Santorini). By 2000 B.C.E. the Minoans had begun to build the vast palace complex at Knossos around which their government was centred. They had their own form of writing, which was used only for administrative purposes such as keeping account of the king's riches. The writing consisted of symbols representing syllables, and pictograms for certain concepts. It was not until the 1950s that this script, known to scholars as Linear B, was deciphered and proven to be a form of Greek. Until that point it was assumed that the art and architecture of Crete was the work of a people who had migrated to the island from the east. Now it seems more likely that the builders of Knossos were Greek-speakers who conquered the island from the mainland.

The Minoan rulers seem to have maintained diplomatic and trading contact with the Egyptian pharaohs across the Mediterranean Sea, and it is possible that they borrowed their religious veneration of the bull from Egypt. This ritualistic bull-cult, together with the huge mazelike palace, probably gave rise to the well-known Greek myth of the Minotaur: a creature that was part man and part bull and lived in a labyrinth. The story (written down centuries later) tells of Athenians who were brought to Knossos as human sacrifices for the bull god, and many historians interpret

THE GREEK PHENOMENON

c. 1850–1600 B.C.E.
Aeolian and Ionian tribespeople, speakers of an early form of Greek, infiltrate Greece.

B.C.E.	3000	2900	2800	2700	2600	2500	2400	2300	2200	2100	2000	1900	1800	1700	1600

c. 3000 B.C.E. Migrant people from Asia Minor occupy the Greek mainland and Crete.

c. 1700–1380 B.C.E.
The Minoan civilisation flourishes on Crete.

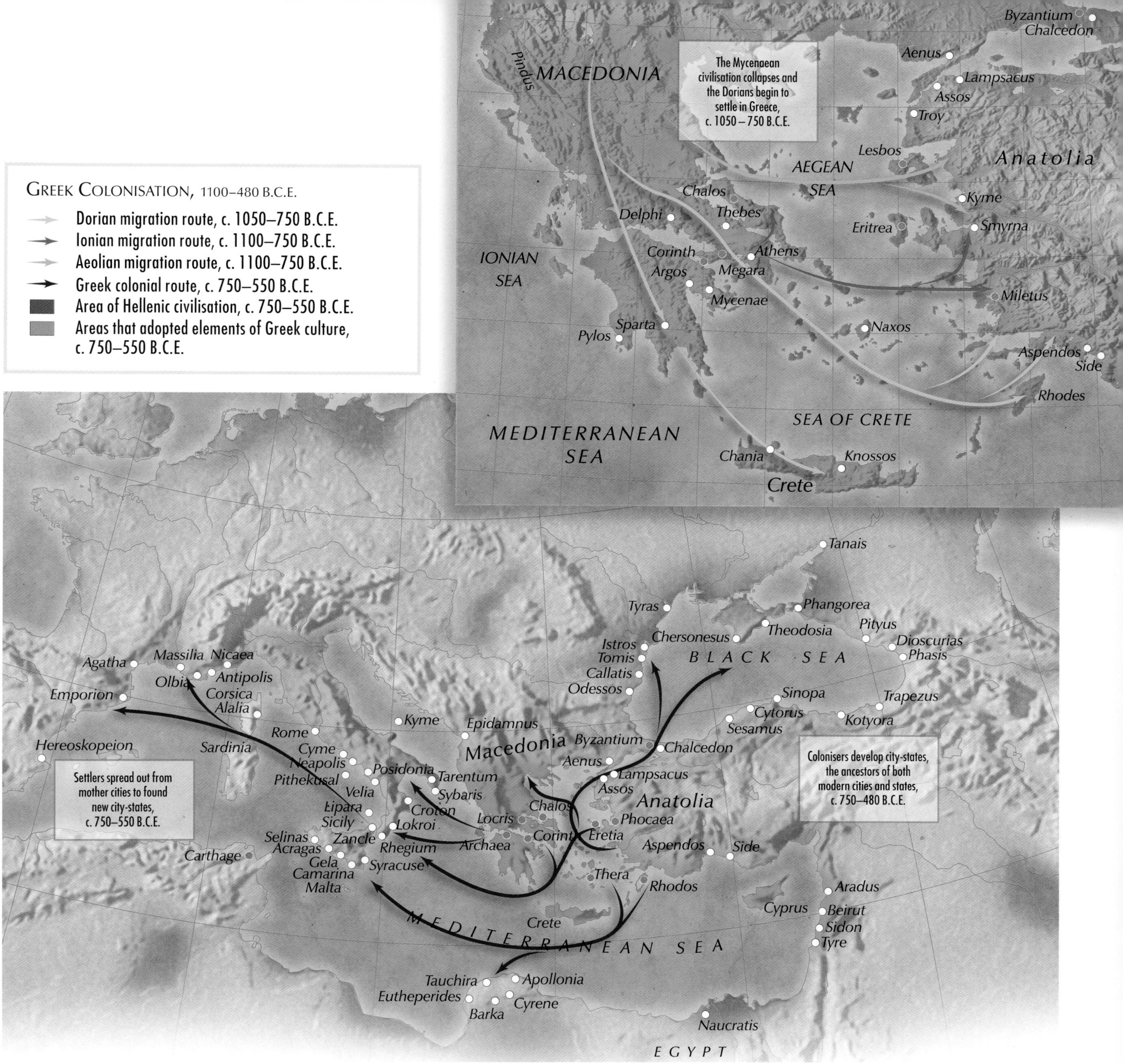

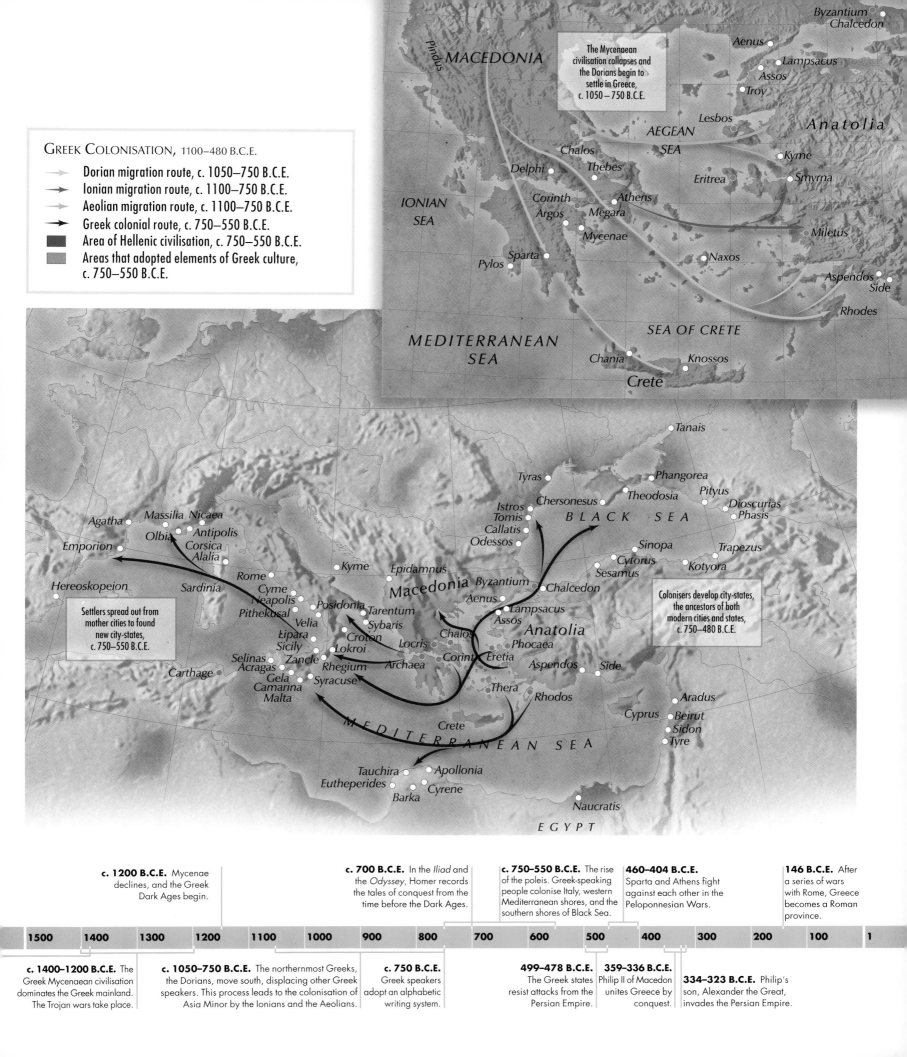

GREEK COLONISATION, 1100–480 B.C.E.
Dorian migration route, c. 1050–750 B.C.E.
Ionian migration route, c. 1100–750 B.C.E.
Aeolian migration route, c. 1100–750 B.C.E.
Greek colonial route, c. 750–550 B.C.E.
Area of Hellenic civilisation, c. 750–550 B.C.E.
Areas that adopted elements of Greek culture, c. 750–550 B.C.E.
The Mycenaean civilisation collapses and the Dorians begin to settle in Greece, c. 1050 – 750 B.C.E.
MACEDONIA
Pindus
Byzantium
Chalcedon
Aenus
Lampsacus
Assos
Troy
Lesbos
AEGEAN SEA
Anatolia
Kyme
Smyrna
Eritrea
Chalos
Thebes
Delphi
IONIAN SEA
Corinth
Argos
Megara
Athens
Mycenae
Miletus
Naxos
Sparta
Pylos
Aspendos
Side
Rhodes
SEA OF CRETE
MEDITERRANEAN SEA
Chania
Knossos
Crete
Settlers spread out from mother cities to found new city-states, c. 750–550 B.C.E.
Colonisers develop city-states, the ancestors of both modern cities and states, c. 750–480 B.C.E.
Tanais
Tyras
Phangorea
Theodosia
Chersonesus
Pityus
Dioscurias
Phasis
Istros
Tomis
Callatis
Odessos
BLACK SEA
Sinopa
Cytorus
Sesamus
Trapezus
Kotyora
Agatha
Massilia
Nicaea
Olbia
Antipolis
Corsica
Alalia
Emporion
Hereoskopeion
Sardinia
Rome
Kyme
Epidamnus
Macedonia
Byzantium
Chalcedon
Aenus
Lampsacus
Assos
Anatolia
Cyme
Neapolis
Pithekusai
Posidonia
Tarentum
Sybaris
Velia
Lipara
Croton
Sicily
Locris
Chalos
Phocaea
Lokroi
Eretia
Corinth
Selinas
Zancle
Acragas
Archaea
Aspendos
Side
Carthage
Rhegium
Gela
Syracuse
Camarina
Thera
Rhodos
Malta
Aradus
Cyprus
Beirut
Sidon
Crete
Tyre
MEDITERRANEAN SEA
Tauchira
Apollonia
Eutheperides
Cyrene
Barka
Naucratis
EGYPT

1500	1400	1300	1200	1100	1000	900	800	700	600	500	400	300	200	100	1

c. 1400–1200 B.C.E. The Greek Mycenaean civilisation dominates the Greek mainland. The Trojan wars take place.

c. 1200 B.C.E. Mycenae declines, and the Greek Dark Ages begin.

c. 1050–750 B.C.E. The northernmost Greeks, the Dorians, move south, displacing other Greek speakers. This process leads to the colonisation of Asia Minor by the Ionians and the Aeolians.

c. 750 B.C.E. Greek speakers adopt an alphabetic writing system.

c. 700 B.C.E. In the *Iliad* and the *Odyssey*, Homer records the tales of conquest from the time before the Dark Ages.

c. 750–550 B.C.E. The rise of the poleis. Greek-speaking people colonise Italy, western Mediterranean shores, and the southern shores of Black Sea.

499–478 B.C.E. The Greek states resist attacks from the Persian Empire.

460–404 B.C.E. Sparta and Athens fight against each other in the Peloponnesian Wars.

359–336 B.C.E. Philip II of Macedon unites Greece by conquest.

334–323 B.C.E. Philip's son, Alexander the Great, invades the Persian Empire.

146 B.C.E. After a series of wars with Rome, Greece becomes a Roman province.

this as evidence that the ruling Minoans received tribute from other Greek communities.

It is not known why the Minoan civilisation fell, although Crete may well have been badly affected by the devastating eruption of a volcano on Thera, c. 1500 B.C.E. It is more likely that the peaceable Minoans were conquered c. 1380 B.C.E. by the Myceneans, who lived on the mainland in the north, and whose civilisation flourished between 1400 B.C.E. and 1200 B.C.E. Their weapons and fortifications show that the Myceneans were a more warlike people than the Minoans. The city of Mycenae was the historical setting of the epics of Homer, which, like the Minotaur myth, were recorded some 700 years after the events that inspired them. In the *Iliad*, Homer states that Mycenae was ruled by Agamemnon, a Greek monarch who was commander-in-chief in the war against Troy. Although there is no other evidence to suggest that the Greek peoples united to fight the Trojans, it is certain that there were great and powerful kings in Mycenae.

The Greek Dark Ages

The exact cause of the decline of the Mycenaean civilisation is unclear, but archaeological evidence reveals that in about 1200 B.C.E. cities across the Greek world were ravaged by fire. Alternatively, the disaster may have been manmade – the result of a war or a seagoing "barbarian" invasion from the east. Troy and Miletus in Anatolia (on the west coast of modern Turkey), Chania on Crete, and Thebes, Mycenae, Pylos, Menelaion and Korakou on the mainland were all ruined. Knossos, the cradle of Greek civilisation, seems to have been destroyed at an earlier date than other cities – but the events leading to this are also obscure.

Following the decline of the Minoans and Mycenaeans, Greece entered a so-called "Dark Age" that lasted for 300 years. Very little is known about this period of Greek history, but what has been deduced with some degree of certainty is that the population of Greece was much reduced, cities and farming were abandoned as people reverted to a pastoral way of life, and the knowledge of writing was lost completely. It is also known that the Dark Ages were a time of migration. Greek-speaking people known as the Dorians, who occupied the Macedonian north, began to move to the south and settle in new areas. The people that they displaced – the Ionians and Aeolians, who, along with the Dorians, were known as the Hellenes – also moved south towards the Mediterranean Sea. Those nearest to the sea took to ships and fanned out through the Aegean islands, sailed back to Crete once more, or pushed on to the eastern

Left: The ritual sport of bull-leaping was a key element of Minoan civilisation. It is not clear what it meant, how it was done or who participated. Most likely, it was a rite of passage for young noblemen. In this fresco, the red figure is male (as is usual in Minoan painting) and the white "bull dancers" are female.

end of the Mediterranean and set up Greek settlements in Asia Minor.

The "domino effect" of this people movement was noted by Herodotus (484–c. 425 B.C.E.), the "father of history". In *The Histories*, written 500 years after the migrations, Herodotus states: "The Spartans were the most eminent of the Dorian peoples, and they were much given to wandering. In the reign of Deucalion they dwelt in Pthithos, and in the age of Doros, son of Hellen, they were in the land lying below Ossa and Olympus. They settled in [the mountains of] Pindos and became known as Macedonians; then they migrated to the Peloponnese, which is where they began to be called Dorians". The changing name of the migrants refers to the successive displacements of people.

Herodotus's account – the first historical report of European migration – was treated with reservation by 19th-century classicists, but the latest thinking is that Herodotus's version of events is fairly accurate: migrants from the north

were the impetus behind the repopulation of Greece in the Dark Ages, and then of the colonisation of the Aegean islands. Migrant groups infiltrated rather than conquered, and they probably made good use of sites and cities abandoned after the collapse of Mycenaean civilisation. By the end of the Dark Ages there were Greek-speaking peoples throughout the islands of the Aegean Sea and all around the surrounding coastline.

Another civilisation that had an important influence on Greek culture was that of the Phoenicians, who came from the eastern end of the Mediterranean Sea. A trading people, they colonised several areas of the Mediterranean, including North Africa, where they founded the ancient city of Carthage. Although the Phoenicians left few written records, their alphabet was adopted by the Greeks.

The Rise of the City-State
Some of the settlements that emerged from the Dark Ages, for example those in Anatolia, were far from the Greek

homeland and vulnerable to attack from neighbouring peoples. To protect themselves, the colonists in these far-flung places built up defensive walls around their cities. Within these boundaries, populations began to develop a strong sense of community and self-reliance. This inward-looking civic attitude led to the development of the poleis, the classic Greek city-state – a notion born outside Greece by colonisers, but then exported back to the Hellenic heartland. Although they were largely independent, individual poleis were bound together by a shared language and culture: citizens knew that they were Smyrnans or Athenians, but they were also very aware that above all they were Greeks. This sense of Greek unity was strengthened by the spread of writing (a highly economical alphabet, far better suited to the Greek tongue than the syllabic Linear B, was adopted shortly after the end of the Dark Ages) and by pan-Hellenic events such as the Olympic games, which were first held in 776 B.C.E.

After 750 B.C.E., many of the stronger poleis (with the notable exception of Athens) began to seed new communities elsewhere. The process of setting up a new colony involved first designating a leader. The chosen individual was called the *oikistes*, which roughly translates as "head settler". The *oikistes* would gather together a group of settlers from the "mother city" – the metropolis – but Greeks from other places were also free to join, and because of the cultural cohesion of the Greek world, they had no trouble fitting in. Many poleis were established in places that would be useful as trade hubs, or where the colonists could produce goods for the metropolis, such as wool, metal, timber and grain.

The establishment of new poleis spread Greek culture all over the known world, most significantly in the country now known as Italy. A Greek settlement called Neapolis – "new city" – eventually evolved into the city of Naples, and the Greeks had a settlement close to the site of Rome in the 8th century B.C.E., not long after the date when, according to tradition, it was founded by the brothers Romulus and Remus. By 500 B.C.E., the Greek settlements had spread around the Mediterranean. The Ionian colony at Massalia became the French city of Marseille, and at the mouth of the Black Sea, Dorian colonists founded the Greek-speaking colony that eventually became Byzantium. Even today the modern name of Byzantium bears witness to its Greek roots: the word "Istanbul" is a corruption of the Greek phrase *eis ten polin* – "to the city". There were also Greek colonies in Sicily, North Africa, and at the far end of the Black Sea.

The founding of poleis continued for 200 years, with colonies being settled as far east as Asia Minor and as far northeast as present-day Ukraine. The Greeks were also not averse to waging war to gain territory. All male citizens had to complete compulsory military service, and city-states periodically fought among themselves. However, their greatest warrior king was Alexander the Great (r. 336–323 B.C.E.), king of Macedon. In the 4th century B.C.E., Alexander led an army of the unified city-states in a war against the Persian Empire. The campaign took him to Egypt, through Phoenicia and Mesopotamia, on to Central Asia, into Punjab, and along the entire coastline of the Persian Gulf and the Arabian Sea. Many of the garrisons he left behind developed into the major cities of the eastern Greek world (Alexandria is just one such example). After his early death in 323 B.C.E., Alexander's successors established Greek cities in lower Mesopotomaia and the Levant as both a means of controlling the region and as a source of soldiers.

When Alexander the Great died, a new major power, Rome, was rising in the west. The Romans borrowed much from the culture of the Greeks who had settled in Italy: the Latin alphabet was adapted from the Greek alphabet and the Greek gods were adopted wholesale, as was Greek science and philosophy. But their respect for Greek culture did not prevent the Romans from attacking Greece itself. In 200 B.C.E. the Romans declared war on Macedonia, and the ensuing conflict continued periodically for the next 50 years. Macedonia was reduced to a Roman province in 150 B.C.E., and the remaining Greek cities were absorbed by Rome in 146 B.C.E. The Greek age was over, and the Roman age was about to begin.

Above: The geometric designs on early Greek vases may be borrowed from the patterns on West Asian textiles. If so, such pottery is evidence of cultural contact and trade between Greece and Asia Minor.

ROME AND ITS EMPIRE

At its peak, the Roman Empire controlled approximately 5.9 million square kilometres (2.3 million square miles) of land. As its borders steadily expanded, colonists from the imperial centre were distributed through the conquered lands. These communities, which promulgated the traditions and policies of Rome, served to spread the influence of Roman rule.

Below: A standard-issue Roman legionary's helmet, dating from the 1st century C.E. Retired legionaries often settled down and lived as farmers in far-flung outposts of the Roman Empire. They were the vanguard of colonisation.

According to Roman tradition, the Roman people are descendants of the Trojan hero Aeneas. As told in the *Aeneid*, written by Virgil in the 1st century B.C.E., Aeneas escaped from the sack of Troy at the end of the Trojan War and travelled – after many adventures – to Latium in Italy, where he founded the royal dynasty that eventually gave rise to the twin brothers Romulus and Remus. Approximately 650 years before the birth of Julius Caesar (r. 49–44 B.C.E.), the twins are said to have founded a city on the west bank of the Tiber River. Centred on the Palatine Hill, this city was named for the older of the two brothers: it was called Roma.

It is perhaps no coincidence that Aeneas is portrayed in Roman mythology as a warrior-turned-colonist. From the time that Rome became a republic at the start of the 6th century B.C.E. until its peak as a world empire 800 years later, Rome protected its borders by the only means at its disposal. It conquered the hostile foreign tribes on the fringes of its territory and then settled the newly-won region with loyal migrants from its heartland. This system became a never-ending process of territorial acquisition, as whenever the Romans absorbed a land and tamed its people, there were usually new enemies beyond the new frontier. However, the driving force behind the expansion of the Roman Empire came not just from the necessity of protecting its conquered territories, but also the continuing need of the military elite to gain military glory in order to further their political careers and personal fortunes.

The Romans invade Britannia in 43 C.E.

CALEDONIA

HIBERNIA

BRITANNIA

Londinium

ATLANTIC OCEAN

GALLI

TRANSALPIN

PROVINCIA

Caesaraugusta   Narbo   Mass

HISPANIA   Barcelor
Tarraco

Seville

Gades   Carthago Nova

MAURETANIA

THE RISE OF ROME

753 B.C.E. According to Roman tradition, Rome is founded by Romulus and Remus.

c. 616 B.C.E. Rome is ruled by Etruscan kings.

c. 400 B.C.E. Rome is engaged in the subjugation of the Etruscans.

B.C.E.	800	750	700	650	600	550	500	450	400	350

c. 800 B.C.E. There is an Iron Age settlement on the Palatine Hill.

510 B.C.E. The Roman Republic is established under two annually elected consuls.

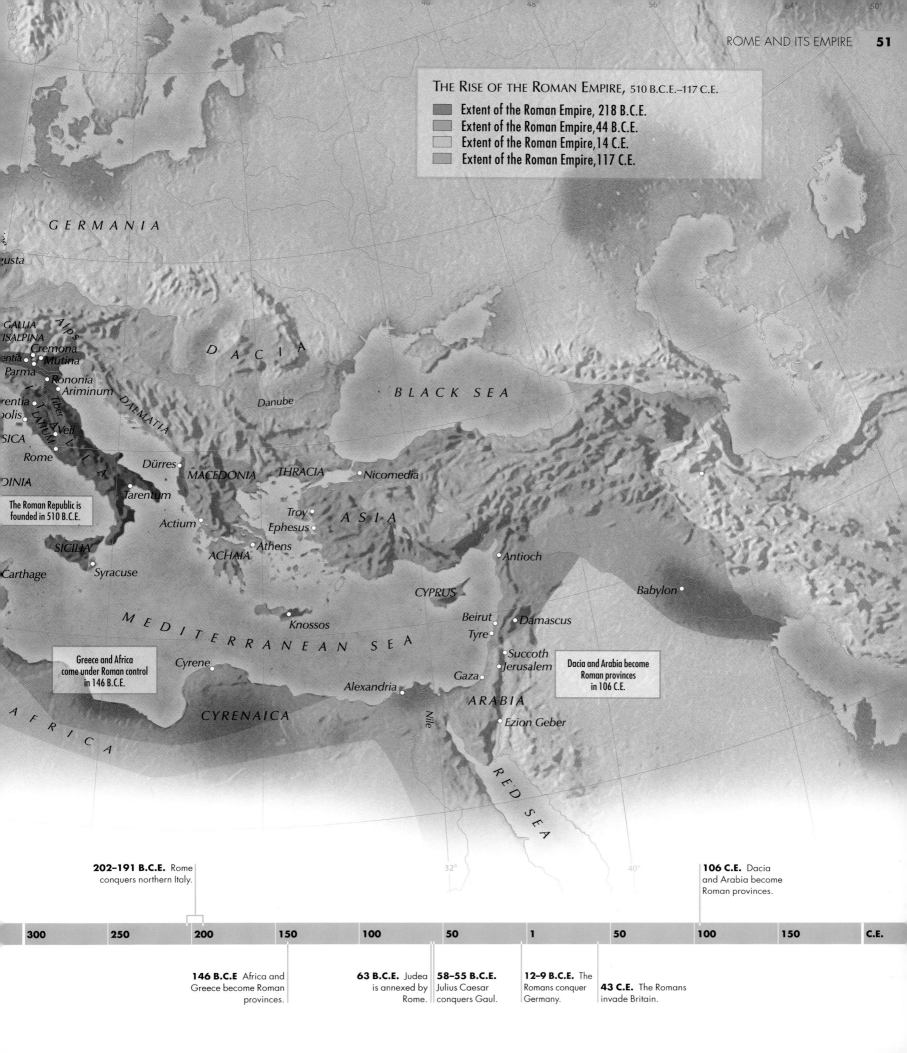

THE RISE OF THE ROMAN EMPIRE, 510 B.C.E.–117 C.E.

Extent of the Roman Empire, 218 B.C.E.
Extent of the Roman Empire, 44 B.C.E.
Extent of the Roman Empire, 14 C.E.
Extent of the Roman Empire, 117 C.E.

GERMANIA

GALLIA
CISALPINA
Cremona
Mutina
entia
Parma
Rononia
Ariminum
rentia
polis
Tiber
Veii
SICA
Rome
DINIA

DACIA

Danube

BLACK SEA

Nicomedia

Dürres
MACEDONIA
THRACIA

The Roman Republic is
founded in 510 B.C.E.

Tarentum

Actium

Troy
Ephesus
Athens

ASIA

ACHAIA

SICILIA

Syracuse

Carthage

Antioch

CYPRUS

Babylon

Knossos

Beirut
Tyre

Damascus

MEDITERRANEAN SEA

Greece and Africa
come under Roman control
in 146 B.C.E.

Cyrene

Succoth
Jerusalem
Gaza

Dacia and Arabia become
Roman provinces
in 106 C.E.

Alexandria

Nile

ARABIA

CYRENAICA

Ezion Geber

AFRICA

RED SEA

202–191 B.C.E. Rome
conquers northern Italy.

106 C.E. Dacia
and Arabia become
Roman provinces.

| 300 | 250 | 200 | 150 | 100 | 50 | 1 | 50 | 100 | 150 | C.E. |

146 B.C.E Africa and
Greece become Roman
provinces.

63 B.C.E. Judea
is annexed by
Rome.

58–55 B.C.E.
Julius Caesar
conquers Gaul.

12–9 B.C.E. The
Romans conquer
Germany.

43 C.E. The Romans
invade Britain.

The Roman Republic was founded in 510 B.C.E., when the city's inhabitants threw off the domination of the Etruscan kings. At that time, the republic governed a hinterland that consisted of around 900 square kilometres (350 square miles) of farmland, and even then, Rome was surrounded by enemies. The Etruscans controlled a network of cities across the region that is present-day Tuscany, Celtic tribes were positioned in the north, the Samnites were in the southeast, and Greek outposts were located in the far south and on the island of Sicily. The Romans won their first major victory over the Etruscans at Veii in 396 B.C.E., and were in control of all of Latium by 340 B.C.E. This brought them into conflict with the Samnites, whom they subdued over the course of three separate wars. A century after the battle at Veii, Rome was in control of the whole width of the Italian peninsula as far south as Naples.

Even at this early stage, the Romans had strategic systems in place to consolidate their gains. They founded colonies in conquered lands and built roads to connect these communities with Rome and other strong points. At the end of a successful conflict the military would first neutralise local opponents of Roman rule by negotiating with the local aristocracy. The civil authorities would also requisition one-third of the conquered territory and hand it over to colonists, who drew lots for plots of land. The colonists would then set about creating a mini-Rome in their new community by erecting civic buildings in the Roman style and installing local governments modelled on that in Rome. Some colonies appointed a magistrate who functioned as an autonomous mayor or governor; others, generally those closest to the capital, were nominally under the aegis of a magistrate in Rome itself – a practice that tended to reinforce the colonists' sense of allegiance to the state.

In the 3rd century B.C.E., Rome extended its influence to the southern tip of Italy. This brought the Romans into conflict with the seagoing empire of Carthage, which claimed ownership of Sicily and was the dominant power in the Mediterranean. In a series of conflicts known as the Punic Wars (264–146 B.C.E.), the Romans defeated the Carthaginians and destroyed Carthage. At the same time, the Roman legions were also pushing north. They ejected or absorbed the Celts who were settled in the Po valley, and established their own colonies: Ariminum (modern-day Rimini) was founded in 268 B.C.E., Cremona in 218 B.C.E. and Parma in 183 B.C.E. By the end of this period of colonisation, the whole of the Italian peninsula was united under Rome, and the border of the Roman state had been extended to a natural boundary: the Alps. All the people of Gallia Cisalpina ("Gaul this side of the Alps") were entirely assimilated as Romans within two or three generations.

The Veteran Colonists

By the 3rd century B.C.E., Rome also had several colonies outside Italy – many of them an incidental consequence of the Punic Wars. The first attempted Roman colony abroad, Colonia Junonia, built in the ruins of the city of Carthage, was unsuccessful. In the Second Punic War (218–202 B.C.E.), the Roman general Scipio Africanus (235–183 B.C.E.) led his troops into the Carthaginian territory of Spain, and at the end of the campaign, left some wounded veterans in a makeshift community near Seville. The Roman Senate later gave their approval for the establishment of a semi-Roman settlement in Spain consisting of the offspring of these Roman soldiers and Spanish women. In the 2nd century B.C.E., more veterans, as well as other Roman citizens, were drawn to Spain by the discovery of silver mines. Slaves could be bought cheaply and made to work as miners, and with luck a demobilised soldier could grow rich.

Army veterans were central to the process of migration and colonisation during the next great period of Roman expansion, which began under Julius Caesar but was at its peak under his successor, Augustus Caesar (r. 27 B.C.E.–14 C.E.). The term of service in the Roman army was 20 or 25 years, and a soldier's life was hard. Compulsory conscription, however, was not found to be necessary, as there were plenty of poor, rural volunteers who were motivated to sign up for service by the prospect of regular pay, the prestige that comes with

Below: The Pont du Gard, an astonishing feat of Roman engineering, still stands 2,000 years after it was built. It is an aqueduct and was constructed to carry water from natural springs to the Roman city of Nemausus (the modern city of Nîmes).

promotion, and the hope of a pension in the form of a grant of land at the end of their service. The land was often located in the Roman province in which the soldier had served, usually some distance from Italy. Although serving soldiers were not allowed to marry, many had "unofficial" wives and families where they were posted, so most were happy to remain in the area once their service was completed. We know from the headstones put up by sons and widows that many of these ex-army farmers did well for themselves. More importantly, they acted as a strong Roman presence in the provinces – both an advertisement for the empire and a veiled threat to would-be insurgents. They also left behind them children who, through their fathers, had acquired the significant benefit of Roman citizenship, although veterans' sons were expected to be available for military service.

The *Coloniae*

Land for veterans was apportioned in the region of a main settlement. This could be an army garrison that, with its accretions of markets, taverns, brothels and temples, might slowly metamorphose into a town. Otherwise, Roman veterans might settle in the region of an established town that had originally been founded by the conquered people. Such places were often granted the official status of a Roman *colonia*, which conferred certain rights on its citizens. Colonists were, for example, freed from the obligation to pay certain taxes, and had the right to return and settle in Rome itself if they chose. One German colony that achieved such status had the long-winded designation Colonia Claudia Ara Agrippinensium, meaning "Claudian colony which is near the altar of the Agrippinenses". The town survived the fall of Rome in the 5th century, but the Roman word *colonia* gradually became its proper name. The Latin word is still visible in its corrupted German form "Köln", and in the purer French form "Cologne".

Julius Caesar established the legal framework within which veteran colonies were subsequently founded, although it was actually the emperor Augustus who founded most of the first settlements, both for his own veterans and for the dispossessed of Italy – young men who had drifted into the city rather than the army. From his point of view, the benefit of these "civilian" colonies was that they reduced the size of the volatile Roman mob. The military colonies set up by Augustus were spread around the Roman world, and include Lyon in France, the Swiss town of Augst (which clearly bears the emperor's name), Barcelona in Spain, Syracuse in Sicily, Knossos in Crete, and Beirut in Lebanon. About 400 towns are known to have been granted the status of *colonia*. The practice continued long after the Augustan age. One of the last towns to become a *colonia* was Nicomedia – the present-day Izmit in Turkey – which was given the title by the emperor Diocletian in around 300 C.E.

Left: Hadrian's Wall marks the northern boundary of Roman influence in Europe. It was built between 122 and 132 C.E. and was manned more or less constantly until the Romans abandoned Britain in the 5th century.

The Romans did not need to go to great lengths to Romanise the original populations of the *coloniae* as the benefits of "going Roman" were so extensive. The children of the defeated peoples understood that, if they were ambitious, speaking Latin and adopting Roman manners were essential to establishing a career within the ruling regime. The colonial communities of Rome had a decentralising effect wherever they took root. Gauls in Narbo (modern-day Narbonne), Spaniards in Caesaraugusta (Zaragoza), and Britons in Londinium (London) assimilated to Roman ways without leaving their native lands. They became Gallo-Romans, Hispano-Romans and Romano-British, and within a couple of generations could easily have held a conversation in Latin with each other.

The cultural unity of the Roman world outlived the political structures of the empire, and the people of former Roman provinces remained Roman long after Roman rule had ceased. They carried on speaking Latin in most of the countries that had belonged to the Western Empire (in the Eastern Empire, Greek had always been the preferred tongue). The language of the Romans did not ever die out – modern Italian is living Latin, and the everyday Latin of the empire has also survived in such languages as French, Spanish, Portuguese and Romanian. These languages are descended from the various local dialects in which Roman soldiers, merchants and colonists spoke to each other – and to their neighbours, the Gauls, Iberians and Dacians, who wanted to benefit from the security and prosperity that Rome had to offer.

THE MEDIEVAL WORLD

I n the 1,000 years following the fall of the Roman Empire, the act of migration was for the most part a violent affair. Migrants were by definition invaders, and the mass relocation of peoples was almost always an effect of war. Beginning in the late 4th century, Asiatic and Germanic tribes began to displace each other steadily, moving west from the eastern steppe until they eventually broke through Rome's imperial walls. The effects of this cultural upheaval were still being felt when the Islamic religion first emerged in the Arabian desert. Islam's message was spread by invasion, settlement and diplomacy, and rapidly became a powerful new force in world politics and human spirituality. At the end of the 8th century, the next major wave of migrants, the seaborne Vikings, were driven from their Scandinavian homeland by a desire for wealth and land. They took to the open water and travelled as far west as North America, and as far east as Kiev and Byzantium. Several hundred years later, Kiev, 'the mother of Russian cities', was one of many that was destroyed and plundered by the unstoppable cavalry of the Mongol hordes – the last and most terrible of the medieval invaders to emerge from the Asian steppeland.

Left: The Catalan Atlas, created by Abraham and Jehuda Cresque in 1375, is considered one of the finest works in medieval cartography. This detail shows a camel train making its way along the Silk Road in Central Asia.

DESCENT OF THE BARBARIANS

In the twilight years of the Roman Empire, Germanic and Asiatic tribes began to uproot and seek new homes elsewhere. The cause of this widespread restlessness remains unknown, but the influence it had on the ethnicity and languages of Europe is still evident today.

Below: The votive crown of King Recesvinth, ruler of the Visigoths in Spain in the 7th century. Rich and sophisticated objects such as this illustrate that the Germanic 'barbarians' were anything but savages.

In the middle of the 4th century C.E., Rome was the only superpower in the world, and the borders of its empire had remained largely unchanged for 200 years. In the north, the boundary was marked by the Rhine and the Danube rivers, and by Hadrian's Wall, which separated Roman Britain from the shaggy, unconquered uplands of Caledonia (modern Scotland). In the east the empire abutted the Sassanid (Persian) Empire at the southeastern tip of the Black Sea. In the south, Rome controlled the entire coast of North Africa from Egypt to Mauritania, and in the west, all of Gaul and Iberia were firmly in Roman hands.

The only substantial loss that the empire had suffered since the reign of Marcus Aurelius (r. 161–180) was Dacia, a province on the northern bank of the Danube, where Romania is today. During a period of political anarchy within the empire in the late 3rd century, it had been abandoned by the Roman legion and occupied by a Germanic people, the Visigoths (that is, western Goths). This internal turmoil had prompted a reorganisation of the empire. In 286, the Emperor Diocletian (r. 284–305) split the unwieldy imperial monolith into four administrative regions, two in the Latin-speaking west, and two in the Greek-speaking east. His successor, Constantine I (r. 306–337), established a new capital in the eastern half of the empire and named this 'second Rome' after himself: Constantinople, or 'Constantine's city'.

CALEDONIA

HIBERNIA

The Angles and Saxons begin to settle in Britain in 450.

ATLANTIC OCEAN

VISIGOTH KINGDOM

LUSITANIA

IBERIA

The Vandals invade Spain in 409.

THE SPREAD OF THE BARBARIANS

330 Constantine establishes a new Roman capital at Constantinople (modern-day Istanbul).

376 The Visigoth tribe crosses the Danube and settles inside the Roman Empire.

406 On New Year's Eve, large numbers of Vandals and Sueves cross the Rhine into Gaul.

409 The Vandals devastate Spain.

429 The Vandals cross into North Africa and establish a capital at Carthage.

452 The Huns invade Italy.

C.E.	300	310	320	330	340	350	360	370	380	390	400	410	420	430	440	450

378 Rome is defeated by Visigoths at the Battle of Adrianople.

370 The Ostrogoths are driven west by the Huns into Visigoth territory.

410 The Romans withdraw from Britain.

410 The Visigoths sack Rome.

435 Attila becomes king of the Huns.

450 The Angles and Saxons begin their conquest of Britain.

455 The Vandals sack Rome.

THE SPREAD OF THE BARBARIANS
300–500 C.E.

→ Hunnic invasion routes

→ Visigoth invasion routes

→ Vandal invasion routes

→ Frankish invasion routes

→ Angle and Saxon invasion routes

▢ Extent of Roman Empire, 300

- - - Border between the Western and Eastern Roman Empires

BALTIC SEA

NORTH SEA

River Rhine

HUNNIC EMPIRE

River Volga

FRANKISH KINGDOM

DACIA

River Danube

The Huns attack the Ostrogoths in 376.

GAUL

OSTROGOTHIC KINGDOM

MOESIA
Adrianople

BLACK SEA

CASPIAN SEA

The Visigoths invade Rome in 410.

Rome

The Visigoths attack the Romans at the Battle of Adrianople in 378.

WESTERN ROMAN EMPIRE

Constantinople

The Vandals invade Rome in 455.

EASTERN ROMAN (BYZANTINE) EMPIRE

Carthage

SASSANID (PERSIAN) EMPIRE

VANDAL KINGDOM

MEDITERRANEAN SEA

ARABIA

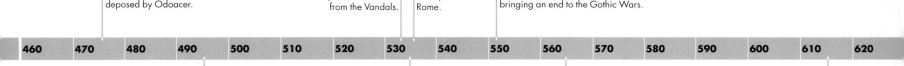

476 Romulus Augustulus, the last Roman emperor, is deposed by Odoacer.

533 Justinian I reconquers North Africa from the Vandals.

536 Justinian I recaptures Rome.

552 Justinian I defeats the Ostrogoths and reinstates imperial rule in Italy, bringing an end to the Gothic Wars.

| 460 | 470 | 480 | 490 | 500 | 510 | 520 | 530 | 540 | 550 | 560 | 570 | 580 | 590 | 600 | 610 | 620 |

495 Clovis, King of the Franks, converts to Christianity.

535 The Gothic War begins, in which Justinian I tries to win back the provinces of Italy lost to the Ostrogoths.

565 Justinian I dies and is succeeded by his nephew, Justin II.

c. 615 The Anglo-Saxon settlement of England is completed.

Occupation and Displacement

By about 100 years later the borders of the Roman Empire were growing increasingly porous. The Visigoths and other Germanic tribes to the north were clamouring for admission to the empire as settlers. These barbarians, as they were known, were not the savages that the modern sense of the word implies: the term 'barbarian' merely meant foreigner. But many of the German barbarians had served Rome as mercenaries, and were thoroughly Romanised. They felt as entitled to the benefits of Roman civilisation, namely social mobility and access to goods, as the citizens within its borders, and they were prepared to fight for these benefits. Raids across the Rhine and Danube were a common occurrence, and a mighty clash of arms seemed inevitable.

Below: Justinian I (in the centre, surrounded by his courtiers) depicted in a mosaic in the Basilica of San Vitale in Ravenna, Italy. Justinian won Italy back from the Ostrogoths in 552, consolidating the Eastern Roman Empire.

When calamity finally came, however, it was from a different direction. A new force in world politics emerged unexpectedly in the east, when warlike nomads – the Huns – appeared on the nearby shores of the Caspian Sea. The Huns had been disturbed by political upheaval in China, which prompted them to migrate west from the flatlands of Mongolia. In 376 the Huns left their Caspian base and attacked the Ostrogoths, the eastern kinsmen of the Visigoths. In response to this attack, the Ostrogoths fled west, driving the Visigoths ahead of them.

The pattern of occupation and displacement acted out by the Germanic barbarians was a recurrent one in this time of wandering nations. Peoples moved en masse, forcing a neighbouring ethnic group to move on themselves and so oust their own neighbour. Eventually, the wave of displaced migrants reached the walls of the Roman Empire, and they began to crumble under the pressure.

Following the Ostrogoths' attack, the leaders of the Visigoths turned to Rome for protection, petitioning the emperor for permission to cross the Danube and take refuge in Moesia (roughly, modern Bulgaria). Permission was reluctantly granted but, as it would on countless subsequent occasions in history, a refugee crisis soon turned into a conflict. The Roman authorities were not equipped to cope with such an influx of new Germanic citizens, and housing and food shortages caused trouble to flare between the Visigoths and the Romans who were policing them. This strife quickly escalated into all-out war, with disastrous consequences for Rome. In 378, angry Visigoths attacked and overwhelmingly defeated the Roman legions at the Battle of Adrianople. Nothing could now stop the western Goths from pushing into the Roman Empire. Thousands of Ostrogoths followed in their wake, as the Huns continued to advance behind them.

The Advance on Rome

After their victory at Adrianople, the Visigoths constituted a dangerous presence inside the dominion of Rome. In 395 they elected a new king, Alaric I (r. 395–410). Until recently Alaric had been a soldier in the service of Rome, acting as a general in an army of German mercenaries. Characteristically for this period, once Rome stopped paying for his services, Alaric's loyalty ceased, and he switched allegiance and fought against the Roman Empire.

Right: Hagia Sophia, built under the supervision of Emperor Justinian I in 537, was considered the jewel of the Eastern Roman Empire. It is one of the greatest surviving examples of Byzantine architecture.

Alaric went on to plunder Macedonia and Greece, where he was opposed by a Roman general named Stilicho (c. 359–408) who, just as characteristically, was also of German stock. From here, in the first years of the 5th century, Alaric turned to the west and led his people into Italy.

The Visigoth invasion of Italy was a profound shock to the Roman authorities. The encroaching barbarians were no longer merely a problem on the distant frontiers of the empire; suddenly they were in the imperial heartland. Their invasion had immediate and dramatic consequences in the northern borderlands of the empire. Troops were withdrawn from the Rhine to bolster the defence of Italy. This tactical move was intended to be a temporary expedient, but it had long-lasting effects. In the deep winter of 406–407, Germanic tribes took advantage of the decreased defences and crossed the frozen Rhine in vast numbers.

Part of this alien wave was made up of Vandals, an eastern German people. They swept through Gaul and down into the Iberian Peninsula, marauding as they went and earning a reputation that made them a byword for wanton destruction. 'The whole of Gaul is smoking like an enormous funeral pyre,' wrote one witness of the Vandals' advance. Within a generation, the Vandals had crossed the Straits of Gibraltar into Africa, leaving nothing behind them but their name: southern Iberia became known as Vandalicia, which the Moors of North Africa pronounced Andalusia.

Moving south side by side with the Vandals were the Sueves, who settled in the western part of the Iberian Peninsula and established a kingdom called Lusitania, which is roughly equivalent to modern Portugal. The land vacated by the Vandals and Sueves was occupied by the Franks in the late 5th century, who established a confederation that subsequently evolved into the so-called Holy Roman

Below: The Battersea Shield was dredged from the River Thames at Battersea Bridge, London, England, in 1857. It is thought that this Celtic artifact was deposited as a ritual gift to the spirits of the river.

Empire in 843. Some Franks became Gallicised but continued to call themselves Frankish (that is, *Français*, or French); others retained their German speech and called themselves simply the *diot* – 'the people' – which is the root of the modern German word for German: *Deutsch*.

Settling Britannia

Two other Germanic tribes, the Angles and the Saxons, who were then residing in what is now northern Germany and southern Denmark, were also caught up in this ethnic and territorial reshuffling. They were infected with the same wanderlust as their southern neighbours, but their travels took them due west and over the sea. In 410, when the Visigoths invaded Rome, the Roman legions withdrew from the far-flung island province of Britannia to support the capital's defences, leaving the territory to the Celtic people they had found there 400 years before. Angles and Saxons began to settle Britannia in large numbers in around 450. The Saxons first established three areas of settlement in southern Britain, which they named geographically in relation to each other: there were West Saxons (Wessex), South Saxons (Sussex) and East Saxons (Essex). Two communities of Angles settled in the eastern protuberance of the island, where they defined themselves as the North Folk (Norfolk) and the South Folk (Suffolk). Their territory as a whole was called Angle-Land, a name that in due course was applied to the whole country: England.

As the German Angles and Saxons spread west and north across England, the Celtic people retreated to the western extremities of the island, to Cornwall and Wales. Some crossed back to mainland Europe and established a community on the sharp triangle of the Cotentin Peninsula in modern-day France. They took their British appellation with them, and thus their new continental home became known as Brittany.

The Fall of the Western Roman Empire

By the mid-3rd century, under the dynamic leadership of Attila (r. 434–453), the Huns had evolved from a loose confederation of warrior-horsemen into a politically organised Asiatic empire that rivalled Rome. At the height of Attila's reign, his empire stretched in a great strip across Europe from the environs of modern Budapest to the River Volga in modern Russia. The potential threat from the Huns was significant enough to force an alliance between the Romans and the Visigoths, who had now moved further west and established a kingdom on the Atlantic seaboard in modern Bordeaux. This alliance defeated Attila in Gaul in 451, but could not prevent his march into Italy the following year, as the Visigoths had done before him. Fortunately for the Romans, the Hunnic army was decimated by a plague, prompting them to retreat across the Danube. Attila himself died in 453, and without his personal authority and terrifying reputation the empire of the Huns dissolved.

By that time, the barbarians of many Germanic tribes had spread throughout the western Roman world, systematically undermining Rome's control. In 476 the last Roman emperor, Romulus Augustulus (r. 475–476), was deposed and replaced by an Ostrogothic general, Odoacer (r. 476–493), who became the first Germanic king of Italy, marking the end of the Western Roman Empire. An Ostrogothic kingdom endured in Italy and the Balkans for some decades, but in 540 it was reconquered by Justinian (r. 527–565), the energetic emperor of the Byzantine (Eastern Roman) Empire.

Germanic invaders or their descendants continued to govern all the remaining former provinces of the once-great Western Roman Empire, each in their own autonomous kingdoms. But despite the change in leadership, Roman customs survived. The new ruling elite slipped naturally into the role of regional administrators. To govern effectively, they adopted well-established Roman customs and laws, as well as the Roman religion – Christianity. The majority of the invaders tilled the land alongside local populations who spoke Latin as their everyday language, and within a generation or two the newcomers were speaking it as well. The vulgar Latin of the farmers, artisans and tradespeople of Western Europe never died out. Its local variants grew into a family tree of distinct but related tongues: French, Spanish and Italian.

By the year 565, when Justinian died, a new status quo had established itself in Europe. The Franks held sway over a territory that covered most of modern France and Germany; the Visigoths ruled modern Spain, and had a foothold on the Cote d'Azur; and the Sueves were clinging to the northwestern corner of the Iberian Peninsula. The Greek-speaking Byzantines, who still considered themselves Romans, were in possession of a vast Mediterranean empire: Italy, Greece, all of the Middle East to the Euphrates and beyond, most of North Africa (which had been wrested from the Vandals in 533), all the islands from Majorca to Cyprus, and a broad band of southern Spain.

Migration within modern Europe did not cease once this new equilibrium had been reached. Far away to the east,

Left: A Visigoth pendant cross. The Visigoths were Christians, but they subscribed to the Arian heresy that Jesus was a being created by God. This made them the implacable enemies of the orthodox Byzantine Empire.

a people known as the Avars were already on a westward march. They, like the Huns before them and the Mongols after them, would wreak havoc for a time. At the other end of the continent, small groups of Scots and Picts, Celtic tribesmen from Ireland, had crossed the water and made a home for themselves in the cold northern reaches of the British Isles. Along the way they had some violent meetings with advancing Saxons – or as they mispronounced it in their Gaelic tongue, the Sassenachs. These encounters were the first skirmishes in a rivalry among neighbours, sometimes friendly but often bloody, that would continue for years to come.

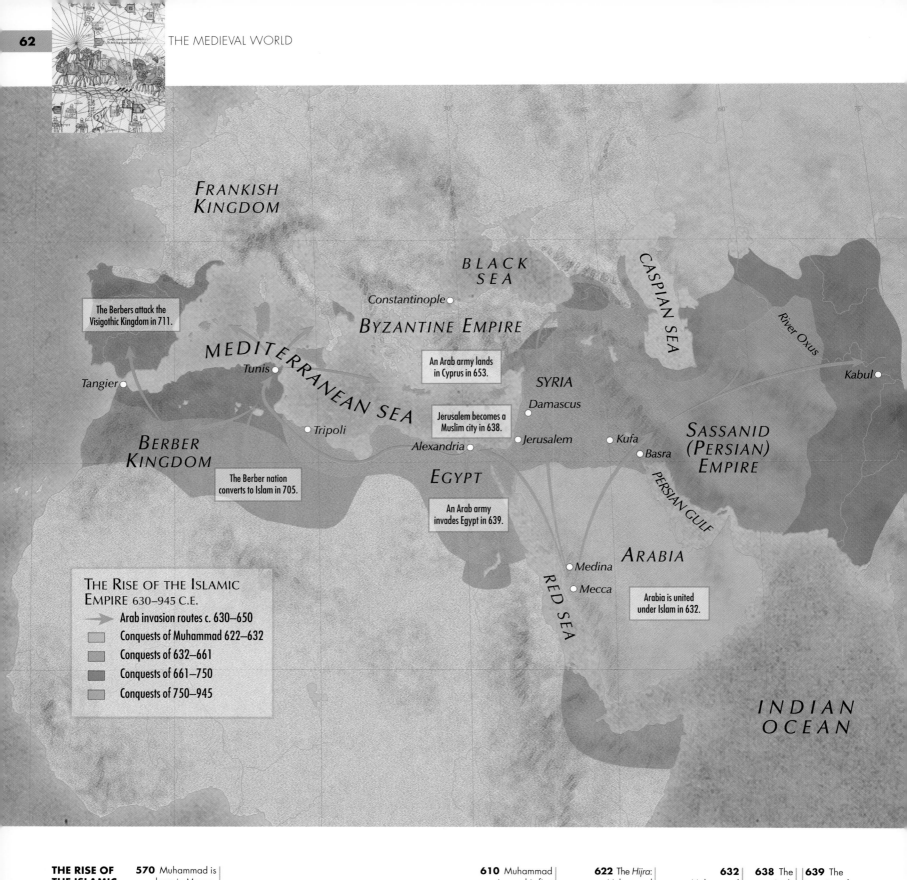

FRANKISH
KINGDOM

BLACK
SEA

Constantinople

CASPIAN SEA

BYZANTINE EMPIRE

River Oxus

The Berbers attack the
Visigothic Kingdom in 711.

MEDITERRANEAN SEA

Tunis

An Arab army lands
in Cyprus in 653.

SYRIA

Damascus

Kabul

Tangier

Jerusalem becomes a
Muslim city in 638.

SASSANID
(PERSIAN)
EMPIRE

Tripoli

Alexandria

Jerusalem

Kufa

BERBER
KINGDOM

Basra

PERSIAN GULF

The Berber nation
converts to Islam in 705.

EGYPT

An Arab army
invades Egypt in 639.

ARABIA

THE RISE OF THE ISLAMIC
EMPIRE 630–945 C.E.

Medina

RED SEA

Mecca

Arabia is united
under Islam in 632.

INDIAN
OCEAN

Arab invasion routes c. 630–650

Conquests of Muhammad 622–632

Conquests of 632–661

Conquests of 661–750

Conquests of 750–945

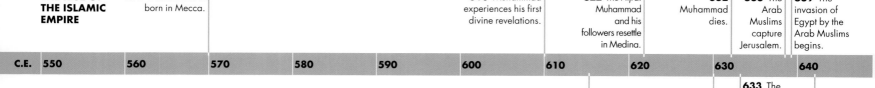

**THE RISE OF
THE ISLAMIC
EMPIRE**

570 Muhammad is
born in Mecca.

610 Muhammad
experiences his first
divine revelations.

622 The *Hijra*:
Muhammad
and his
followers resettle
in Medina.

632
Muhammad
dies.

638 The
Arab
Muslims
capture
Jerusalem.

639 The
invasion of
Egypt by the
Arab Muslims
begins.

C.E. | 550 | 560 | 570 | 580 | 590 | 600 | 610 | 620 | 630 | 640

615 The first Muslims
emigrate to Abyssinia
to escape persecution.

630 Muhammad
returns to Mecca with
an army to impose the
will of Allah.

633 The
conquest of
Persia by
Arab Muslim
armies begins.

642 The Arab
Muslims conquer
the Berbers.

THE WORD OF THE PROPHET

At its height the Islamic Empire extended from modern Spain in the west to Central Asia in the east. The word of the Prophet Muhammad was carried out of Arabia by invading armies and Muslim settlers, but the history of Islam, and the spread of the faith, began with the forced migration of the Muslim people.

In the year 610 C.E. Muhammad, a 40-year-old merchant from the city of Mecca, reported that he had received revelations from God, delivered through the Archangel Gabriel. Among these was the message that there was only one God, and that submission (*islam* in Arabic) to Him was the true path. Some people, mostly Muhammad's own friends and relations, immediately adopted this theology. They called themselves 'those who submit' – *Muslims*.

The monotheism that Muhammad preached was far removed from the pagan tradition that was prevalent in Mecca at the time. Every year, Arabian tribesmen, the nomadic Bedouin and inhabitants of other cities travelled to the Kaaba in Mecca, a cube-shaped shrine surrounded by over 360 idols, to worship and offer animal sacrifices to the tribal gods on the revered Black Stone housed within. Many of Mecca's citizens had grown rich on the commerce generated by these pagan pilgrimages and, angered by the economic threat that Muhammad's preaching represented, they began to persecute his sect. In the year 622, 12 years into his ministry, this persecution had intensified to a point that Muhammad and his followers left Mecca and relocated to the city of Medina, where Muhammad led the first avowedly Muslim community. This event is known to history as the *Hijra* – the settlement – and is so central to the story of Islam that the compilers of the Muslim calendar later took it as the starting point of a new era: 622, when the first migration of the first Muslims took place, is Islam's Year 0.

United under the Banner of Islam

In Medina, Muhammad's teaching won new converts at a fantastic rate. He quickly emerged as the leader of a theocratic city-state – becoming far more influential than the local visionary he had been in Mecca during the first years of his mission. In 630, Year 8, his following was strong enough that he could march back into Mecca at the head of an army and impose the will of Allah on the city's idolaters. Muhammad removed all the idols from the environs of the Kaaba and rededicated it to Allah.

Muhammad refrained from taking vengeance on the wealthy merchants of Mecca who had vilified him. On the contrary, he took many of the most influential Meccans into his inner circle – once they had agreed to adopt Islam. His magnanimity made a great impression on the tribal clans. They began to come and pledge their fealty to Muhammad, who accepted them into Islam with the injunction that tribal rivalries and vendettas were against God's law. Henceforth the *umma*, that is, the Islamic community as a whole, was to be considered a higher authority than the tribe, and the head of the *umma* was Muhammad himself, God's prophet on Earth.

Muhammad reinforced his message by careful diplomacy: he took wives from among the womenfolk of influential tribes, made gifts of land and money, and occasionally waged war against recalcitrant tribal leaders. Islam's powerful religious message was introduced to the nomadic Bedouin alongside the economic benefits that submission to Muhammad's leadership could provide, as the Muslim faith was by now bound up in the marketplaces on which the Bedouin depended for their livelihood.

Muhammad's leadership was so successful that by the time of his death in 632 (Year 10), he had united a large part of Arabia under the banner of Islam. For the first time in their history, the desert peoples resembled a cohesive nation. And the energies that for generations had been frittered away on fratricidal bickering could now be used in the cause of glorifying the One God.

649 Arab troops invade modern-day Tunisia.

670 50,000 Bedouins are resettled in the eastern Persian province of Khurasan. Arab armies advance across northwest Africa.

711 Tariq ibn Ziyad, a Berber Muslim, invades Spain from North Africa.

712 Arab armies in the east advance beyond the Jaxartes (Syr-Darya) to the Chinese frontier.

650	660	670	680	690	700	710	720	730	740

653 The Arab Muslim army makes landfall on Cyprus and Rhodes.

696 Arabic is declared the official language of the Muslim Empire.

705 The Berbers convert to Islam.

732 Arab armies are defeated by the Franks at Tours, marking the end of the Muslim advance in Europe.

The Spread of Islam

Muhammad's first successor (*kalifa* in Arabic, whence 'caliph') was his friend and father-in-law, and one of the first converts to Islam, Abu Bakr (r. 632–634). The new ruler made it clear from the start that he had taken on Muhammad's political authority only. Muhammad was seen as the 'seal of the prophets', that is, the final culmination of the line of prophets that stretched back through Jesus and Moses. But Abu Bakr's religious beliefs were strong, as was his political and military expertise. Under his leadership, Arab Muslim armies burst out of the Arabian desert and invaded modern Iraq, then part of the Sassanid (Persian) Empire. They also pushed north into the Byzantine province of Syria. The Byzantines and the Sassanids were weakened by war with each other, and ripe for conquest. Syria fell to the Arabs in 636, and Palestine yielded soon after. Jerusalem withstood Bakr's attacks, but not for long: it became a Muslim city in 638. The Sassanids, meanwhile, were defeated at a decisive battle at Qadisiya in c. 637. In the 650s, the Arab Muslims extended their frontiers beyond the eastern borders of Persia, fighting their way to the River Oxus (the modern Amu Darya in Uzbekistan), to Kabul and to the northern edge of India.

All of these conquests were carried out by small armies made up of nomadic Arab tribesmen. The successful conclusion of military campaigns triggered mass migrations of tribal peoples who travelled to join their soldiering family members. North of Arabia, the Arab Muslim army congregated in two camps where they built a mosque and a residence for the commander. Once the soldiers were joined by their families, the camps rapidly grew into cities. Reed tents were replaced by mud-brick houses, and suburbs were founded to house the overspill as the civilian population increased. One of the camps was Kufa, where each tribe was assigned its own district according to the size of their contribution to the campaign. The other was Basra – which went on to become a major city in the modern state of Iraq.

In Syria, Muslim settlers made their homes in established towns rather than newly built barracks. This was probably due to the fact that a large part of the Greek-speaking population of towns such as Damascus took to the road as refugees as the Arabs advanced, leaving their homes invitingly empty. In other instances the invaders made treaties with townspeople, whereby they promised to leave cities intact so long as half the properties were handed over as homes for Arabs, and half the churches were given over for conversion into mosques. In this way, Muslim custom and Arab populations took root in the new Islamic Empire.

Left: The Kaaba, pictured here using time-lapse photography in 1996, is circled seven times by Muslim worshippers during their Hajj, or annual pilgrimage to Mecca. It was here in 610 that Muhammad first preached submission to Allah – a message that spread rapidly through the Middle East and Africa.

As well as grafting their communities onto occupied land, Muslim invaders also instilled the precepts of Islam into the minds of conquered peoples. Everywhere they attacked, Muslim armies gave three options to the peoples they defeated: convert to Islam, retain your own religion but pay a poll tax, or stand and fight. Some people always chose to convert in order to preserve their wealth. If these pragmatists were not committed to Islam, their children and grandchildren often became so, in the same way that the children and grandchildren of emigrants to new countries become naturalised citizens of their new communities.

Jews and Christians who chose to keep their faith were left in peace, partly because Muhammad himself had always been well disposed towards the 'people of the Book' (Abyssinian Christians had sheltered Muslim refugees from Mecca even before the *Hijra*), but mostly because they were a valuable source of revenue. The caliphate did not want too many converts, because that would have undermined the tax base. The new Islamic rulers were careful to set the tax of adherents to other faiths below the rate that they had paid under the Byzantine and Sassanid empires – thereby guaranteeing the goodwill of the non-Muslim population. Those who resisted the new regime militarily, or chose to rise up in revolt, were usually crushed.

The policies of the Muslim conquerors made for a stable government, but more importantly it created the conditions in which the very principles of Islam were perpetuated by migration. The teachings of Muhammad entered the minds and souls of men at the same time as the armies of Muhammad's successors were overrunning the land.

Further Conquests

In 639, an Arab army marched into Egypt, which at the time was a Byzantine possession. The advancing Muslims swiftly took possession of Alexandria, and forced the Byzantine army to quit the country altogether, while offering the usual terms to the Jews and the Coptic Christians who resided there. In 649, the Arabs advanced into modern Tunisia and fought off an attempt by the Byzantines to retake Egypt from the sea. This experience prompted the Arabs to create a navy of their own, and though these men of the desert were never at home on the water they did achieve significant victories at sea. In 653, Arab troops landed on Cyprus and Rhodes, where they found the remains of the fabled bronze Colossus, one of the seven wonders of the world. They sold the metal to a Jewish merchant for scrap.

After driving the Byzantines out of North Africa, the Arabs came into contact with the Berbers, the indigenous African people of the region, in 642. They proved to be a fierce enemy but were eventually subdued. In 705, the entire Berber nation converted to Islam, adopting the religious zeal of the Arab Muslims. A Berber Muslim general, Tariq ibn Ziyad (r. 711–712), at the head of a Berber Muslim army, crossed the narrow straits from Tangier to modern Spain. He landed on the rock of Gibraltar, the name of which is a corruption of the Arabic words *jabal Tariq* – Tariq's mountain – and claimed it for Islam.

Tariq smashed the Visigothic army that came to meet him in Spain, and rapidly subdued the entire Iberian Peninsula. The Moors, as the African converts to Islam became known, were a presence in Spain for more than 700 years – and they left their mark on everything from the food to the architecture of the home they made in Europe. By this time, the *umma*, the community of Muslims, had grown so large that political strife became inevitable. Rival caliphs fought each other for the honour of being known as the Prophet's true successor, and the unity of the faith was lost to factionalism. The growth of Islam was also inhibited by the fact that no Arab army had managed to subdue Constantinople, the citadel of the great Byzantine enemy, which remained the capital of a Christian empire until 1453, when it finally succumbed to the Turkish Ottomans.

By that time Muhammad's people, and Muhammad's message, had spread far and wide. In the steppelands of Central Asia and China, and throughout India and the Malayan Peninsula, there were people who knew nothing of Arabia and its deserts, but who nevertheless turned their faces towards Mecca five times a day, in order to pray.

THE MEN OF THE NORTH

At the end of the 8th century, seaborne raiders – known to history as Vikings – began to swarm out of Scandinavia. At first they were content to raid foreign coasts and steal loot from monasteries. But good land was as precious to them as ecclesiastical silver – and in time the Norse pirates became intrepid explorer-colonists.

In 793, a seaborne Viking party from Norway landed on the Northumbrian coast of England. It proceeded to the monastery at Lindisfarne, slaughtered the monks, smashed the holy relics and carried off all the precious church ornaments. News of the attack spread quickly to the court of Emperor Charlemagne (r. 768–814), whose Holy Roman Empire in central Europe was soon to experience Viking aggression firsthand. Alcuin of York (c. 735–804), an English scholar in Charlemagne's employ, was appalled by the news from home: 'Never before has such a terror appeared in Britain,' he wrote in a letter to the king of Northumbria. 'Nor was it thought that such an inroad from the sea could be made.' Alcuin's remark highlights the particular skill that made the Vikings such a daunting enemy: until now, such a landing had indeed not been possible. The Vikings' mastery of shipbuilding and seamanship had made it so. It carried them to England – and it would take them far beyond.

The Scandinavian homeland of the Vikings is a great peninsula that hangs over Western Europe like a dragon's head. In the western half, modern Norway, the coast is riven with deep, sheltered inlets. In the centuries before they set out to sea, the Vikings learned their boatcraft among these fjords. The eastern half – roughly modern Sweden – was home to the Viking tribes known as the Varangians. To the south, in the Baltic isles and the bud-shaped peninsula of Jutland, lived the Danes.

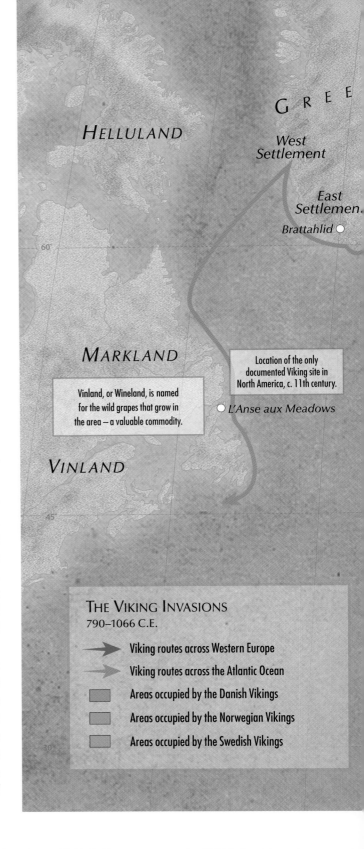

GREE...

HELLULAND

West Settlement

East Settlemen...

Brattahlid ○

MARKLAND

Vinland, or Wineland, is named for the wild grapes that grow in the area – a valuable commodity.

Location of the only documented Viking site in North America, c. 11th century.

○ L'Anse aux Meadows

VINLAND

THE VIKING INVASIONS
790–1066 C.E.

→ Viking routes across Western Europe

→ Viking routes across the Atlantic Ocean

▭ Areas occupied by the Danish Vikings

▭ Areas occupied by the Norwegian Vikings

▭ Areas occupied by the Swedish Vikings

THE VIKING INVASIONS

798 The Vikings reach Ulster in Ireland and the Hebrides.

799 The Vikings attack the coast of Aquitaine in the Holy Roman Empire.

c. 830 The Vikings begin to settle in Britain.

834 Danish Vikings attack the Frisian coast.

c. 870 The Vikings' colonisation of Iceland begins.

876 The Vikings establish a kingdom at *Jorvic*, modern-day York in England.

c. 900 The first sighting of Greenland is recorded. Danelaw – the Viking territory in the north of England – is established.

C.E.	770	780	790	800	810	820	830	840	850	860	870	880	890	900	910	920

793 Lindisfarne is raided by Norwegian Vikings.

795 The Vikings plunder Skye and Iona in modern Scotland.

841 A Viking harbour is established at Dublin.

845 Viking ships sail up the Seine and besiege Paris.

862 Rurik gains control of Novgorod.

878 Alfred the Great defeats a Viking army at Edington in southern England.

911 The West Franks make a treaty with Hrolf, granting his Vikings land around the mouth of the Seine and Rouen.

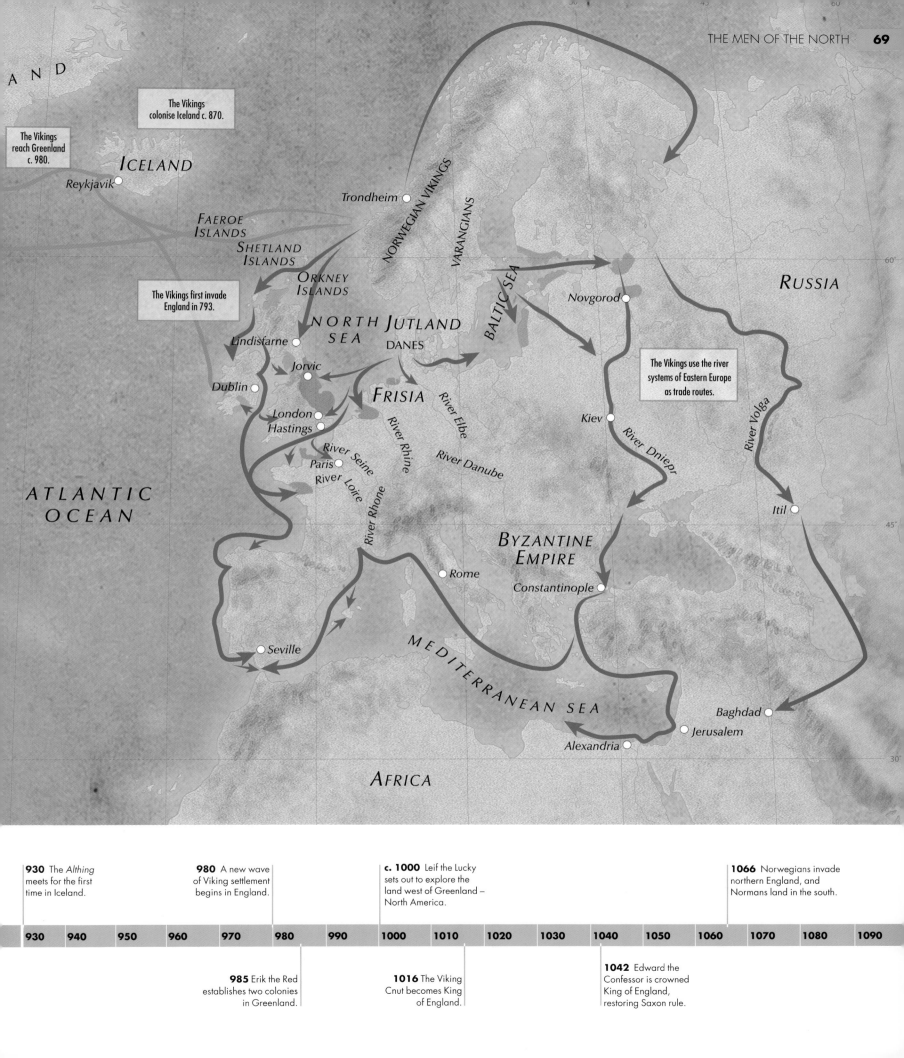

The Vikings
colonise Iceland c. 870.

The Vikings
reach Greenland
c. 980.

ICELAND

Reykjavik

The Vikings first invade
England in 793.

*FAEROE
ISLANDS*

*SHETLAND
ISLANDS*

*ORKNEY
ISLANDS*

Trondheim

NORWEGIAN VIKINGS

VARANGIANS

RUSSIA

Novgorod

The Vikings use the river
systems of Eastern Europe
as trade routes.

*NORTH
SEA*

JUTLAND

DANES

BALTIC SEA

Lindisfarne

Jorvic

Dublin

FRISIA

River Elbe

London
Hastings

River Rhine

River Seine

Paris

River Loire

River Danube

Kiev

River Dniepr

River Volga

*ATLANTIC
OCEAN*

River Rhone

Itil

*BYZANTINE
EMPIRE*

Rome

Constantinople

Seville

MEDITERRANEAN SEA

Baghdad

Jerusalem

Alexandria

AFRICA

930 The *Althing*
meets for the first
time in Iceland.

980 A new wave
of Viking settlement
begins in England.

c. 1000 Leif the Lucky
sets out to explore the
land west of Greenland –
North America.

1066 Norwegians invade
northern England, and
Normans land in the south.

| 930 | 940 | 950 | 960 | 970 | 980 | 990 | 1000 | 1010 | 1020 | 1030 | 1040 | 1050 | 1060 | 1070 | 1080 | 1090 |

985 Erik the Red
establishes two colonies
in Greenland.

1016 The Viking
Cnut becomes King
of England.

1042 Edward the
Confessor is crowned
King of England,
restoring Saxon rule.

In England, the raid on Lindisfarne proved to be merely a prelude of things to come. In the years that followed there were more assaults in the northeast, and for a generation from 835 onwards, Viking pirates attacked the south of England as regularly as summer storms. Southampton was targeted in 840; Romney Marsh in 841; London in 842 – and so on, year in and year out. The attackers usually left each autumn, but some years they chose to winter in England – usually on offshore islands such as Sheppey, off the coast of modern-day Kent, or on the Isle of Wight, where they were untouchable.

In 865, however, the nature of the Viking attacks changed. A Danish army landed in East Anglia, and this time its intent was not to pillage and plunder, but to conquer English lands. This army, bolstered by a continual influx of Danish newcomers, fought the Angles for 20 years. The Vikings conquered all the north of England, making good use of horses and the still-intact Roman roads to do so. They established their own capital at *Jorvic* – modern York.

But the Danes were unable to entirely subdue Wessex, which resisted the Viking advance under the leadership of the scholar-king Alfred the Great (r. 871–899). In 878, a treaty was reached and Britain became a partitioned island. Broadly speaking, north of the Roman road called Watling Street, which ran from modern Dover to London, the country was Danelaw and Norse-speaking. As part of the treaty, the Viking leader of the Danelaw, Guthrum (r. 874–890), converted to Christianity, but many of his subjects retained their pagan beliefs and practices, or merely accepted the Christian God alongside their own. South of this medieval Green Line were the English-speaking, Christian Saxons.

While the Danes were battling and settling in Middle England, their Norwegian cousins were making their way across the North Atlantic. Late in the 8th century, in sea-going ships called *knorrs* (which were broader and larger than the swift and shallow longships used by the raiding Viking parties), they travelled up the east coast of Scotland, and went on to occupy the Orkney, Shetland and Faeroe islands. Some voyagers made their way down the western side of the British Isles, making landfall on the Isle of Man off the coast of Wales, and on the Irish coast. They waged war on the native Irish and, as in England, some of the invaders eventually became settlers. A purely Viking town was founded on the coast at a place the local people called the Black Pool. It still bears this old Gaelic name: *Dubh Linn* – Dublin.

Running Riot
At the start of the 9th century, shortly after the Norwegian Viking attack on Lindisfarne, the Danish Vikings sailed out of Denmark in search of loot. In their serpentine ships they went marauding along the coastline and through the river systems of Western Europe. They ravaged Frisia (modern Belgium and the Netherlands); they sailed up the River Seine and besieged Paris; they headed down the coastline of Spain (where they were soundly repulsed by a Moorish army at Seville); and they sailed across the Mediterranean as far as Jerusalem. Christian churches were frequently targeted during these raids. Monasteries were typically both wealthy and poorly defended, and the gold and silver treasures they housed could be translated into personal wealth and power at home. Civilians were captured to be held for ransom, or to be sold as slaves later.

Above: This 7th-century helmet was found at Sutton Hoo, an Anglo-Saxon cemetery in Suffolk, England, in 1939. It resembles 6th-century helmets of Scandinavian design, and may be connected to the royal dynasty of Sweden.

Discovering New Worlds

Late in the 9th century, Norwegian Vikings began the systematic colonisation of the empty island known to the ancient Greeks and Romans as Thule. This rocky isle had been disparagingly dubbed 'Ice-Land' by one Viking navigator who spent a cold winter there alone. But overpopulation and political strife in the Norwegian homeland meant that there were plenty of disaffected men ready to uproot their families and venture to a virgin land – even one with such a reputation for being inhospitable.

Over the course of two generations as many as 15,000 Norwegian Vikings migrated to Iceland. Many of the womenfolk were the Irish wives and concubines of Dublin Vikings. The brave new Icelanders had no king; instead they submitted to the authority of the 'First Settler', Ingolf Arnarson (r. 877–930), who led the colony from the homestead he called Reykjavik, or 'Steamy Bay'. After his death, the second-generation Icelanders summoned a general assembly made up of the representatives of settlers from all corners of the island, who gathered to decide on legislation and dispense justice. This exercise in democracy was purely an Icelandic institution, replacing the tribal and autocratic systems of Scandinavia. The *Althing*, as it was known, first met in June of 930.

By the latter half of the 10th century, all the farmable land in Iceland was spoken for and some of the settlers were looking to move on. When Erik the Red (950–1003) was banished from Iceland for three years in the 980s, he set off to explore a land in the northwest that had been spotted some years before by a storm-lost Viking. Erik, motivated more by prudent salesmanship than geographic accuracy, named this new country Greenland, and after his exile he returned to Iceland to organise an expedition. Lean harvests in Iceland meant that there was no shortage of interested parties. This new generation of colonists founded two communities in Greenland, prosaically called the East Settlement and the West Settlement. They lasted for 500 years before, unaccountably, dying out.

Other Viking explorers pressed still further west of Greenland. Norse sagas, stories about ancient Scandinavian and Germanic history and early Viking voyages, tell of Erik's son, Leif the Lucky (c. 980–c. 1020), who sailed from Greenland past Helluland (Baffin Island) and Markland (Labrador) and found a new country endowed with a commodity as desirable as silver coin: grapes. The fruit was

growing abundantly in the wild, and inspired the Viking name for this far-flung territory: Vinland – Wineland.

There is no doubt that Vinland is North America – and that the Vikings were therefore the first Europeans to reach the New World. The stretch of coast described in the sagas has been identified as anywhere from Florida to Boston, but no one will ever know exactly where Leif and his compatriots came ashore and celebrated their discovery with new wine. The only documented Viking site in North America is an 11th-century settlement at L'Anse aux Meadows, on the northern tip of modern Newfoundland. This community seems to have been short-lived, perhaps even deliberately temporary. At any rate, the Vikings did not settle in North America. Their encounters with the indigenous people – *Skraelings* or 'ugly wretches' as the Vikings called them – were antagonistic and violent. The Vikings were outnumbered, and withdrew from this westernmost outpost to safer territory.

While Norwegian Vikings explored the far west, Swedish Norsemen had made inroads in the east. The Varangians – known to their Finnish neighbours as the *Ruotsi*, an obscure word that may have meant either 'fair-headed' or 'rowing people' – were no less warlike than their Norwegian kinsmen, but they found that amicable trade with other peoples was just as advantageous as hostile confrontation. The mercantile expeditions of the Varangians took them south and east, along the great rivers of the East European plain, into the territory of the eastern Slavs. According to Russian chronicles, some of these Slavonic people made an attractive proposition to the leader of the Varangians, Rurik (r. 862–879): 'Our land is great and fruitful, but there is no order in it. Come and reign over and govern us.' The political reality was doubtless more complex than that, but at any rate the Varangians established a principality based around the Slavic town of Novgorod –

meaning 'new city'. The new Varangian authority became known among the Slavs by a version of its Finnish name: *Ruotsi* was transformed into *Rus*, which is the root of the word 'Russia'.

Rurik's compatriots continued south along the river routes and founded a separate dynasty at Kiev, on the River Dniepr. His grandson, Svyatoslav (r. 942–972), whose name, unlike his Norse predecessors', is indisputably Slavic in origin, ruled in Kiev and grew rich through trade with the great Byzantine city of Constantinople. In 988 Svyatoslav's son Vladimir (r. 980–1015) broke with the pagan heritage of the Norsemen and adopted the Byzantine version of the Christian rite. Thus Kievan Rus became a Greek Orthodox state, and grew apart from the Catholic peoples of the west – a factor that would go on to have a great influence on Russia's history.

A Viking Empire Emerges

In the early 10th century, Alfred the Great's son, Edward the Elder (r. 899–924), established rule over Danelaw, incorporating it into his Kingdom of England. But in the 980s, the uneasy peace that existed between the Danes and Saxons broke down. New waves of Viking invaders harried the south, and the English king, Ethelred the Unready (r. 978–1016), unwisely tried to buy them off with 'Danegeld'. The Danes accepted the king's silver, but kept returning for more. Waves of armies from Denmark were aided and supported by the Anglo-Scandinavian population of Danelaw, who remained loyal to their Norse heritage. The long war came to an end only in 1016, when Ethelred died and was succeeded by a conquering Danish prince, the 22-year-old Cnut (or Canute, r. 1016–1035). Within 10 years Cnut had also succeeded to the thrones of Denmark and Norway. He was now master of a Viking empire that extended in a great arc from Dublin through the British Isles to the Baltic. Anglo-Saxons and Anglo-Danes alike became subjects of a supreme Norse monarch.

One Viking enclave that was not part of Cnut's empire was an area in West Francia, at the mouth of the Seine, where there had been a Viking presence for 150 years. In 911 Charles the Simple (r. 898–929), King of the West Franks, granted to the local Vikings the lands that they already occupied – provided that their leader Hrolf (Rollo to the French, r. 911–933) was baptised. As in Russia, these newly Christian Norsemen became assimilated with the local population. But although they adopted French as their own tongue, they kept their ancestral name for their territory: this corner of France was known as 'Norseman-land' – Normandy.

The French-speaking descendants of these Vikings took a keen interest in English affairs, as did the rulers of Norway. Following the deaths of Cnut's sons, Harold Harefoot (r. 1035–1040) and Harthacanute (r. 1040–1042), Edward the Confessor (r. 1042–1066) succeeded to the English crown, restoring Saxon rule in England. When Edward died, there were three claimants to the throne: Harold Godwinson, Earl of Essex; William, Duke of Normandy; and Harald III of Norway, who in his youth had served in the 'Varangian Guard', the Viking bodyguard of the Byzantine Emperor. Both Harald and William invaded England, where the Englishman Harold had declared himself king. It was William's good fortune that Harald of Norway got there first. The English marched north and defeated Harald's army, but then had to race back to the south to face William at Hastings. The battle in the north and the marathon march to the south had left the English tired and depleted. William duly conquered Harold's forces and opened the gates of England to a new wave of settlers: aristocratic Normans – knights, courtiers and bishops – were given land in the conquered country and became the new ruling class in England.

Norman England is one of the Vikings' indirect legacies; the first Russian state is another. But perhaps their most enduring mark is the fiercely independent republic of Iceland, which exists as a state only because the Vikings ventured to its frozen shores. The Icelandic people, who still speak a language that is directly descended from the tongue of their Norse ancestors, proudly claim that their parliament is the world's oldest. It dates back to the *Althing*, which first met on a bleak volcanic plain near Reykjavik more than 1,000 years ago.

Below: The Vinland map, a Viking chart depicting the eastern seaboard of North America, is believed to be a forgery. But the remains of a Viking settlement in Newfoundland prove that they did make landfall on the far side of the Atlantic.

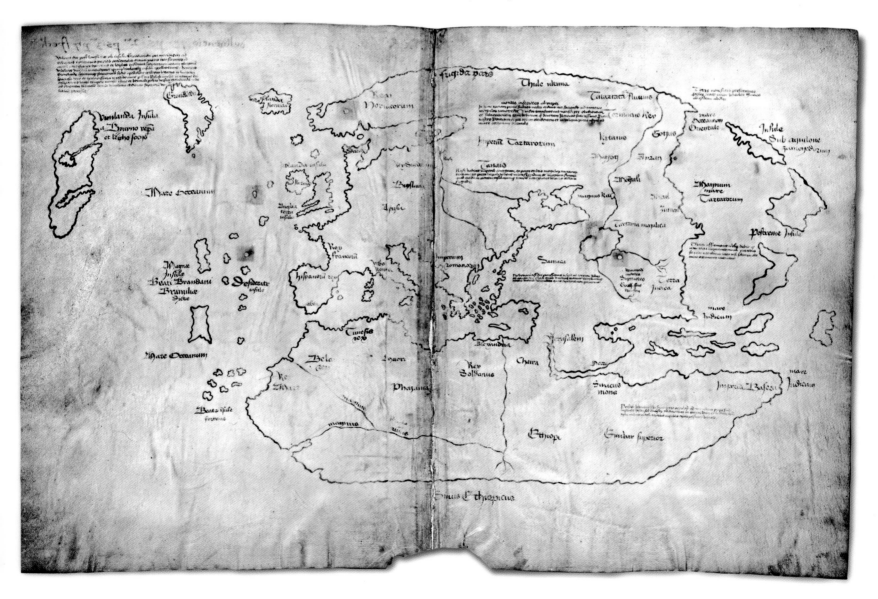

CONQUERORS OF THE WORLD

The Mongols were the last and most successful of the nomadic tribes of Central Asia. In the space of one lifetime they created the largest contiguous land empire in the history of the world. More remarkably, their bloodthirsty triumphs were largely the achievement of one man: the military and political genius Genghis Khan.

The Mongols emerged as an ethnic group in the 12th century. Prior to that time, the peoples who would come to make up the Mongol nation consisted of a collection of tribes – some Asiatic and some Turkic, but all of them warlike, illiterate and prone to feuding among themselves. Their society was strictly hierarchical: each tribe had a dominant clan, and each clan had its head. The clan leaders formed a kind of aristocracy, one that placed great emphasis on wealth, which was measured by the number of carpets, horses, silver, cattle, wives, sons and slaves in one's possession.

The tribes lived a nomadic existence, shuttling back and forth in an area between Lake Baikal and the Altai Mountains in modern Mongolia. This was hard territory, and it made the tribespeople hard, too. Boys learned from a young age to ride the sturdy little horses of the steppe, and to hunt on them using short and powerful bows. By the time they reached adolescence, all young men had acquired a formidable set of soldierly skills.

The Rise of Genghis Khan
Temujin, the boy who became known to history as Genghis Khan (r. 1206–1227), had a particularly tough upbringing.

The Mongol army invades Kiev in 1240

Kiev

BLA

MEDITERRANEAN SEA

THE MONGOL INVASIONS

1162 Temujin is born.

1213 The Mongols invade northern China and destroy the Jin dynasty.

C.E.	1140	1150	1160	1170	1180	1190	1200	1210

1206 Temujin, having united the Mongol tribes, takes the title Genghis Khan, which means 'universal ruler'.

1218 Genghis Khan sends an envoy to the Khwarezmid Empire to open up trade relations.

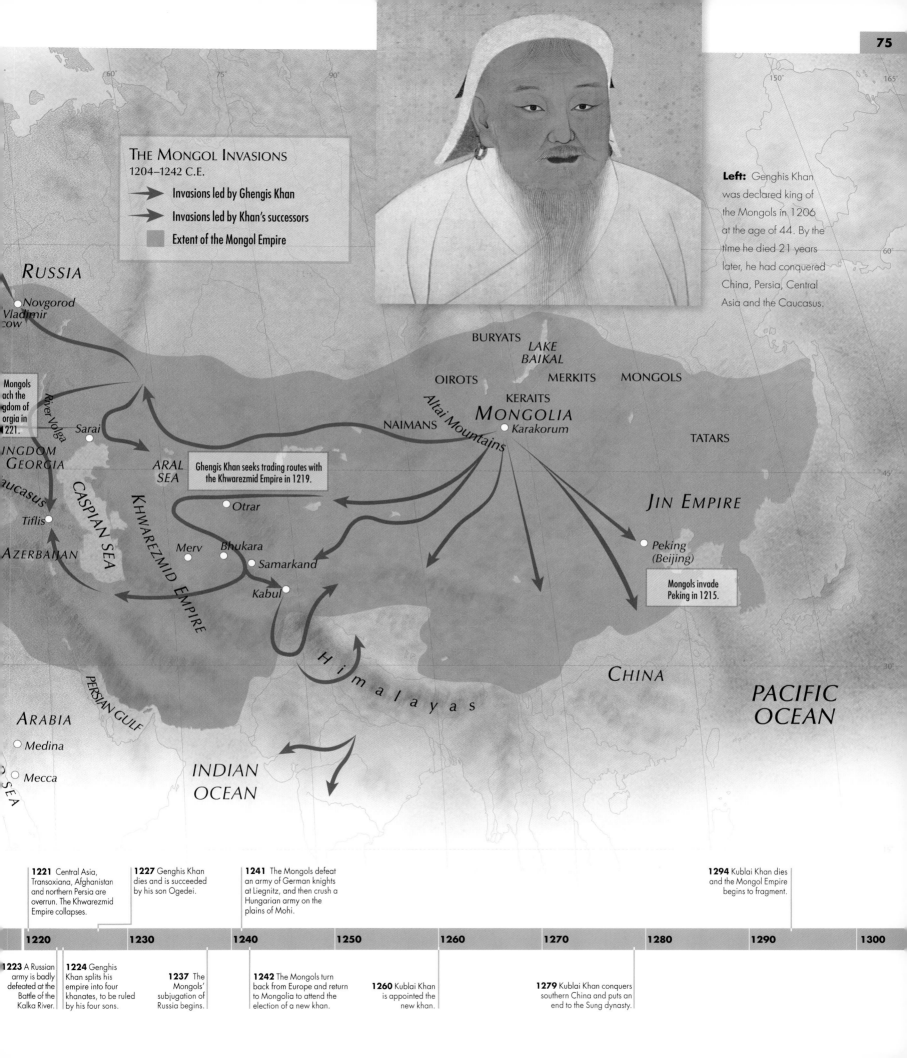

THE MONGOL INVASIONS
1204–1242 C.E.

→ Invasions led by Ghengis Khan
→ Invasions led by Khan's successors
■ Extent of the Mongol Empire

Left: Genghis Khan was declared king of the Mongols in 1206 at the age of 44. By the time he died 21 years later, he had conquered China, Persia, Central Asia and the Caucasus.

RUSSIA

Novgorod
Vladimir
cow

Mongols
ach the
gdom of
orgia in
221.

River Volga

Sarai

INGDOM
GEORGIA

ucasus

Tiflis

AZERBAIJAN

CASPIAN SEA

ARAL SEA

KHWAREZMID EMPIRE

Ghengis Khan seeks trading routes with the Khwarezmid Empire in 1219.

Otrar

Merv

Bhukara

Samarkand

Kabul

BURYATS
LAKE BAIKAL

OIROTS
MERKITS
MONGOLS

KERAITS
MONGOLIA
Karakorum

NAIMANS

Altai Mountains

TATARS

JIN EMPIRE

Peking (Beijing)

Mongols invade Peking in 1215.

H i m a l a y a s

CHINA

PACIFIC OCEAN

PERSIAN GULF

ARABIA

Medina

Mecca

SEA

INDIAN OCEAN

1221 Central Asia, Transoxiana, Afghanistan and northern Persia are overrun. The Khwarezmid Empire collapses.

1227 Genghis Khan dies and is succeeded by his son Ogedei.

1241 The Mongols defeat an army of German knights at Liegnitz, and then crush a Hungarian army on the plains of Mohi.

1294 Kublai Khan dies and the Mongol Empire begins to fragment.

1220	1230	1240	1250	1260	1270	1280	1290	1300

1223 A Russian army is badly defeated at the Battle of the Kalka River.

1224 Genghis Khan splits his empire into four khanates, to be ruled by his four sons.

1237 The Mongols' subjugation of Russia begins.

1242 The Mongols turn back from Europe and return to Mongolia to attend the election of a new khan.

1260 Kublai Khan is appointed the new khan.

1279 Kublai Khan conquers southern China and puts an end to the Sung dynasty.

Right: This 14th-century Persian miniature shows the Mongols sacking Baghdad in 1258. Adhering to their taboo on spilling royal blood, the Mongols executed the caliph by rolling him in a carpet and trampling him to death with their horses.

His father, a minor clan leader, was killed by enemies when Temujin was nine and the boy, abandoned by his tribe, spent some years living in exile with his family, without the protection that a clan provided. In these years he quickly learned the diplomatic and martial arts of survival – skills that would come to serve him well. When he was 16 he married the wife who had been promised to him in childhood, and became assimilated into her tribe. In his 20s and 30s he rose to prominence, and by forming shrewd alliances and choosing his fights with great care, he gained respect as a war leader and managed to unite the Merkits, Naimans, Tatars, Uyghurs, Keraits, Mongols and other smaller tribes under his rule. They became known collectively as the Mongols, and in 1206 Temujin was declared 'ruler of all who live in felt tents' at a tribal assembly and took the title 'Genghis Khan'.

If Genghis Khan had achieved nothing more in his life, he would still be ranked as one of the great leaders of the medieval era. He rose from nowhere to unite the restless and diverse tribes of his homeland, a great feat that he consolidated by codifying a set of laws for the Mongol nation. The Mongol book of law was called the Yassa, but the supreme law was unwritten: total and unquestioning deference to the khan. The principle of obedience was applied with utter ruthlessness to the Mongol army, which in effect included the entire male population, and dissent or disloyalty on the part of a soldier was punishable by death. Genghis Khan had managed to harness all the warlike energies of his countrymen, which for centuries had been expended on intertribal conflict, under one banner. The khan was now in a position to turn this unstoppable belligerence against the settled peoples of Asia and Europe.

Building an Empire

The Mongols' first target was the Jin Empire of northwest China, whose riches were an irresistible attraction. Genghis Khan was not interested in usurping the throne of the Celestial Empire, merely in stripping it of its assets.

to obtain the surrender of a city, and then promptly break it once the gates were opened. Civilians were often ordered out of the invaded city and systematically slaughtered, with each Mongol warrior being assigned 300 to 400 people to kill. The only people spared were nubile women, who were sent to Mongolia as booty, along with artisans or scholars, who had valuable skills that the Mongols could use. Children were slaughtered indiscriminately unless they were deemed to have value as slaves.

In 1215, after a laborious campaign, the Jin capital of Peking (modern Beijing) fell to the Mongols. They spent a month denuding it of its wealth – silks, books, artworks and precious metals – which were sent back to Mongolia on an endless camel train. The Chinese capital, one of the largest and most refined cities in Asia, was reduced to rubble and hills of rotting corpses.

Leaving the further conquest of China in the capable hands of his generals, Genghis Khan now turned his acquisitive gaze towards the west. The Khwarezmid Empire of Shah Muhammad II (r. 1200–1220) encompassed the lands lying southeast of the Caspian Sea and included the trade cities of Bukhara, Merv and Samarkand, and all of modern Afghanistan. In 1218, recognising the commercial advantages of establishing trade ties with Khwarezmia, the khan sent a caravan to the empire laden with valuable goods and accompanied by several hundred men and an ambassador. The caravan was intercepted by the governor of the eastern Khwarezmid province of Otrar, who confiscated the goods and executed all the envoys as spies.

His cavalry rode into China in 1213, first terrorising the countryside, laying waste to the fields and massacring everyone they encountered. Once these open spaces were under their control, the Mongol columns turned their attention to China's walled cities – whose populations had heard of their advance and were thoroughly terrified.

At first, the Mongols were not skilled in siege warfare (although they later learned useful techniques from their Chinese subjects). Their tactic was to make any promise

This gross affront provided the Mongols with a *casus belli*, and Genghis Khan personally led a four-pronged attack on the shah's empire. For two years Mongol columns went on a murderous rampage through the empire, leaving behind a trail of misery and destruction. When the Mongols reached the capital in 1221, the shah fled rather than surrender. The Mongols hunted him relentlessly throughout his crumbling and devastated domain, but the shah died before they could catch up with him. The governor of Otrar, who had so offended the Great Khan, was not so lucky. He was captured alive by the Mongols, who saw fit to punish his greed by pouring molten silver into his eyes and ears.

By this time, news of the fall of the Khwarezmid Empire had reached the rulers of Christendom in central Europe, who wondered whether the formidable Mongol army might also be Christian, and therefore an ally in their crusade to recapture Jerusalem and the Holy Land from Muslim rulers. But when the first encounter between a Christian nation and the Mongols took place, it was a much less friendly meeting than had been hoped for in Europe. In 1221, having completed its plunder of Khwarezmia, a Mongol force rounded the southern tip of the Caspian Sea, ravaged Azerbaijan, and crossed the Caucasus range into the Kingdom of Georgia. The Georgian cavalry, with the king at its head, took to the

field south of Tiflis (Tbilisi), but could not hold off the invaders for long.

The Mongol force carried on into southern Russia, where they raided the Black Sea coast in 1222 and smashed a large Kievan army on the River Kalka in 1223. The Mongols did not follow up on this crushing victory – not yet at least – but turned east and fought their way to the River Volga and then back to the main Mongol army north of the Aral Sea. This brilliant campaign, which had taken a small, unsupported army on a complete circuit of the Caspian Sea, was only a small part of the larger Mongol achievement. In 15 years, their invincible cavalry had carved out an empire that extended from the Pacific Ocean to the shores of the Black Sea. Temujin, the insignificant orphan, was now the ruler of half the known world.

The Mongol Legacy

Genghis Khan spent the last years of his life reconquering rebellious corners of China. He died in 1227 and was succeeded by his son Ogedei (r. 1227–1241), who initiated a new phase of expansion. Although Ogedei was not as gifted a leader as his father, the imperial momentum built up by Genghis Khan seemed unstoppable: the Mongols could no more keep themselves from the business of conquest than their victims could withstand them.

Below: The Mongolians were nomads rather than settlers. During battles they lived in 'yurts' – easily dismantled felt tents that are still used throughout Mongolia today.

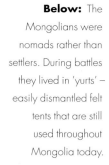

In 1237 a Mongol army under the leadership of Batu Khan (r. 1205–1235), grandson of Genghis and nephew of Ogedei, returned in force to Russia. The first areas to fall were the small city-states in the north: Ryazan, Suzdal, Vladimir and Moscow. Kiev was then sacked and burned in 1240. Novgorod alone was spared when an unseasonal thaw stranded the Mongols in a sea of mud, forcing them to turn back. Unlike subsequent invaders, including Napoleon in 1812 and Adolf Hitler in the 1940s, the Mongols were happy to wage war in the Russian winter. The frozen rivers were used as open highways, directing the Mongol cavalry to the very walls of one town after another.

After razing Kiev to the ground, Batu Khan led his army west into Poland and Hungary. Krakow, Wroclaw and Pest all fell, and the atrocities that had become the hallmark of the Mongol forces were inflicted on the civilian population. In the spring of 1242 Batu stood at the gates of Vienna, and the Mongols seemed poised to infiltrate Western Europe. But at this moment, news reached Batu of the death of his uncle, the Great Khan Ogedei, and he decided to abandon the campaign and return to Mongolia to take part in the election of a new khan.

In this manner, Western Europe was spared the torment of Mongol occupation, but the reprieve came too late for Russia, where the 'Tatar yoke' as Mongol rule became known, had taken hold. Batu had established his capital at Sarai, east of the River Volga, and from here the descendents of his original Mongol warriors continued to govern Russia. The territory was called 'the Golden Horde'. Although Russian principalities each had their own grand dukes, they ruled only with the approval of the khan of the Golden Horde. Generations of Russian princes were little more than glorified tax collectors, who travelled to Sarai in person to pay tribute to the khan each year. The Mongol legacy in Russia remained even after the nation grew strong enough to throw off the Tatar yoke in the late 15th century. Mongol rule meant that the Eastern Slavs were cut off from the west, and the advancements that developed there during the Renaissance and Enlightenment periods passed the region by.

The Muslim world, on the other hand, recovered more quickly. The ravaged areas were repopulated and rebuilt, while the unity of the Mongol Empire made it possible for trade and ideas to travel swiftly and unimpeded from one end of their domain to the other. Inventions such as printing, paper money and gunpowder swiftly made their way from China to the Near East via the Silk Road, an interconnected series of routes through Central Asia.

Whether the Mongols could have extended their empire any further into Europe is a much-debated question. At the end of the 12th century, their armies ground to a halt in Vietnam and Japan. Possibly they would have had a similar fate in Western Europe. By the time that Kublai Khan (r. 1260–1270), grandson of Genghis Khan, took control of the empire, it was in the process of disintegrating into smaller khanates. Mongol rulers of different parts of the empire eventually assimilated to local culture, becoming Muslims in the Near East and Buddhists in China.

But the Mongols remain a lively presence in folk memory, above all among the Eastern Slavs. 'Look at your room,' Russian mothers say to their untidy children. 'It looks like the Tatars have been through here.'

Above: A 16th-century illustration of Timur the Lame (Tamerlane, r. 1369–1405) attacking a walled town. In the 14th century, the Turco-Mongol warlord Timur tried to rebuild the Mongol Empire, conquering vast lands in the Middle East, Central Asia and India.

THE EXPANDING WORLD

The explorers who followed Columbus to the new lands in the West were driven as much by avarice as they were by the spirit of adventure. Many voyaged to the Americas in a search for gold. They found it in abundance, but Europeans also realised that there were even more lucrative ways to make money in the New World. Chief among these was the slave trade, which lasted for almost 400 years and involved the shipment of countless Africans to North and South America and to the Caribbean. While the American colonies were under British control, they also become home to tens of thousands of English criminals. Following American independence, Britain's convicts were dispatched to Australia where they became the founding fathers of a new nation. Other "founding fathers" – austere and pious men and women from the flatlands of East Anglia in England – chose Cape Cod in Massachusetts as the place to establish a simple, God-fearing community, a "beacon on a hill" for Christian souls everywhere. Although this particular migration was small, it became firmly engrained in American mythology.

Left: A 17th-century print depicts the departure of Christopher Columbus and his little fleet for the New World. As the explorer's ships fire a salute, King Ferdinand and Queen Isabella wave them off from the shores of Spain.

IN SEARCH OF EL DORADO

In 1492 the explorer Christopher Columbus (c. 1450–1506) sailed west from Spain hoping to find an unimpeded trade route to the Indies. After 61 days at sea he made landfall in the Bahamas, and was sure that he had arrived at the eastern seaboard of Asia. In fact, Columbus had reached the Americas. His journey was one that would be traced by millions of future immigrants.

When Columbus arrived in the Bahamas, he fully expected to be ushered into the presence of the Hongzhi Emperor (r. 1487–1505), ruler of China, and be showered with the precious spices and priceless jewels that he had read about in the travel writing of Marco Polo (1254–1324) and other traders and explorers. This, however, did not happen. The greatest discovery of the millennium was a disappointment to the man who made it, and it remained so all his life. Columbus made three successive voyages across the Atlantic, in 1493, 1498 and 1502, during which he explored the Caribbean and the northern coastline of South America. In 1506, Columbus

Left: Christopher Columbus's great mistake was to underestimate the distance from Europe to the Indies. He believed that Asia was no more than 5,000 kilometres (3,000 miles) west of the Canary Islands. This miscalculation led him to believe that he was in China when he reached the Bahamas.

DISCOVERING AMERICA

1492 The Genoese navigator Christopher Columbus discovers "West India" while sailing in the opposite direction to Dias.

1498 Vasco da Gama reaches India via the Cape of Good Hope.

1500 Pedro Cabral discovers Brazil; Columbus, on his third voyage, lands on the South American mainland for the first time in Venezuela.

C.E.	1475	1480	1485	1490	1495	1500	1505

1487 Bartholomeu Dias reaches the Cape of Good Hope, opening the way for an easterly sea route to India.

1494 Pope Alexander VI divides the New World into Spanish and Portuguese domains.

1497 John Cabot encounters the North American continent.

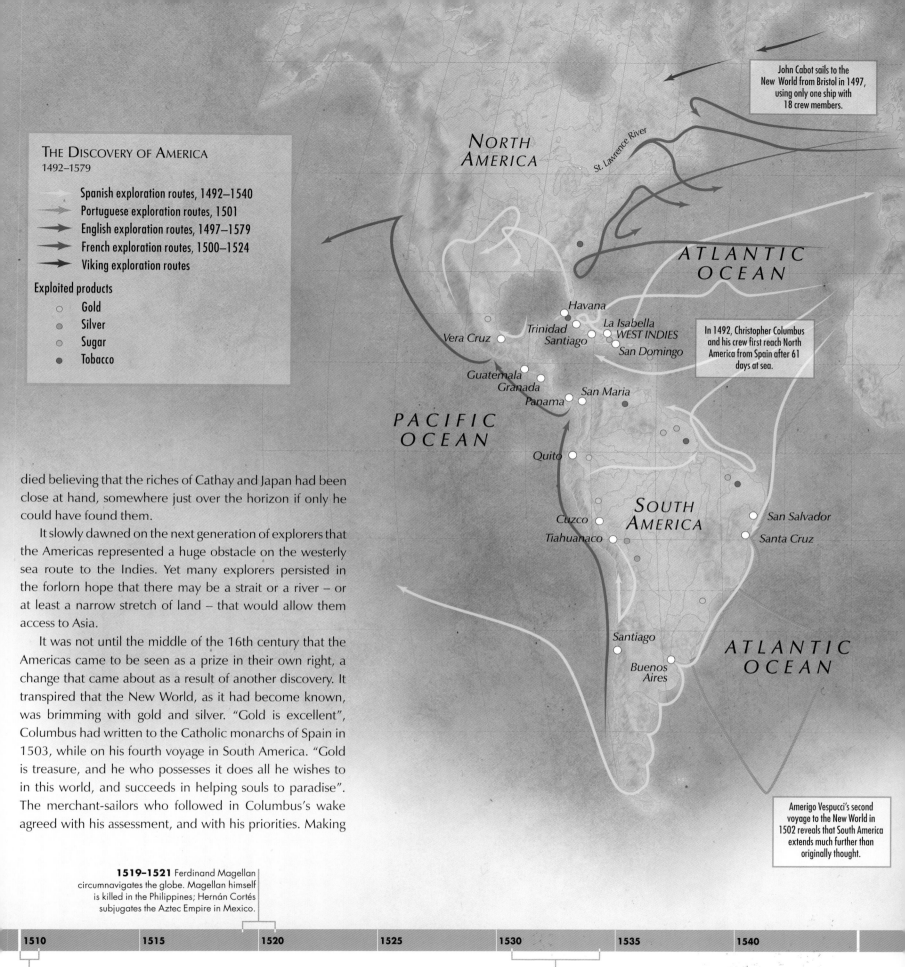

The Discovery of America
1492–1579

→ Spanish exploration routes, 1492–1540
→ Portuguese exploration routes, 1501
→ English exploration routes, 1497–1579
→ French exploration routes, 1500–1524
→ Viking exploration routes

Exploited products
○ Gold
◑ Silver
○ Sugar
● Tobacco

John Cabot sails to the New World from Bristol in 1497, using only one ship with 18 crew members.

In 1492, Christopher Columbus and his crew first reach North America from Spain after 61 days at sea.

Amerigo Vespucci's second voyage to the New World in 1502 reveals that South America extends much further than originally thought.

NORTH AMERICA

St. Lawrence River

ATLANTIC OCEAN

Havana
Trinidad
Santiago
Vera Cruz
La Isabella
WEST INDIES
San Domingo

Guatemala
Granada
Panama
San Maria

PACIFIC OCEAN

Quito

SOUTH AMERICA

Cuzco
Tiahuanaco
San Salvador
Santa Cruz

Santiago
Buenos Aires

ATLANTIC OCEAN

died believing that the riches of Cathay and Japan had been close at hand, somewhere just over the horizon if only he could have found them.

It slowly dawned on the next generation of explorers that the Americas represented a huge obstacle on the westerly sea route to the Indies. Yet many explorers persisted in the forlorn hope that there may be a strait or a river – or at least a narrow stretch of land – that would allow them access to Asia.

It was not until the middle of the 16th century that the Americas came to be seen as a prize in their own right, a change that came about as a result of another discovery. It transpired that the New World, as it had become known, was brimming with gold and silver. "Gold is excellent", Columbus had written to the Catholic monarchs of Spain in 1503, while on his fourth voyage in South America. "Gold is treasure, and he who possesses it does all he wishes to in this world, and succeeds in helping souls to paradise". The merchant-sailors who followed in Columbus's wake agreed with his assessment, and with his priorities. Making

1519–1521 Ferdinand Magellan circumnavigates the globe. Magellan himself is killed in the Philippines; Hernán Cortés subjugates the Aztec Empire in Mexico.

| 1510 | 1515 | 1520 | 1525 | 1530 | 1535 | 1540 |

1510–1511 African slaves begin to be imported to the New World.

1531–1534 Conquistador Francisco Pizarro destroys the Inca Empire in Peru.

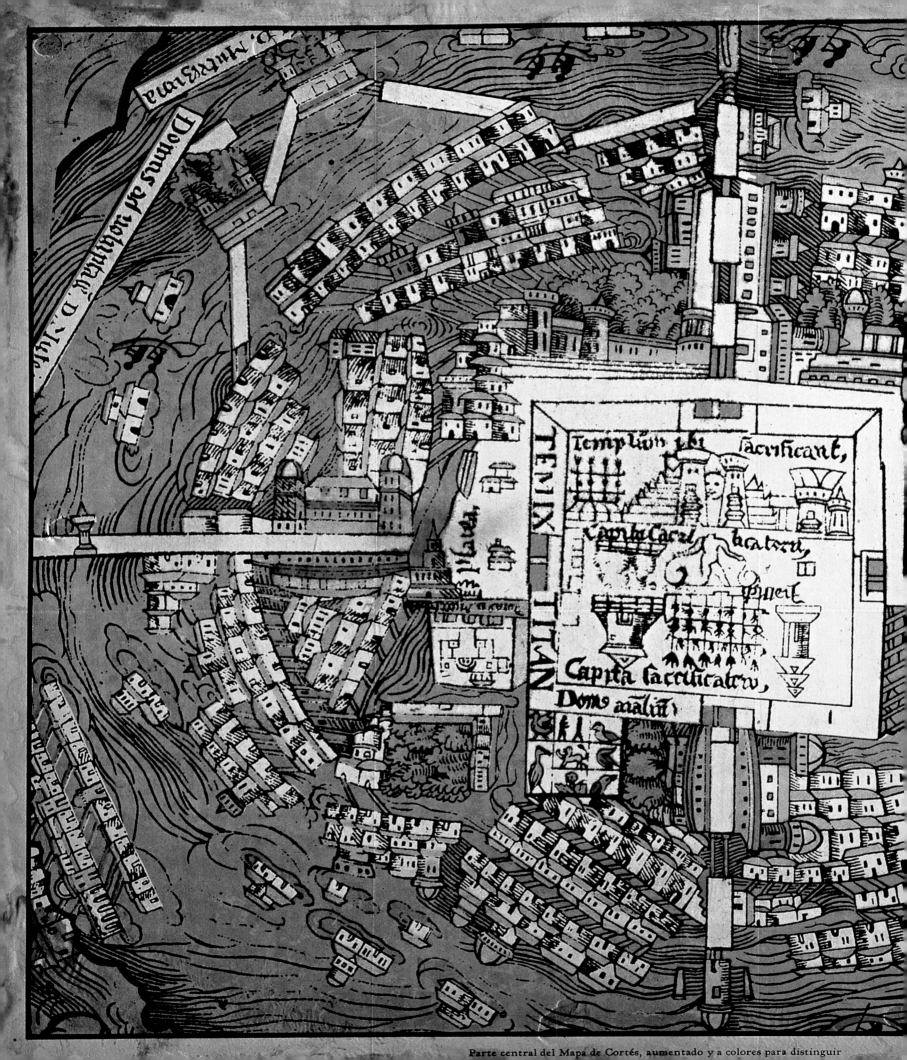

Parte central del Mapa de Cortés, aumentado y a colores para distinguir

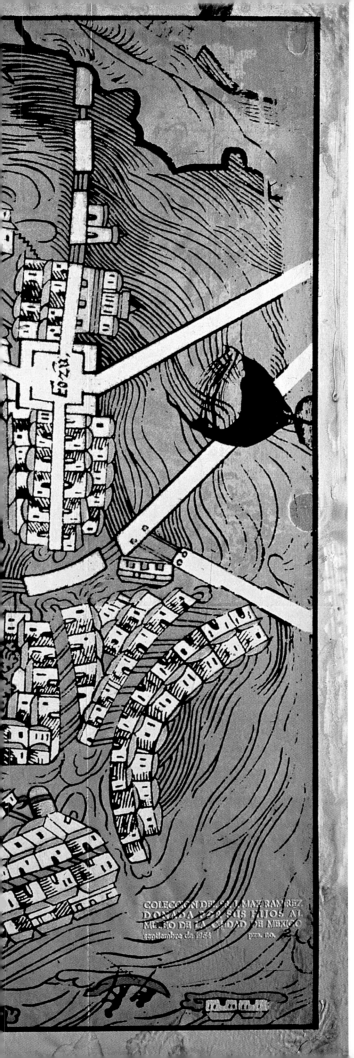

money was the main driving force behind their exploration of the Americas. The secondary purpose – to save the souls of the benighted "Indians" (as the Europeans persisted in misnaming them) – constituted the unilateral bargain that the Old World struck with the New. The European interlopers took earthly treasures from the natives they encountered, the Aztecs and the Incas, and in return they showed these "heathens" how, through faith in Christ, they could store up treasure in heaven. The European sea captains and adventurers, though, knew who was getting the better part of the deal.

The Treasures of the New World

Spain was the innovator in the exploitation of the Americas. On Columbus's first voyage in 1492 one of his ships ran aground on an island he called Hispaniola – "little Spain". Making a virtue of a necessity, Columbus left the crew on the island to form an impromptu colony, the first European community in the New World. By the time Columbus returned the following year, all of the settlers had been killed by the local Taino peoples, but a colonial base was nevertheless established: Hispaniola was the starting point for the exploration of the Caribbean Sea. In the early 1500s, Spanish explorers conquered the islands of Cuba and Puerto Rico and then made landfall on the North American mainland (something Columbus never did). Florida, or "the land of flowers", was found and named in 1513, and in the 1520s Spanish expeditions made their way up the eastern seaboard of North America as far as Labrador in present-day Canada.

The Spanish, however, were much less interested in the cold and barren shores to the north than they were in the Aztec kingdom of Mexico where, they had heard, gold was as common as grass. In 1519, the Spanish conquistador Hernán Cortés (1485–1547) led an expedition of 600 men to invade

Left: Tenochtitlan, capital of the Aztecs, was one of the largest cities in the world at the time the Spanish found it. It was also one of the most civilised: there were private houses with toilets, a town planner, an army of street cleaners, a botanical garden and a zoo. All of this was destroyed by the Spanish.

Mexico from Cuba. The Aztec emperor, Moctezuma II (r. 1502–1520), was alarmed by the approach of this army and its unknown weapons – war dogs, horses, muskets and cannons. He invited Cortés and his men into his capital, Tenochtitlan. The city, which was built on an island in the middle of a lake, was magnificent beyond anything the Spaniards had ever seen. The architecture was as stunning as it was colourful, and the immense wealth of the empire was plain to be seen. "These great towns and pyramids and buildings arising from the water, all made of stone, seemed like an enchanted vision", wrote Bernal Diaz del Castillo (c. 1492–1584), who served under Cortés. "Some of our soldiers asked whether it was not all a dream".

The conquistadors' dream quickly turned into a nightmare for the Aztecs. The Spaniards took Moctezuma prisoner, besieged his great city, and after months of fighting reduced it to rubble, killing thousands of Aztecs in the process. Thousands more were beginning to die of the diseases that the Europeans had brought over from the Old World. Imported pathogens – smallpox, measles and typhus, but also relatively mild conditions such as chickenpox and whooping cough – combined to devastate

the inhabitants of the New World, who had no immunity against these foreign diseases. Deadly epidemics followed wherever Europeans came into contact with native peoples, and the pattern of pandemic was repeated when the conquistadors invaded the Inca Empire in Peru in 1532. Disease made the conquerors' job easy, and by the mid-16th century almost all of South America had become a large and lucrative Spanish possession (the region that became Brazil had been awarded to Portugal in 1494 in the Treaty of Tordesillas).

Spain was intent on settling all the land where the Spanish flag was planted, and the business of colonising was seen as an important operation. As the Spanish historian Francisco López de Gómara (c. 1511–1566) put it, "Without settlement there is no good conquest, and if the land is not conquered, the people will not be converted. Therefore the maxim of the conqueror must be to settle". In the course of the 16th century about 250,000 Spaniards settled in the New World. Most of the emigrants were men – the dangers and hardships of life in the Americas were held to be too great to be undertaken by women. As time went by, many Spanish colonisers took wives from

Below: Objects like this turquoise serpent convinced the Spanish that the Aztec Empire was ripe for plunder. It took Cortés and his small army less than three years to destroy Aztec civilisation and to obliterate the magnificent city of Tenochtitlan.

among the native population, and the mixed race offspring of the next and subsequent generations were known as *mestizos*.

When African slaves began to be imported to South America in large numbers in the early 1500s, female slaves were also taken as concubines by the ruling Spaniards. Children of Afro-Hispanic parentage were known as *mulattos*. In the absence of an established aristocracy, colonial Spanish society came to be organised according to a careful and legally sanctioned grading of skin colour. "Pureblood" Spaniards were at the top of the social pyramid, native Amerindians and black-skinned Africans were at the bottom, and all the varieties and shades of mestizos and mulattos occupied the middle levels. This organised system of discrimination is another example of how the "discoverers" of America came to dominate the New World's old inhabitants.

Above: The Incas were skilled goldsmiths. But the Spanish invaders were not interested in Inca workmanship, only in Inca treasure, and they melted down most of what they stole. This sun plate is one piece that escaped their attention.

" I found very many islands filled with people innumerable, and of them all I have taken possession for their Highnesses, by proclamation made and with royal standards unfurled, and no opposition was offered to me. They do not have arms and they are all naked, and of no skill in arms, and so very cowardly that a thousand would not stand against three [armed] Spaniards. And so they are fit to be ordered about and made to work, plant, and do every thing else that may be needed, and build towns and be taught our customs and to go about clothed. "

Christopher Columbus's thoughts on the first encounter between Europeans and the natives of the New World, 1492

THE MIDDLE PASSAGE

Over the course of 400 years, from the beginning of the 16th century to the end of the 19th century, around 11 million Africans were removed from their homelands against their will and shipped to North and South America, and to the islands of the Caribbean to live out their lives as slaves. Known as the Atlantic slave trade, this transport of humans constitutes the largest forced migration in history.

Below: Slaves wait in chains to be sold at the market in Zanzibar, East Africa. The African slave trade was abolished by most countries by the 1850s.

The traffic of Africans involved all the main European trading nations (Spain, Portugal, the Netherlands, France and Britain) at one time or another. It also relied heavily on African tribal leaders and kings, who brought a ready supply of slaves from the continent's interior to the ports of West Africa, from where European traders operated. For the victims of the slave trade, the experience was an unimaginable trauma. The voyage from Africa to the Americas – the "middle passage", as it became known – was cruel, degrading and brutal. It has been calculated that, on average, 15 per cent of enslaved Africans died in transit, either from disease or from maltreatment. More surprisingly perhaps, as many as one-third of all Africans imported to the Americas died within three or four years of arrival. To this death toll must be added the incalculable number – millions more, certainly – who died en route from the African interior to the coast while the trade lasted.

The Beginnings of the Slave Trade

The Spanish and the Portuguese were the pioneers of the slave trade. From as early as the 15th century, these European nations bought slaves in the ordinary course of commerce with Africa. Some slaves were transported to work in the gold mines of South America by the conquistadors, and it was noted that Africans were much hardier and more efficient workers than the local Amerindians, who were also enslaved by the Spanish at the time. The Portuguese used African slave labour on their sugar plantations in the Atlantic islands of Madeira, Cape Verde, Sao Tome and the Azores. These first slaves, however, were generally incidental acquisitions and they were few in number. The first organised transport of slaves to the Americas was undertaken by Spanish traders in 1518. Once the Portuguese had set up sugarcane production in their new acquisition of Brazil (discovered in 1500), there was both a

THE ATLANTIC SLAVE TRADE

1518 The first transport of slaves from Africa to the New World takes place.

1627–28 Britain takes possession of Barbados.

1655 Britain takes possession of Jamaica.

C.E.	1500	1510	1520	1530	1540	1550	1560	1570	1580	1590	1600	1610	1620	1630	1640	1650	1660	1670	1680	1690

1500 Eastern Brazil is discovered by Pedro Cabral of Portugal.

1619 Black slaves are sold in Jamestown, Britain's first permanent colony in America.

mid 1600s The American colonies begin to use slave labour to work on tobacco and rice plantations.

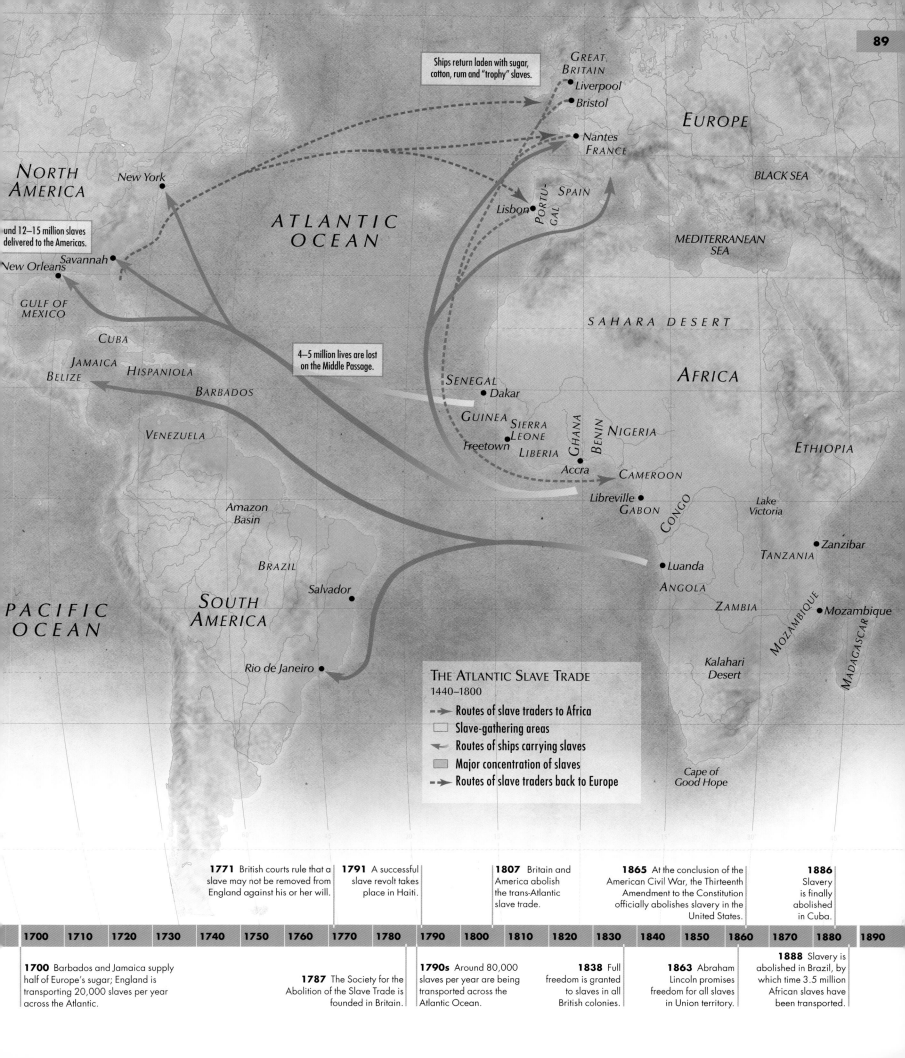

Ships return laden with sugar, cotton, rum and "trophy" slaves.

GREAT BRITAIN
• Liverpool
• Bristol

EUROPE

BLACK SEA

NORTH AMERICA

New York

ATLANTIC OCEAN

Nantes
FRANCE

PORTU-
GAL
Lisbon

SPAIN

MEDITERRANEAN SEA

...und 12–15 million slaves delivered to the Americas.

Savannah

New Orleans

GULF OF MEXICO

SAHARA DESERT

AFRICA

CUBA

JAMAICA
BELIZE
HISPANIOLA

BARBADOS

4–5 million lives are lost on the Middle Passage.

SENEGAL
• Dakar

GUINEA
SIERRA LEONE
Freetown
LIBERIA

GHANA
BENIN
NIGERIA

ETHIOPIA

VENEZUELA

Accra

CAMEROON

Libreville •
GABON

CONGO

Lake Victoria

Amazon Basin

• Zanzibar

TANZANIA

BRAZIL

PACIFIC OCEAN

SOUTH AMERICA

Salvador •

• Luanda

ANGOLA

ZAMBIA

• Mozambique

MOZAMBIQUE

MADAGASCAR

Kalahari Desert

THE ATLANTIC SLAVE TRADE
1440–1800

- - → Routes of slave traders to Africa
☐ Slave-gathering areas
← Routes of ships carrying slaves
▨ Major concentration of slaves
- - → Routes of slave traders back to Europe

Rio de Janeiro •

Cape of Good Hope

1771 British courts rule that a slave may not be removed from England against his or her will.

1791 A successful slave revolt takes place in Haiti.

1807 Britain and America abolish the trans-Atlantic slave trade.

1865 At the conclusion of the American Civil War, the Thirteenth Amendment to the Constitution officially abolishes slavery in the United States.

1886 Slavery is finally abolished in Cuba.

1700	1710	1720	1730	1740	1750	1760	1770	1780	1790	1800	1810	1820	1830	1840	1850	1860	1870	1880	1890

1700 Barbados and Jamaica supply half of Europe's sugar; England is transporting 20,000 slaves per year across the Atlantic.

1787 The Society for the Abolition of the Slave Trade is founded in Britain.

1790s Around 80,000 slaves per year are being transported across the Atlantic Ocean.

1838 Full freedom is granted to slaves in all British colonies.

1863 Abraham Lincoln promises freedom for all slaves in Union territory.

1888 Slavery is abolished in Brazil, by which time 3.5 million African slaves have been transported.

market for African slaves in place and a means of delivering them to buyers. By 1550 Brazil was the world's largest exporter of sugar and a major importer of Africans, and this link between sugar and slaves went on to last as long as the trade itself.

The sugar industry came to depend on slave labour wherever it took root. In Barbados and Jamaica, which became British possessions in 1627 and 1655 respectively, tobacco was at first the main cash crop and plantation workers were mostly indentured immigrants from Britain itself. Sugarcane, however, was found to be more profitable, and once the plantation owners began to grow this product in the late 1600s they also adopted the Brazilian practice of using slave workers. Dutch merchants specialised in supplying the slaves from Africa, and they also had the means to take the sugar harvested in the Americas to market in Europe. This arrangement, which was convenient for all the businesspeople involved, constituted the "Atlantic Triangle", a term used to describe the flow of goods along the slave trade routes of the 18th century.

The first side of the triangle was represented by the traders' voyage from Europe to West Africa, where goods such as guns and gunpowder, Indian cloth, copper or iron bars and cowrie shells were traded for slaves. The slaves were then carried – sometimes on the same ships – to the Americas along the infamous "middle passage", the second side of the triangle. To complete the triangle, American-made produce, including sugar, rum, molasses, coffee and cotton, were ferried back to willing buyers in Europe. Not all voyages, or all trade, followed this pattern – much of the commerce between Brazil and the Slave Coast in Africa, for example, was bilateral – but these three connecting routes constituted the practical workings of the slave trade: the trade channel that provided the means of buying slaves, the paths along which slaves flowed, and the transport of the goods that slave labour produced.

Collecting Slaves

The African slave markets were spread all along the concave coast of Africa, from the Senegal River in the north to Luanda in the south. Slaves were just one of many commodities to be found in Africa, and Europeans named stretches of the seaboard after the main export the area had to offer. The Ivory Coast (Côte d'Ivoire) retained its European name when it became an independent nation in the 20th century. To the east of this was the Gold Coast (present-day Ghana), and further east still was the Slave Coast (modern-day Togo, Benin and western Nigeria). European traders rarely penetrated far into the African interior. The risk of contracting sickness was high and there was also the danger of hostility from local tribes. Instead, traders waited for slaves to be brought to them on the coast. The slaves carried to market were often prisoners-of-war who had been enslaved by their tribe's enemies. European traders were always heartened to hear that a conflict was brewing between two African tribes or peoples, because war guaranteed a rich harvest of fresh slaves. "The battle is expected shortly", wrote one English trader on Cape Coast in 1712. "After which 'tis hoped the trade will flourish".

James Penny, another experienced British slaver, described the slave-buying process to a parliamentary

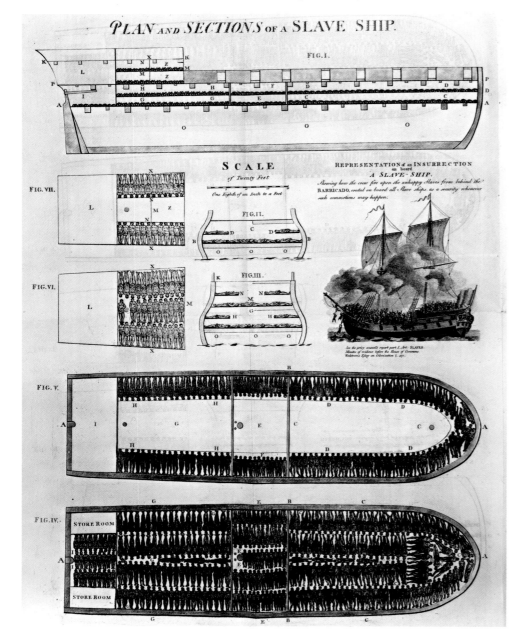

" There came a merchant from the Gold Coast. He traded with the inhabitants of our country in ivory. He said, if my parents would part with me for a little while, and let him take me home with him, it would be of more service to me than any thing they could do for me. I cannot recall how long we were in going from Bournou to the Gold Coast. It was upwards of a thousand miles. I was heartily rejoic'd when we arrived at the end of our journey. I was conducted by my friend, the merchant, to the King. It pleased God to melt the heart of the King. He took me upon his knee and wept over me. He sat me down and blest me; and added that I should not go home, but be sold for a slave, so then I was conducted back to the merchant's house. The next day he took me on board a French brig; but the captain did not chuse to buy me; he said I was too small. A few days after, a Dutch ship came into the harbour, and they carried me on board in hopes that the Captain would purchase me. As they went I heard them agree that if they could not sell me then, they would throw me overboard. I was in extreme agonies when I heard this. The Dutch Captain bought me for two yards of check, which is of more value there than in England. "

James Albert Ukawsaw Gronniosaw, who was sold into slavery in the 1720s

committee in 1789: "At Bonny traders go up into the country to purchase slaves … At the head of two rivers there is a mart for trade where the black traders purchase these slaves of other black slave traders, who bring them from the interior country". Once they had been bought and paid for, slaves were branded with a hot iron on the breast or shoulder and kept in the European forts until it was time for them to be loaded onto the trade ships. Pairs of slaves were chained together at the ankle, and herded below decks by sailors with whips. The slavers generally had no idea about the tribal provenance of the slaves, and often a slave would find himself yoked to a speaker of a different language, or to a member of a tribe with which he had until recently been at war.

Life on the Middle Passage

The terrible hardships of the middle passage tended to erase African enmities. The spaces below deck on slave ships were rarely more than 1.5 metres (5 feet) high, so it

Origins of Enslaved Africans

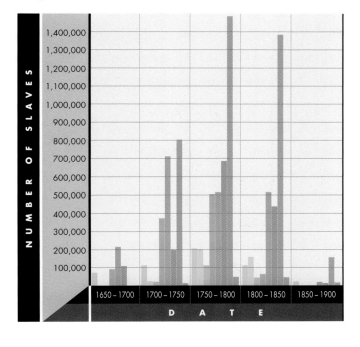

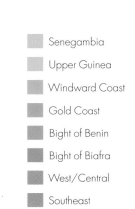

- Senegambia
- Upper Guinea
- Windward Coast
- Gold Coast
- Bight of Benin
- Bight of Biafra
- West/Central
- Southeast

Right: The first generations of African slaves in America tended the tobacco plantations of Virginia. Later the slaves tended the cotton fields of the South. The most dangerous and debilitating slavework was harvesting sugar cane in the Caribbean and on the South American coast.

was impossible for the captured slaves to stand up straight. Their beds were narrow shelves on which they were made to lie down "spoonways" – head to toe and toe to head – to maximise the number of people that could be squeezed into the available space. Conditions below deck quickly became unsanitary to the point of being deadly, particularly as the slaves were confined there for the week or so that it took to sail out of sight of land. By that time dysentery and other diseases were rife. All eyewitness accounts speak of the unbelievable stench of slave ships, which could be smelled downwind several kilometres away.

It was not in the interests of the ships' captains to deliberately harm slaves – to damage the goods, so to speak – since their profit depended on delivering fit and healthy workers to the plantations of Cuba and Brazil. Many slaves were mistreated, however, in order to prevent rebellion and thereby protect the overall investment. Discipline was harsh, and beatings and floggings were commonplace. During the long voyage slaves were periodically made to "dance" on deck to give them some fresh air and exercise, but as they were bound in manacles this often amounted to a form of torture. Slaves who refused to eat were force fed – sometimes with the help of an instrument, such as a pair of tongs that was used to prise the jaws apart and hold them open. Women (who were a minority on the slave routes, since the main market was for strong male field workers) were in constant danger of being abused or raped by the ship's crew.

The mortality rate on slave ships varied over time and from place to place, but generally speaking, it decreased over the years. As many as 40 per cent of slaves died during the middle passage in the 16th century; by the 19th, this figure was between 5 and 10 per cent. Gastrointestinal illness was, not surprisingly, the main cause of death among slaves, and smallpox and malaria were also prevalent. In 1790, however, one English ship's surgeon suggested that that most deaths on board ship were due to *banzo* – a Portuguese slaving term that is usually translated as "mortal melancholy" or, even more chillingly, "involuntary suicide".

But not all enslaved Africans descended into melancholy; some reacted to their plight with vengeful fury and rose up against their captors, an event that was dreaded by every ship's captain. It has been estimated that 10 per cent of ships experienced some form of revolt, and there are at least 133 recorded instances of rebellions. A further 140 slave ships simply disappeared, and it may be that some of these were taken over by their human cargo, who then perished because they did not now how to navigate the boat. In some instances slaves managed to take control of the ship and force the crew to sail back to Africa, but these were very few. Most revolts ended in failure, and failure was invariably followed by the most bloody and sadistic reprisals against the rebel slaves.

The Slave Markets

In the 18th century, the voyage from Africa to the Caribbean lasted about 14 weeks, and on arrival slaves were quickly

Left: A flamboyant slaver pays for his human purchases on the coast of West Africa. His ships are waiting offshore to take his goods on the gruesome "middle passage" to the Americas or the islands of the Caribbean.

" I was soon put down under the decks, and there I received such a salutation in my nostrils as I had never experienced in my life: so that with the loathsomeness of the stench and the crying together, I became so sick and low that I was not able to eat. I now wished for the last friend, death, to relieve me; but soon, to my grief, two of the white men offered me eatables, and on my refusing to eat, one of them … laid me across I think a windlass, and tied my feet while the other flogged me severely. The stench of the hold was so intolerable that it was dangerous to remain there for any time … The shrieks of the women and the groans of the dying rendered the whole scene of horror almost inconceivable. "

Ouladah Equiano, who was kidnapped as a small boy in Nigeria in the 1750s and shipped to Barbados

sold. They were either passed on to a pre-arranged buyer, sold at auction like cattle, or sold in what was known as a "scramble" – in which prospective buyers rushed on board ship and simply grabbed the people they wanted to buy.

Once bought, a slave's chance of any kind of decent life depended on where he found himself and the work he was put to. The hardest labour and worst regimes were found on the sugar plantations of Brazil and Cuba. Many slaves died after a few years of this work, which is why these sugar states continued to import slaves illegally long after the trade was banned by the British and Americans in 1807. Although the hardships that slaves in America endured were also great, a slave's life was generally better in the United States than in the Caribbean or Brazil. Work

on the tobacco plantations of Virginia was less arduous, and the estates were smaller, which meant there was a greater opportunity for slaves to develop settled communities. American slaves could form families and have children, and in that sense avoid the total dehumanisation experienced by South American slaves. Indeed, in America, the slave population grew by natural reproduction, rather than further imports from Africa.

Despite the ill treatment that slaves received at the hands of their masters, they did not lose the knowledge of their own self-worth as human beings rather than human chattel. After centuries of living in harsh conditions, slaves were able to throw off their chains when slavery was finally abolished in the Americas in the late 19th century.

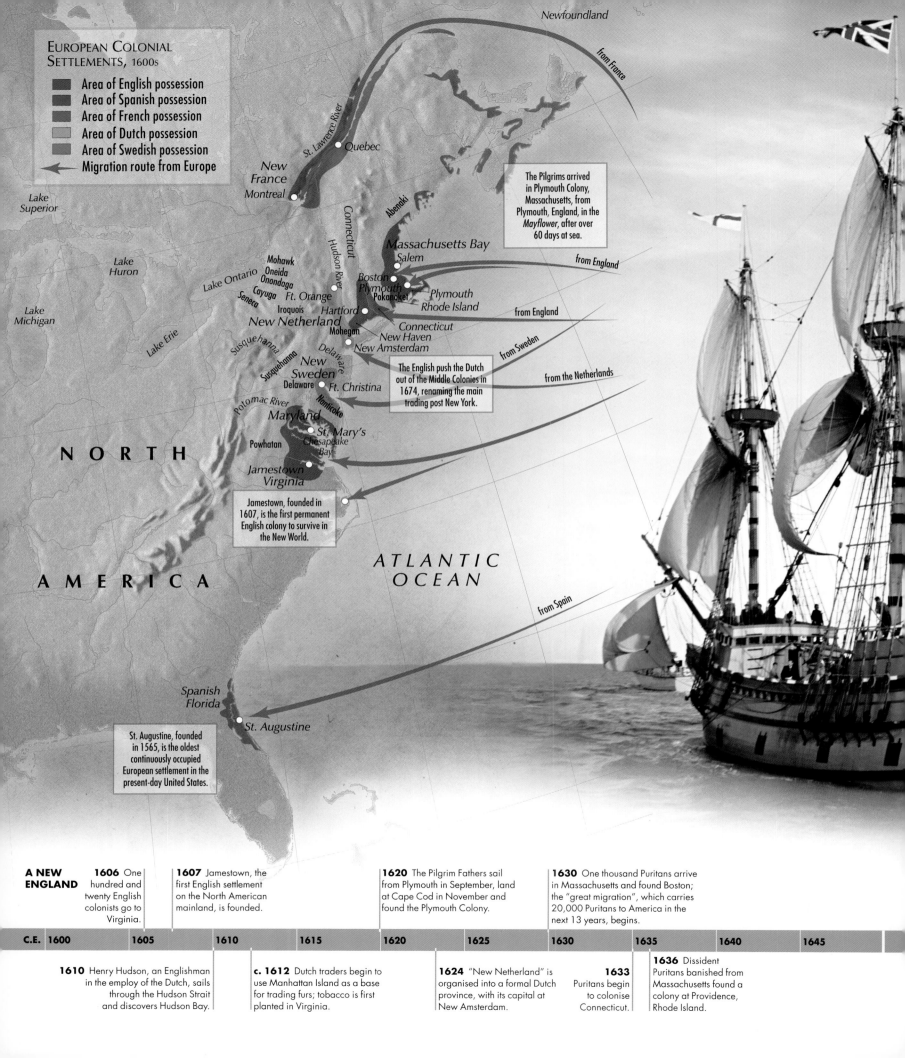

EUROPEAN COLONIAL SETTLEMENTS, 1600s

- Area of English possession
- Area of Spanish possession
- Area of French possession
- Area of Dutch possession
- Area of Swedish possession
- → Migration route from Europe

Newfoundland

from France

Lake Superior

Lake Huron

Lake Michigan

Lake Ontario

Lake Erie

St. Lawrence River

New France
Quebec
Montreal

Connecticut

Abenaki

Massachusetts Bay
Salem

Mohawk
Oneida
Onondaga
Cayuga
Seneca
Iroquois
Ft. Orange

Hudson River

Boston
Plymouth
Pokanoket
Plymouth
Rhode Island

Hartford

New Netherland
Mohegan
New Haven
New Amsterdam

Connecticut

from England

from England

from Sweden

from the Netherlands

The Pilgrims arrived in Plymouth Colony, Massachusetts, from Plymouth, England, in the *Mayflower*, after over 60 days at sea.

The English push the Dutch out of the Middle Colonies in 1674, renaming the main trading post New York.

Susquehanna

New Sweden
Delaware
Ft. Christina

Susquehanna

Delaware

Nanticoke

Potomac River

Maryland
Powhatan
St. Mary's
Chesapeake Bay

Jamestown
Virginia

Jamestown, founded in 1607, is the first permanent English colony to survive in the New World.

N O R T H

A M E R I C A

ATLANTIC OCEAN

from Spain

Spanish Florida
St. Augustine

St. Augustine, founded in 1565, is the oldest continuously occupied European settlement in the present-day United States.

A NEW ENGLAND	**1606** One hundred and twenty English colonists go to Virginia.	**1607** Jamestown, the first English settlement on the North American mainland, is founded.	**1620** The Pilgrim Fathers sail from Plymouth in September, land at Cape Cod in November and found the Plymouth Colony.	**1630** One thousand Puritans arrive in Massachusetts and found Boston; the "great migration", which carries 20,000 Puritans to America in the next 13 years, begins.

C.E.	1600	1605	1610	1615	1620	1625	1630	1635	1640	1645

1610 Henry Hudson, an Englishman in the employ of the Dutch, sails through the Hudson Strait and discovers Hudson Bay.

c. 1612 Dutch traders begin to use Manhattan Island as a base for trading furs; tobacco is first planted in Virginia.

1624 "New Netherland" is organised into a formal Dutch province, with its capital at New Amsterdam.

1633 Puritans begin to colonise Connecticut.

1636 Dissident Puritans banished from Massachusetts found a colony at Providence, Rhode Island.

A NEW ENGLAND

In 1497, five years after Christopher Columbus (c. 1450–1506) planted the Spanish flag on a "West Indian" island in the Caribbean, John Cabot (c. 1450–1499) made landfall on the North American continent and claimed it for the English Crown. While the southerly parts of the New World continued to be influenced by Iberian nations – they became the possession of Spain and, to a lesser extent, of Portugal – the northern reaches became an area of activity for the British, Dutch and French sea powers.

Cabot, like Columbus, had been seeking a route to Asia when he came upon the impassable landmass of North America. Unlike Columbus, Cabot realised that he had arrived at a previously uncharted coast, and he called his discovery New-Found Land. Cabot was unaware that the Vikings had discovered this very land some 500 years previously: Newfoundland was the island sprawling with grapes that pioneering Norsemen had named Vinland – "Wineland".

The Spanish did not recognise England's or anyone else's right to make use of the North American continent. They had been the first to explore the lands north of Mexico and they made a point of rooting out any attempts to intrude on their new empire. In 1565, for example, Spanish troops destroyed a colony of French Huguenots that had settled in Florida. Nevertheless, by the late 1500s several intrepid Englishmen were exploring the American coast. Martin Frobisher (c. 1535–1594) made three voyages to North America in the 1570s in search of a "northwest passage" to China, and gained much useful knowledge

Left: A modern reconstruction of the *Mayflower*, the famous ship that transported the Pilgrim Fathers from Plymouth, England, to Plymouth Colony, Massachusetts, in 1620.

| 1650 | 1655 | 1660 | 1665 | 1670 | 1675 | 1680 | 1685 | 1690 | 1695 | 1700 |

1681 William Penn founds Pennsylvania as a refuge for Quakers.

of the continent. In 1580, Francis Drake (c. 1540–1596) returned to England from a three-year voyage that had taken him around the world, following a route that passed through the heart of Spanish overseas dominions. Tension between Spain and England had been growing since the 1560s due to economic competition over Atlantic trade, and Drake's achievement was so daring and so politically sensitive that it was a closely guarded state secret until after the English defeated the Spanish Armada (the Spanish fleet) in 1588 in the battle of Gravelines in the North Sea.

The Virginia Colony

In the 1580s, England had begun to make plans to colonise America's eastern seaboard. Although the battle of Gravelines signaled the end of Spanish hegemony in the New World, the British still felt it was prudent to settle areas that were as far away from Spanish territory as possible. "Beside the portion of land pertaining to the

the Spaniards", wrote the Elizabethan geographer Richard Eden, "There yet remaineth an other portion of that main land reaching toward the north-east, thought to be as large as the other, and not yet known but only by the sea coasts, neither inhabited by any Christian men … In this land there are many fair and fruitful regions". This description was more idealistic than accurate, but it was enough to tempt the inveterate adventurer Walter Raleigh (c. 1552–1618), a favorite courtier of Queen Elizabeth I (r. 1558–1603), to organise an expedition. After an exploratory expedition a year earlier, in 1585 Raleigh dispatched more than 100 men from England to colonise "Virginia", named in honour of Elizabeth I, the "Virgin Queen".

The colonists settled on the island of Roanoke, but they were ill-equipped to make the community a success. The

Above: A 17th-century woodcut depicts the departure of religious dissenters for the New World. Behind them they left a history of persecution, represented here by the unhappy figure being burned at the stake.

soil was poor, and the native peoples soon grew tired of the Englishmen's requests for food. When the hungry colonists took their maize by force, the natives simply removed themselves and left the white men to their fate. They were starving when they were picked up by English ships in 1586 and ferried home. Raleigh dispatched another group of colonists in 1587, and this time sent women as well as children. He had chosen a more hospitable site for the colony further north on Chesapeake Bay, but the sailors who carried the colonists to North America unceremoniously left them on Roanoke once more. No English ship approached the settlement for three years, and the first visitors to the colony found it empty. There was no sign of a struggle or any kind of catastrophe: what became of the second Roanoke colony remains a mystery.

The third English attempt to colonise Virginia got off to an equally unpromising start. Three ships set sail for Virginia in 1606 under the auspices of the Virginia Company, a pair of English joint stock companies chartered in the same year by the new king, James I (r. 1603–1625), with the purpose of founding colonies in North America. The 105 colonists on board arrived in Virginia in the spring of 1607 and made a base for themselves, Jamestown, 100 kilometres (60 miles) inland along the James River on Chesapeake Bay (both the town and the river were named in honour of James I). Here they were well hidden from Spanish marauders, but it soon emerged that the real hazard was their own ineptitude and inexperience. By Christmas, all but 38 of the Jamestown colonists were dead of disease or hunger. The Virginia Company sent more settlers to the colony year after year, but the rate of attrition was such that most died during the harsh winters. Over the course of 15 years, 10,000 men and women made the voyage to Jamestown, but by 1622 there were only 2,000 people living in the community.

The Jamestown colony managed to subsist, but only just. Its survival was due to the military regime introduced by Captain John Smith (c. 1580–1631), the leader of the colony during its early, hungry years. He forced the colonists to work like prisoners in a penal colony, and this tough regime probably assured the survival of at least the fittest. (John Smith's fame also rests on an incident in 1607, when he claimed he was captured by Native Americans and subjected to a mock execution in which his life was ritually spared by "princess" Pocahontas, c. 1595–1617.) In the longer term, the salvation of the colony was the introduction from the West Indies of a lucrative cash crop – tobacco. In 1612, a colonist named John Rolfe (c. 1585–1622, the husband of Pocahontas) learned how to plant the crop and

"The Duke's Plan"

A · DESCRIPTION · OF · THE
TOWNE · OF · MANNADOS
OR · NEW · AMSTERDAM
as it was in September 1661
lying in Lattitude 40 and 40
Anno Domini
1664

Governours Garden

· Hudsons · River ·

THE · MAINE · LAND

·This Scale of Fiue Hondred yeardes is for the Toune·

| 50 | 100 | 200 | 300 | 400 | 500 |

---

taught the techniques to other colonists. The shareholders of the Virginia Company, who for years had failed to see a return from the money they had invested in the struggling colony, saw the potential of this new and exciting product. They freely gave land to the colonists, and encouraged them to grow as much tobacco as they could. The dried weed was shipped east from the settlement, and profits flowed back to the colony and into the pockets of the company men. At last, Virginia became a land of prosperous plantation owners.

The Plymouth Colony

To the north of Virginia, beyond the Hudson River, the coastal country was more temperate. It was too cold to grow tobacco in the region, but not cold enough to support

the animals that sustained the fur trade further north. John Smith, who had explored the coast in 1614, named it "New England" because it struck him that the climate was very similar to that of the mother country. A very different kind of settlement took root in New England at the same time that Virginia began to flourish. In 1620 a group of religious dissenters, known to history as the Pilgrim Fathers, set sail from Plymouth in southwest England and voyaged to the natural harbour of Cape Cod in Massachusetts. Within its sheltered bay they founded a religious colony called Plymouth, and for 10 years they were the only permanent community of Europeans in New England.

The Pilgrims (not a term they used to describe themselves) were émigrés twice over. They had been brought together

Above: New Amsterdam in 1661, three years before it was acquired by the British and renamed New York. The Dutch colony was confined to the southern tip of Manhattan. A single Native American trail, known to the Dutch as "the broad way" ran north through the island.

Their greene corne.

Corne newly sprong.

Their sitting at meate.

The place of solemne prayer.

The house wherin the Tombe of their Herounds standeth.

SECOTON

A Ceremony in their prayers wth strange gestures and songs dansing abowt posts carued on the topps lyke mens faces.

Left: This sketch of an orderly Native American village was made by an Englishman, John White, who sailed with Sir Walter Raleigh's expedition of 1585.

" This bay is a most hopeful place … Monday, the 18th day [December, 1620], we went a land … We marched along the coast … but saw not an Indian nor an Indian house; only we found where formerly had been some inhabitants, and where they had planted their corn. We found … running brooks of very sweet fresh water … Many kinds of herb we found here … sorrel, yarrow, carvel, brooklime, liverwort, watercresses, great store of leeks and onions. [Also] … innumerable store of fowl … and cannot but be of fish in their seasons: skate, cod, turbot, and herring we have tasted of; abundance of mussels … crabs and lobsters in their time, infinite. "

William Bradford, one of the Pilgrim Fathers, describes the first landing at Cape Cod Bay in 1620

between 1586 and 1605 by their common belief in the ideas promoted by Richard Clyfton of the All Saints Parish Church in Nottinghamshire, England. In 1608, many of them had fled to Holland, where they hoped they would be able to practise their form of Christianity free from persecution by the Church of England, which they believed to be too hierarchical and ritualistic – much like the Roman Catholic Church from which it had broken away. Some of the Separatists, however, found it difficult to create their ideal community within the confines of a settled society. They considered returning to England, but this seemed like a step backwards, and in any case England was in the grip of an economic recession. After much soul-searching and prayer, the group decided to journey to America and found "a city on a hill" – their vision of a Bible republic that would act as an example to old England and the rest of the world of how to live alongside one's fellow man in a Christ-like way.

The broadly democratic outlook of the Pilgrim Fathers, along with their scorn for wealth and their relish for hard work, stood them in good stead during their first years in North America. They were less disdainful of the Native Americans than most other European settlers, and they even formed friendships with some individuals (as long as they first converted to their religion.) Their "city on a hill", however, did not endure for long. In the 1630s, the Pilgrims were eclipsed by a great migration of Puritans – a distinct sect within the Protestant fold. Over the course of the decade, about 20,000 Puritans travelled from England to New England, where they founded the city of Boston in 1630.

The Puritans were a radical left-wing group within the Church of England who rejected the popery that they felt had been introduced to the church in the early 17th century and instead sought a "purity" of worship and doctrine. They

were stricter and less tolerant than the Separatist Pilgrims, and were more hostile to other dissenting sects such as Quakers and Baptists, who had also migrated to the colonies of America. The Puritans acted as a spur to migration within New England itself. Several new colonies – notably that on Rhode Island – were set up by splinter groups who found that their views on theology differed from the majority. For a short time in the 1630s, Rhode Island was probably the most open society in the world. Its spiritual leader was a charismatic and idealistic woman named Anne Hutchinson (1591–1643), and its policy of religious toleration encompassed not only other non-Conformists, but even extended to Jews. Maryland, meanwhile, was a haven for Catholics, who were made unwelcome in the Puritan commonwealth of Massachusetts.

During the reign of Charles II (r. 1660–1685), Britain took control of the "Middle Colonies" (the present-day mid-Atlantic states), which had been in the possession of the Dutch since 1614. This united under one flag and one language the lands between the two English enclaves of New England and Virginia. New Amsterdam, the Dutch trading post on the Hudson River, was renamed in honour of the king's brother, the Duke of York. It was as New York that the town grew through the 18th century to become the greatest city in English-speaking North America – and later still, the focus of a turbulent century of European immigration to the United States. The many millions of immigrants that would travel to the New World in the 19th century were attracted by the values that the Pilgrim Fathers had used to build their "city on a hill": an instinctive respect for one's fellows, an idealistic belief in advancement through honest toil, and a refusal to be denied the liberty of conscience.

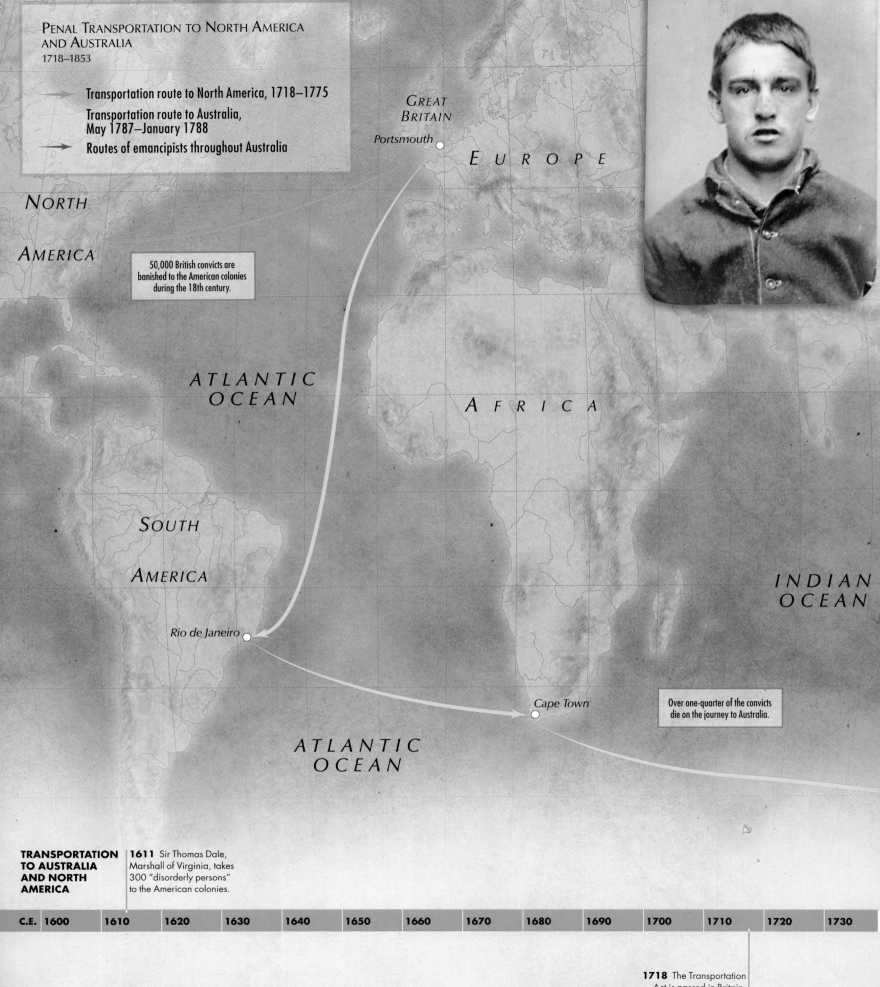

PENAL TRANSPORTATION TO NORTH AMERICA
AND AUSTRALIA
1718–1853

→ Transportation route to North America, 1718–1775

→ Transportation route to Australia,
May 1787–January 1788

→ Routes of emancipists throughout Australia

NORTH

AMERICA

50,000 British convicts are
banished to the American colonies
during the 18th century.

GREAT
BRITAIN
Portsmouth

EUROPE

ATLANTIC
OCEAN

AFRICA

SOUTH

AMERICA

INDIAN
OCEAN

Rio de Janeiro

Cape Town

Over one-quarter of the convicts
die on the journey to Australia.

ATLANTIC
OCEAN

**TRANSPORTATION
TO AUSTRALIA
AND NORTH
AMERICA**

1611 Sir Thomas Dale,
Marshall of Virginia, takes
300 "disorderly persons"
to the American colonies.

C.E.	1600	1610	1620	1630	1640	1650	1660	1670	1680	1690	1700	1710	1720	1730

1718 The Transportation
Act is passed in Britain.

ROGUES, VAGABONDS AND STURDY BEGGARS

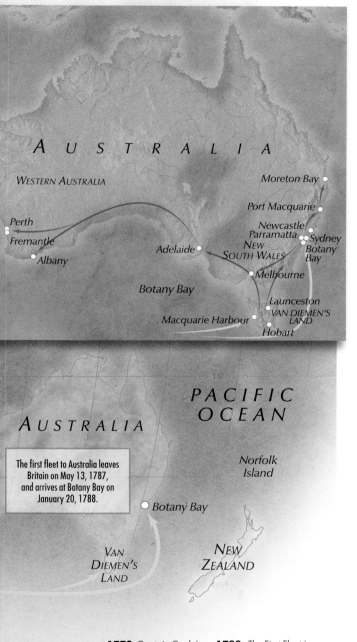

The first fleet to Australia leaves Britain on May 13, 1787, and arrives at Botany Bay on January 20, 1788.

Exile is an ancient form of punishment. It was used by Roman emperors, who sent their enemies and rivals to rot on barren rocks in the Mediterranean Sea. The medieval Scottish courts sentenced offenders to banishment from the burgh or county, or worse still, to England. And in Elizabethan England, a Vagrancy Act passed in 1597 stated that "Rogues Vagabonds and Sturdy Beggars" were liable to be "conveyed to parts beyond the seas".

In the 17th century, the "parts beyond the seas" referred to the British colonies in North America. Prisoners who had been condemned to death by the English courts could potentially have their sentences commuted to deportation and be shipped to the New World to bolster the colonial population. Many of the deportees were common criminals, but political dissidents were also disposed of in this fashion, and it was a frequent form of punishment for Irish prisoners-of-war following the English Civil War (1642–1651). The war involved a series of conflicts between Royalists (supporters of King Charles I, r. 1625–1649) and Parliamentarians (led by, among others, Oliver Cromwell, 1599–1658), who believed that the king was attempting to rule without the consent of Parliament. In 1649, Cromwell, who had gained control of England and Scotland, led Parliamentary forces to reconquer Ireland, which had been in the control of the Irish Confederate Catholics (an ally of the Royalist party) since 1641. Before the English Civil War, about five

Far left: Thomas Nevin, a 19-year-old convict about to begin his sentence at Port Arthur, Tasmania. This prison was the harshest and most feared in Australia. Close by was Port Puer, a jail for juvenile criminals. The prison closed in 1877.

1770 Captain Cook discovers Australia and in 1774 sights Norfolk Island.

1788 The First Fleet arrives in Botany Bay under Arthur Phillip, a British naval officer and colonial administrator.

1815 The Napoleonic Wars in Europe come to an end, and the rate of transportation rises rapidly.

1820s Number of convicts transported to Australia reaches 33,000.

1830s Number of convicts transported to Australia reaches 50,000.

1853 Transportation to Van Diemen's Land comes to an end.

1740	1750	1760	1770	1780	1790	1800	1810	1820	1830	1840	1850	1860	1870

1775 The American Revolution begins, putting a stop to transportation to Virginia and Maryland.

1810s More than 17,000 British and Irish convicts are transported to Australia.

1822 The Macquarie harbour penal station is built in Van Diemen's land.

1824 A colony for the "worst … convicts" is founded on Norfolk Island.

1833 In one year, 6,779 prisoners are transported to Sydney and Van Diemen's Land.

1868 The last convict ship, loaded with 60 Irish political prisoners, lands at Fremantle.

people a year on average were exported to the Americas, but Cromwell's defeat over Ireland produced a large number of exiles, and in the second half of the 17th century the rate of outflow of convicts to the colonies reached an average of just under 100 a year.

After Cromwell's death and the restoration of the monarchy in England in the late 1650s, King Charles II (r. 1660–1685) continued to use banishment as a form of criminal punishment, directing it against anti-monarchists, Catholics who refused to worship in Anglican churches and Quakers who refused to take oaths of allegiance to the Crown. Charles II also formalised the practice of granting pardon to criminals if they agreed to leave the country for a fixed term. Prisoners were sent to Virginia or Maryland to work on the tobacco plantations, where they were a valuable source of labour until the growing number of slaves exported from Africa made them economically unnecessary.

Finding a Place for Britain's Criminals

In 1718, Britain passed a Transportation Act, which established a seven-year banishment to North America as a possible punishment for lesser crimes, and also stated that capital punishment could be commuted to banishment by royal action. Over the course of the century systematic exile became a central part of England's justice system. As a form of punishment, transportation was thought to be advantageous for everybody involved. It was considered to be more humane than executing or flogging the criminal, and (in the opinion of the authorities) it offered the possibility of moral rehabilitation and then freedom afterwards. For the state, exile was beneficial because it rid the populace of dangerous individuals and deterred others who might be tempted to commit crimes. It was also felt that the colonial settlements into which these undesirables were thrown were bettered because, as the Act said, "in many of his Majesty's colonies and plantations in America there is a great want of servants". Colonisation, or the forced migration of labour for the greater good of the empire, was one of the aims of transportation from the moment it became a formal penal tool.

Transportation to North America under the 1718 Act continued for nearly 60 years, but then ceased abruptly in 1775, when the American colonies rose in revolt against the British crown. By that time, more than 40,000 criminals had been shipped to the New World – a fact that freeborn Americans had come to resent. This particular grievance against the British was eloquently and bluntly expressed by Benjamin Franklin (1706–1790) in 1751. "In what can *Britain* show a more Sovereign Contempt for us", he wrote in *The Pennsylvania Gazette*, "Than by emptying their *Jails* into our Settlements; unless they would likewise empty their *Jakes* [chamber pots] on our Tables?" The British authorities would have agreed with Franklin that transportation was an exercise in exporting human filth. The only difference was, Britain believed it had a perfect right to dump its waste wherever it chose. "The political body, like the human body, has vicious humours which should be often evacuated", wrote one English commentator of the time, making slightly more delicate use of the same simile as Franklin. "The proper use of banishment is to send the criminal from the country he has infested into another".

The American push for independence, however, presented Britain with an urgent problem. Once America refused to accept further shipments of convicts, England's prisons began to fill up and overflow. Britain's first response was to accommodate the excess prisoners in "hulks", decommissioned merchantmen and warships. This was meant to be an entirely temporary measure – the ships were somewhere to put convicts until the American colonies could be brought back into line – but the floating prisons became a looming gothic presence on the River Thames and along the south coast of England for decades to come. Once it became apparent that the new United States of America was here to stay, the British government began to look for somewhere else to send its felons. As a first resort, the British asked the US whether, independence notwithstanding, they would take on some more convicts; the Americans refused. Canada was considered next, but then rejected. The West African coast was another option, but when surveys were carried out, it was decided that sending felons to the region's malarial swamps would be tantamount to a death sentence.

The most appropriate location, it was concluded, was New South Wales in Australia, which had been discovered less than 10 years before by Captain James Cook (1728–1779). No one had visited the land since, and very little was known about it except that it was empty (in the eyes of Britain, the native aboriginal peoples did not count), it was an extremely long way away, and all signs suggested that it was commercially useless. Despite its lack of monetary value, the British government did not want France to take possession of the land, so the proposal to use it as a penal colony seemed to make strategic as well as judicial sense

"[We were] chained two and two together and confined in the hold during the whole course of our long voyage … We were scarcely allowed a sufficient quantity of victuals to keep us alive, and scarcely any water; for my own part I could have eaten three or four of our allowances, and you know very well that I was never a great eater … When any of our comrades that were chained to us died, we kept it a secret as long as we could for the smell of the dead body, in order to get their allowance of provision, and many a time have I been glad to eat the poultice that was put to my leg for perfect hunger. I was chained to Humphrey Davies who died when we were about half way, and I lay beside his corpse about a week and got his allowance. "

Thomas Milburn, transported to Australia in the notorious Second Fleet in 1790, writing to his parents

Above: A prison ship in Portsmouth Harbour, England, sketched in 1828. Such hulks were an economic use of decommissioned naval ships. They were conveniently sited in ports and on rivers such as the Thames, where they functioned as holding prisons for convicts awaiting transportation to Australia.

– it was a good way to make use of an otherwise worthless possession. The vast Australian continent would become an enormous, escape-proof jailhouse.

The First Fleet

The first group of ships transporting convicts to Australia, known as the First Fleet, set off from England in May 1787. The fleet consisted of 11 ships carrying 736 prisoners from the hulks, including 188 women. Most of the convicts were Londoners, and they were all petty criminals – by modern standards their crimes were very petty indeed. One, Thomas Chaddick, had been jailed for picking 12 cucumber plants from a garden; Elizabeth Beckford, aged 70, had stolen 12 pounds of Gloucester cheese; and the youngest convict, a 7-year-old chimney sweep named John Hudson, had been sentenced to seven years confinement for purloining a pistol and a cloak.

It took the fleet 252 days to reach its destination. The long, crowded voyage was a punishment in itself, and over 40 convicts died en route. The ships arrived in Botany Bay in Sydney, New South Wales, in January 1788, within an hour of each other. The motley crew of petty thieves and their jailers went ashore, where they were greeted by a hostile group of Aborigines shouting, in their own language, "Go away!" It was soon realised that Botany Bay was not as ideal as Cook's accounts had made it seem. The bay was open and unprotected, fresh water was scarce, and the soil was poor. The intruders did leave, but they did not go far: the penal colony moved a short distance to the north, to a harbour lined with pink eucalyptus trees. The governor named the area Sydney Cove, and it was here that the convicts set about building their own jail. They did not know that they were also building a city and a new nation.

Australia's Thief Colonies

For these first convicts, merely being in Australia was a punishment. Life was extremely hard; the prospect of starving to death was never far away, and conflicts with the Aborigines often ended in bloodshed and murder on one side or the other. A second fleet of prisoners arrived at Botany Bay in 1790, but the convicts on what became known as the "Death Fleet" were so badly treated that more than a quarter died during the voyage, and the majority of those who survived the journey were too ill to work on their arrival.

As the "thief colony" took root, however, it gradually began to flourish. Army officers, the wardens of the jail, were encouraged to take land and were given 10 convicts each to work it. Some of the convicts became farmers themselves once they had served their sentence and became "emancipists". These free colonists were then given the opportunity to take on other convicts on "assignment". Free Australians used the convicts as cheap labour – some might say slave labour – during the term of their sentence. Though Sydney Cove was a prison, the system on which it operated bore a close resemblance to the open prisons of modern times: the convicts worked in the community, and this prevented the stirring up of trouble and disorder that could potentially have arisen if they had been cooped up together.

Nevertheless, conditions within the colony were harsh, and the regime grew more difficult as the number of convicts grew. To maintain order the penal colonies were organised into various circles and zones. For example, on the island of Van Diemen's Land (present-day Tasmania) there was a camp for children at Point Puer (puer being the Latin for "boy"). There were also punishment camps for incorrigibles at Macquarie Harbour on the far side of the island. Particularly dangerous convicts – repeat offenders against the prison regime – were sent to Norfolk Island, 1,600 kilometres (1,000 miles) to the east of Australia in the Pacific Ocean. Life on the island was so difficult that it was not uncommon for a man confined

there to kill a fellow convict so that he could be sent to Sydney and hanged: murder as a form of suicide.

In the 1830s, the penal colony's peak years, around 3,000 convicts arrived in Australia each year. At the same time, objections to the system began to be made by people in both Britain and Australia. By now there were free emigrants living in Australia, rich men who had made the journey to take advantage of the promise of cheap land and labour, and had then made fortunes in sheep farming. These and other free citizens (including a good many former convicts) worried, like the Americans before them, that the colony of criminals in their midst would have a negative influence on the country. In Britain, social reformers were concerned by the brutal excesses of Norfolk Island, and by the arbitrary nature of transportation in principle. Their outrage was best expressed by the English social and legal reformer, jurist and philosopher, Jeremy Bentham (1748–1832), who wrote in parody of a judge handing down a sentence of transportation: "I sentence you, but to what I know not; perhaps to storm and shipwreck, perhaps to infectious disorders, perhaps to famine, perhaps to be massacred by savages, perhaps to be devoured by wild beasts. Away – take your chance; perish or prosper, suffer or enjoy; I rid myself of the sight of you".

Bentham helped convince legislators that model prisons on British soil were the best and most economic way to hold and mould criminals. Transportation was an unusual punishment after the 1860s (although the French continued to transport political prisoners) – the last convict ship left Britain for Australia in 1868. The precise records kept by the British legal authorities tell us that by that time 161,021 men and 24,900 women had made the long lonely voyage "to the Bay".

Left: Some convicts made a life for themselves after prison, but few were as successful as George Barrington. After serving a sentence for theft, he rose to become chief constable of Parramatta in New South Wales. He died a wealthy man and a model citizen in 1804.

THE INDUSTRIAL WORLD

I ndustrialisation and colonialism – the two great historical processes of the 18th and 19th centuries – both involved the mass movement of populations. The new machines developed during the Industrial Revolution drew workers out of the countryside, prompting the rapid growth of vast, crowded cities. The trend towards urbanisation began in England at the turn of the 18th century, but it was repeated the world over. The late 19th century, for example, saw the start of the Great Migration of African-American people from the United States' rural south to the industrial north, as they searched for work and fled racial persecution. This movement followed another epic story of migration in the US: the westward journey to colonise new American states. The wagon trains and the long march of the Mormon pioneers, and the dash to California during the Gold Rush, are all part of the legend surrounding imperial America. In Europe, meanwhile, empires were carved out of other continents, and some of Europe's hardiest citizens went to serve as administrators in Asia or Africa, living a life of voluntary, semipermanent exile.

Left: In the 19th century, thousands of hardy Americans trekked westward in covered wagons such as these. The wagon trains that made their way across the flat plains were like flotillas of ships crossing the open sea.

FARM AND FACTORY

Below: This photograph, taken in 1909, presents a rather sanitised view of working conditions in the Lancashire cotton mills. Certainly for most of the 19th century, they had been noisy, dirty and downright unpleasant places to work.

In the 100 years between the end of the Napoleonic Wars (1799–1815) and the outbreak of World War I (1914–1918), Great Britain saw one of the most profoundly long-lasting migrations in history. The advent of the Industrial Revolution prompted thousands of people to move out of the countryside and into British towns, utterly transforming their way of life in the process.

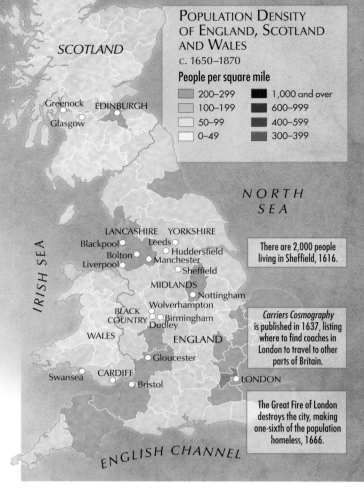

POPULATION DENSITY OF ENGLAND, SCOTLAND AND WALES
c. 1650–1870

People per square mile

200–299	1,000 and over
100–199	600–999
50–99	400–599
0–49	300–399

There are 2,000 people living in Sheffield, 1616.

Carriers Cosmography is published in 1637, listing where to find coaches in London to travel to other parts of Britain.

The Great Fire of London destroys the city, making one-sixth of the population homeless, 1666.

The development of James Watt's steam engine in 1765 was the most important innovation of the Industrial Revolution. The use of steam, fuelled primarily by coal, to power machines triggered the rapid development of efficient, semiautomated factories. This had a dramatic effect on the British economy, changing it from one based on manual labour to one that was supported by large-scale manufacturing. Industrial towns, unlike anything that had been seen in Britain before, began to spring up in the north of England. These towns were positioned for the convenience of the factories (or rather the factories' owners) rather than the good of the cities' inhabitants. The new industrialists understood that it made sound economic sense to site their mills close to the sources of coal in the north that drove the steam engines. Traditionally marketplaces were the economic and geographical focus of English towns, but now machines and the tall, brick buildings that housed them became the hub

of new cities. Workers seeking employment began to flood into the cities from the English countryside, and market villages of the south went into slow decline as the factory towns of the north boomed.

The rise of British factory towns largely began in the 19th century, but there were several early examples of the industrial cities that would come to dominate the northern landscape. The population of Sheffield, for instance, rose from around 2,000 people in 1616 to more than 10,000 by 1740. By that time the city's defining industry, the manufacture of cutlery, was already in place. Eighteenth-century Sheffield was covered in a permanent pall of smoke from the many smithies' furnaces, and the sound of hammering was inescapable – it was a small foretaste of the grime and graft that was to come. The population growth

THE RISE OF URBAN ENGLAND

1761 The Bridgewater Canal, Britain's first entirely artificial waterway, is completed.	**1779** The first cast-iron bridge is built at Ironbridge in Shropshire.	**1812** The population of Manchester passes 100,000.	**1825** The first public railroad opens between Stockton and Darlington.	

C.E.	1750	1760	1770	1780	1790	1800	1810	1820	1830

1765 James Watt develops a working model of his steam engine.

1816 Luddites stage protests against the technology that is making them redundant by destroying machinery.

1833 The Factory Act introduces regulations against child labour.

1801

SCOTLAND

Greenock
Glasgow
EDINBURGH

NORTH SEA

There are 16.5 million people living in Britain in 1801.

IRISH SEA

LANCASHIRE YORKSHIRE
Blackpool   Leeds
Bolton   Huddersfield
Liverpool   Manchester
                Sheffield

MIDLANDS
Nottingham
Wolverhampton
BLACK
COUNTRY   Birmingham
           Dudley

WALES   ENGLAND

Gloucester

Swansea CARDIFF
         Bristol   LONDON

The population of Leeds triples between 1700 and 1770, to almost 18,000 people.

James Watt develops the idea of using steam to power machines in 1765. His steam engine replaces most natural power sources in factories.

ENGLISH CHANNEL

1870

SCOTLAND

Greenock
Glasgow
EDINBURGH

NORTH SEA

The population of Britain in 1861 is 33 million, and two-thirds live in a city.

IRISH SEA

LANCASHIRE YORKSHIRE
Blackpool   Leeds
Bolton   Huddersfield
Liverpool   Manchester
                Sheffield

MIDLANDS
Nottingham
Wolverhampton
BLACK
COUNTRY   Birmingham
           Dudley

WALES   ENGLAND

Gloucester

Swansea CARDIFF
         Bristol   LONDON

The population of London exceeds 3 million, c. 1868.

The Great Western Railway is founded in Bristol in 1833. Its lines connect the countryside with many industrial towns.

ENGLISH CHANNEL

in nearby Leeds was another early sign of the incipient Industrial Revolution. Here the number of inhabitants tripled between 1700 and 1770, rising from about 6,000 people to almost 18,000. Leeds' new residents were already a visible urban proletariat, living in small cottages and workshops crowded beneath the factory walls, and depending entirely on the woolen industry for their livelihood. This symbiotic relationship – whereby the industry relied on the community for manpower, and the community relied on the industry for its livelihood – was to become the basis of urban cities across Britain, from the coal mine towns of South Wales to the shipyard cities of Belfast and the Clyde.

Much of the massive population redistribution that occurred in Britain as a result of the Industrial Revolution happened in the first half of the 19th century. In 1801, there were 16.5 million people in Britain, and London was the only city that was home to more than 100,000 inhabitants: the vast majority of Britons lived in the country. By 1861, Britain's population had doubled, and two-thirds of Britons were city-dwellers.

Leaving Home

For many migrants, the move from countryside to town involved enormous social upheaval, but the process was unavoidable and unstoppable. The population in rural areas had increased to a point whereby the local economy could not sustain it. Employment became scarce, and in the age-old manner, sons and daughters left home and sought work elsewhere – which inevitably meant in the city. The story of Dick Whittington, an archetypal figure in British pantomime, tells of a poor country boy who sets out to London, attracted by the siren call of Bow Bells, to make his fortune. But most new city-dwellers were summoned to the capital by the less romantic but more pressing clamour of spinning mules and steam pistons. They were not looking to make a fortune or find streets paved with gold; they

1842 The Mines Act bars women and female children from working in the pits.

1858 The 'Great Stink' of London, in which the smell of untreated sewage almost overwhelms the people in the capital, highlights the problem of sanitation in large cities.

1913 Henry Ford introduces the moving production line in his automobile factory in Detroit, Michigan.

1840	1850	1860	1870	1880	1890	1900	1910	1920

c. 1845 The population of London exceeds 2 million.

1848 11,000 kilometres (7,000 miles) of railroad have now been laid in Britain, facilitating the drift of population from the countryside to the town.

1868 The population of London exceeds 3 million.

1885 Gottlieb Daimler invents the first gasoline-driven vehicle in Germany.

merely sought to make a living in the cold, hard cobble-stoned alleyways of industrial England.

These first migrants did not travel far, but the territory that they considered to be their 'country' often extended for a radius of only 16 kilometres (10 miles) around their home village. In the late 18th century, many people never travelled beyond that boundary and felt thoroughly uprooted when they had to leave for good. One young migrant, Benjamin Shaw, recalling his family's transplantation to a Lancashire mill town in 1791, reveals the emotional trauma that such a move provoked: 'This leaving our own Countery was a great cross to my mother, for she was greatly attached to her Native town, & had she known what would follow, I am sure that she never would have left her relations and countery on any account.' The Shaw family had in fact moved barely 50 kilometres (30 miles).

The arrival of the railroads in the 19th century sped up the process of migration to the cities. Trains carried workers from rural villages into the growing urban centres of London, Manchester, Glasgow and Liverpool. The population that drained out of the country was redistributed in a ribbon of built-up territory that ran diagonally from Lancashire in the northwest, through the Midlands and the Black Country, to London in the southeast. A similar belt of dense population straddled Scotland at its narrowest point, from Greenock to Edinburgh. For some migrants, the process of adopting an urban life involved an altogether longer journey. Thousands of Scottish and English citizens escaped rural poverty by voyaging by ship for New York. These early emigrants preceded the spectacular exodus from the British Isles that was brought on by the Irish potato famine in 1845. Throughout the 19th century, the emigration of English and Scottish rural folk to the United States was in effect the same urbanisation process that was occurring in Britain, only the move from the country to the city was carried out across high seas and national borders.

Life in the City

The great irony of urbanisation was that it gave a better life to very few of the millions of people who undertook to leave their country homes. The cities thrown up by the Industrial Revolution were, by any modern standards, dreadful places in which to live. They were phenomenally unhygienic and unhealthy. Sanitary arrangements were unbelievably filthy, and the presence of stinking heaps of sewage on city streets was a universal fact of life until the sewer-building programs of the 1860s. Mountains of rotting faeces were a common country practice that was brought into the town, but there

is a world of difference between a hill of manure sitting in a fallow field, where it is open to the cleansing effects of wind and rain, and one in an enclosed, airless courtyard, situated metres (yards) from where people eat and sleep.

Recurrent epidemics were a natural result of the overcrowding and appalling sanitation in industrial cities. Cholera and other fatal diseases were rife, and for much of the 19th century the death rate in British cities exceeded the birth rate by as much as 10 per cent. But this rate of attrition did not discourage incomers; on the contrary, it merely created constant new vacancies for the next wave of migrants.

Social strife was another inescapable consequence of life in the city. Overcrowding and poverty led to endemic crime, political unrest and juvenile delinquency. At first, the machines themselves were held to blame for the ills of industrial life. The Luddites, a social movement of English textile workers of the early 1800s, protested – often by destroying machines – against the social changes brought about by the Industrial Revolution. The Luddites hoped that by destroying factory machines they could effect a return to rural production methods, and with it the country way of life wherein a man and his family worked a loom at home for money, and grew their food on a private plot. Riot was the Luddites' main weapon, but sometimes they resorted to blackmail, and to methods that today would be called terrorism. In 1812, for example, the owner of a wool factory in Huddersfield was sent the following letter, signed by Ned Ludd, the Luddites' professed leader: 'Sir, Information has just been given in, that you are a holder of those detestable Shearing Frames, and I was desired by my men to write to you, and give you fair warning to pull them down … If they are not taken down by the end of next week, I shall detach one of my lieutenants with 300 men to destroy them, and furthermore take notice that if you give us the trouble of coming thus far, we will increase your misfortunes by burning your buildings down to ashes, and if you have the impudence to fire at any of my men, they have orders to murder you …'

Slaves of the Factory

The real social evil, of course, was not the machines but the conditions under which they were operated. Harsh working conditions – spending long hours in unhealthy environments – were prevalent in Britain long before the Industrial Revolution, but the exploitation of workers reached new heights in the 1820s and 1830s. The worst manifestation was the universal use of child labour. Most children of working-class parents began to work from the age of five, and they

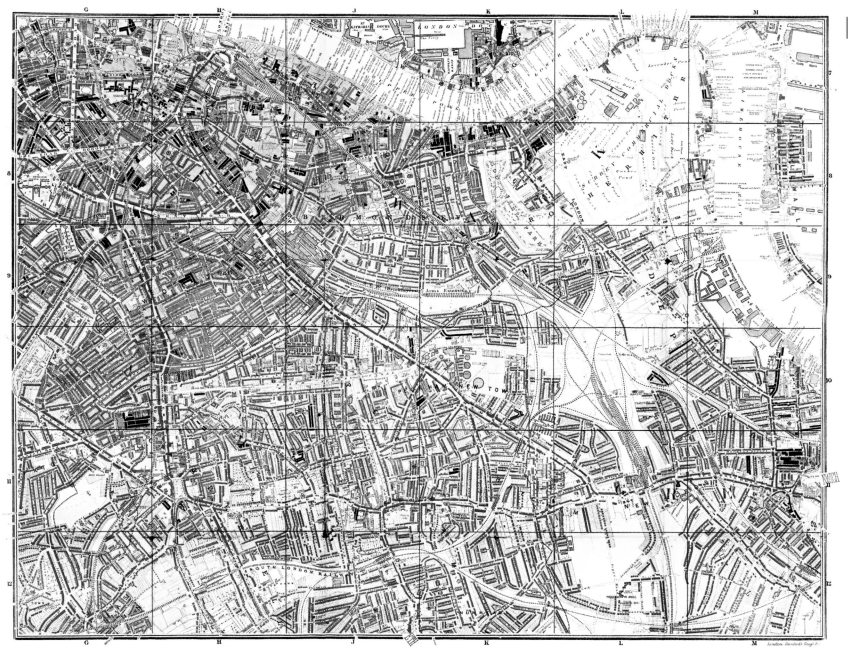

were popular with employers because they could be paid less than an adult worker. Richard Oastler, a campaigner against the employment of children in Yorkshire mills, documented some of the worst abuses against young factory workers, including the vicious beating of children who fell asleep on the job or appeared to be slacking. In 1830, he went before a parliamentary committee and reported that children were dragged from their beds seven days a week to go to the factory, where they worked 13 hours with only a half-hour break. Although there was steady improvement in the rules governing the age of child workers and the amount of hours they could work, the statistics are still shocking by today's standards. The Factory Act of 1833, the first law to be passed against child labour, stated that children under nine could not work in textile factories, children could not work at night, and children between nine and 13 years old could not work for more than nine hours a day. The 1842 Mines Act banned the practise of sending girls underground,

and stated that boys had to be at least 10 years old to hold such employment.

In his efforts to bring an end to child labour, Richard Oastler related to parliament a conversation he had had with a man who ran a plantation worked by slaves in the Caribbean and three Yorkshire factory-owners: 'On one occasion I was in the company of a West India slave master and three Bradford spinners; they brought the two systems [of labour] into fair comparison, and the spinners were obliged to be silent when the slave-owner said: "Well, I have always thought myself disgraced by being the owner of black slaves, but we never, in the West Indies, thought it was possible for any human being to be so cruel as to require a child of nine years old to work twelve and a half hours a day." ' In many ways, a child worker in an English mill was more thoroughly a slave than a black West Indian who was his master's property. The only difference was, the child had travelled a shorter distance to be so enchained.

Above: In the 1890s, the reformer Charles Booth colour-coded maps of London's social structure. Middle-class areas were coloured in red; 'very poor' or 'vicious; semicriminal' were blue or black — so on this map the slums of Southwark, on the south bank of the Thames, show up like specks of soot.

EMPIRE BUILDERS

Between 1800 and the outbreak of World War I in 1914, the European powers – Britain, France, Germany and to a lesser extent the Netherlands – added more than 40 million square kilometres (15 million square miles) of land to their colonial portfolios. The golden age of imperialism was the impetus for a variety of people movements, as migrants travelled abroad while empires grew, or returned to the motherland when they inevitably fell.

The frenzied acquisition of new land by European countries was carried out by bureaucrats and soldiers, migrants and missionaries. Countless thousands of Europeans left their homelands in Britain, France, Germany and Holland and travelled to India, Africa, Southeast Asia, America or Australasia. Most of these migrants were going overseas to earn a living – in the first instance as soldiers or administrators. This is particularly true of the young British men who spent their lives as 'district officers' or 'political officers' in India and other British colonies. Their role was to maintain Britain's civil control within the conquered country and facilitate the exploitation of its natural wealth – foodstuffs, minerals, precious metals and manpower – for the good of the empire. The ideal district

At its peak, the British Empire comprised about one-quarter of the Earth's land area and population, and included territories on every continent.

CANADA

UNITED STATES

MEXICO

CENTRAL AMERICA

PACIFIC OCEAN

St. Pierre and Miquelon (French)

Bermuda (British)

Bahamas (British)

CUBA

HAITI

Puerto Rico (US)

Virgin Islands (US)

JAMAICA (British)

Curaçao (Dutch)

Lesser Antilles (British, French and

Trinidad (British)

VENEZUELA

COLOMBIA

BRITISH GUIANA

SURINAM

FRENC GUIAN

Palmyra Island (US)

Jarvis Island (US)

Galapagos Islands (Ecuadorian)

ECUADOR

PERU

BRAZIL

BOLIVIA

Manihiki Islands (British)

Marquesas Islands (French)

Tuamotu Islands (French)

Society Islands (French)

Pitcairn Islands (British)

Cook Islands (British)

Austral Islands (French)

PARAGUAY

CHILE

ARGENTINA

URUGUAY

Falkland Is (British

South Orkney Isla (British

THE AGE OF EMPIRE

1788 Britain establishes a penal colony in Australia.

1830 The French begin to occupy Algeria. They retain control until 1962.

1849 The Punjab province is annexed to British India.

C.E.	1780	1790	1800	1810	1820	1830	1840	1850	1860

1815 The Napoleonic Wars come to an end.

1840 Britain declares sovereignty over New Zealand.

1857 The Indian Mutiny against British rule occurs.

SPITZBERGEN

ARCTIC OCEAN

COLONIAL EMPIRES, c. 1940

United States
Great Britain
France
Italy
Spain
Portugal
Netherlands
Belgium
Soviet Union
Japan
Mandated areas shown in lighter tints

NORWAY
SWEDEN
FINLAND

ELAND

Faeroe Islands
(Danish)

ESTONIA
LATVIA
LITHUANIA

GREAT
BRITAIN
DENMARK

IRELAND
NETHER-
LANDS

POLAND

SOVIET UNION

Sakhalin

BELGIUM
GERMANY
FRANCE
HUNGARY
SWITZER-
LAND
ROMANIA
YUGO-
SLAVIA
ITALY
BULGARIA

The total area of land in the Soviet Union
is 22.4 million sq kilometres (8.5 million sq miles).

Mongolia (under Soviet mandate)

Manchukuo

PORTUGAL SPAIN
GREECE TURKEY

CHINA

KOREA
JAPAN

PACIFIC
OCEAN

Gibraltar
(British)

aдеira
guese)
Islands
panish)

MALTA
(British)
CYPRUS
PALESTINE
SYRIA
IRAQ
TRANS-
JORDAN

IRAN

AFGHAN-
ISTAN

MOROCCO
TUNISIA

DE ORO

ALGERIA
LIBYA

EGYPT

SAUDI
ARABIA

INDIA

BURMA

Macao
(Portuguese)

FORMOSA

Mariana Islands
(Japanese)

The total area of land under
French sovereignty reached
12.8 million sq kilometres
(4.9 million sq miles).

YEMEN

Kiu
(Portuguese)

Yanaon
(French)

Hong Kong (British)
Kwangchowan (French)

HAINNAN

ANGLO-
EGYPTIAN
SUDAN

YEMEN
ADEN

Goa
(Portuguese)

Pondicherry
(French)

THAILAND
FRENCH
INDO-
CHINA

Guam
(US)

Marshall Islands
(Japanese)

FRENCH WEST AFRICA

GAL
BIA
NCH
INEA
A LEONE
LIBERIA

NIGERIA

GOLD
COAST

Socotra
(British)

Mahe
(French)
Karikal
(French)

Andaman
Islands
(British)
Nicobar Islands
(British)

PHILIPPINE
ISLANDS

FRENCH EQUATORIAL AFRICA

ITALIAN
EAST AFRICA

Laccadive Islands
(British)
Maldives
(British)

CEYLON

Caroline Islands
(Japanese)

IVORY
COAST
CAMEROONS

KENYA

Seychelles Islands
(British)

MALAY
STATES

SUMATRA

Singapore (British)

BORNEO

Bismarck Archi-
pelago (British)
NEW
GUINEA

Gilbert Islands
(British)

Nauru Island
(British)

Ascension Island
(British)

BELGIAN
CONGO

TANGAN-
YIKA

Zanzibar
(British)

Amirantes
(British)

Chagos Islands
(British)

INDIAN
OCEAN

NETHERLANDS INDIES

JAVA

Solomon Islands
(British)

Comoro Islands
(French)

Cocos
(British)

Christmas Islands
(British)

Ellice Islands
(British)

St. Helena Islands
(British)

ANGOLA
RHODESIA

MOZAMBIQUE

MADAGASCAR

Mauritius
(British)

Rodrigues
(British)

New Hebrides
(British and French)

Samoa Islands
(British)

New Caledonia
(French)

Fiji Islands
(British)

SOUTHWEST
AFRICA

BECHUANA-
LAND

Reunion
(French)

Tonga Islands
(British)

ATLANTIC
OCEAN

UNION OF
SOUTH
AFRICA

AUSTRALIA

Lord Howe Island
(British)

Norfolk Island
(British)

Kermadec Islands
(British)

Tristan da Cunha
(British)

New Amsterdam Island
(French)

NEW
ZEALAND

Gough Island
(British)

St. Paul Island
(French)

Chatham Islands
(British)

Crozet Islands
(French)

Prince Edward Island
(French)

Kerguelen
(French)

Auckland Island
(British)

Antipodes Island
(British)

Campbell Island
(British)

Macquarie Island
(British)

1880s The 'Scramble for
Africa': European powers
rush to claim various territories
on the African continent.

1898 The US occupies
Manila in the Philippines.

1914–1918 World War I
results in the collapse of the
Austro-Hungarian and the
Ottoman empires.

1945 World War II leaves
the USSR in control of all of
Eastern Europe; Britain begins
to dismantle its empire.

1870	1880	1890	1900	1910	1920	1930	1940	1950

1889–1902 The Boer War
takes place between Britain and
Afrikaner settlers.

1933–1939 Hitler sets about creating
a Reich (empire) that will embrace all
ethnic Germans in Europe.

1882 Britain takes
control of Egypt.

officer was, according to one governor of the Punjab province of India, 'a hard, active man in boots and breeches, who almost lived in the saddle, worked all day and nearly all night, ate and drank when and where he could, had no family ties, and no wife or children to hamper him'.

The British Empire was run by such men, many of whom had been schooled in institutions such as the East India Company College, which specifically prepared young men nominated for overseas civil service for a life abroad. Often these men would leave Britain in their teens and spend their entire working lives as the local viceroy of some small patch of empire. In many cases they never returned to England. It is estimated that, by 1900, two million Britons lay buried in India. This seems like a large tally, but in fact the ratio of Britons in India to the indigenous population was always tiny. Throughout the 19th century – the heyday of the British Empire – their influence was out of proportion to their numbers. This was due as much to their energy and commitment to what they saw as a civilising mission as it was to the political power invested in them.

Europeans Abroad

The belief of the British in India – and in Africa, too – that they were helping to 'civilise' the country in which they were stationed points to the fact that they were occupiers rather than settlers. The poor and dispossessed European emigrants who travelled to the United States in droves throughout the 19th century saw the New World as one that was superior to that from which they had come, and wanted to raise their own status by becoming a part of it as quickly as possible. But British administrators looked down on the peoples they governed, and generally viewed their postings not as a new life but a job, at the end of which they would return home. Although some came to feel at home in the places where they were posted, as a rule expatriates always remained outside the culture of the countries they ran. In fact, they went out of their way to preserve their European way of life as much as possible – especially if they had a wife and family with them – and they invariably sent their children back to England to be schooled.

French administrators took an analogous approach to their possessions in Southeast Asia, governing in small numbers and retaining their European values. The French colonised modern Vietnam in the mid-19th century, introducing Christianity to the local society and developing a plantation economy for the export of tobacco, indigo, tea and coffee. At first the French presence east of the Mekong River consisted mostly of merchants, missionaries and a handful of local

Right: The first Britons in India must have seemed strange to the indigenous people. The man at the centre of this early 19th-century picture is James Todd, who was a sympathetic admirer of all things Indian, but here he looks like a comically pompous outsider.

Left: In the 1830s and 1840s, Dutch-speaking Boers undertook a 'great trek' out of the zone of British influence in South Africa. The crossing of the Orange River, depicted here in a painting made 100 years after the event, entered the mythology of white Afrikaner nationalism.

officials. It was not until 1858 that French troops occupied the Saigon Delta in present-day Vietnam – an action taken to protect French Catholic missionaries from persecution by an anti-Christian Vietnamese emperor. Similarly, Cambodia was occupied in the 1880s, and Laos and Siam in the 1890s. Together this region was known as French Indochina, with Saigon as its capital. Although the French formally left the local rulers of each country in place, they acted as figureheads only, and the real power remained in French hands.

But rule by a small caste of occupiers was bound to fail. Both the British and the French found that sooner or later the indigenous people of the regions they governed demanded the right to run their own countries, and this invariably led to political strife – or open war – and then to independence for the countries concerned. Indochina dissolved in the 1950s when the French came into conflict with the Viet Minh, an organisation of Communist Vietnamese nationalists, and at the same time, nationalist movements in French North African colonies led to losses by the empire. Similar patterns played out in India, which gained independence from Britain in 1947, and the British African colonies.

Peopling the Empire

Empire building was more successful when it involved the phenomenon of mass migration. Immigrants in British Canada, for example, were settlers rather than sojourners. As pioneers in uncharted territory, they were not preoccupied with preserving their European traditions or promoting the interests of the empire, but merely wished to carve a better life for themselves out of the wilderness around them. The emigrants who travelled to Canada may have come from Britain in the first instance, but within a generation or two they were Canadians first and British subjects second. Their lifestyle was naturally shaped by their new country and, as in the United States, this meant the incremental settlement of less crowded lands – at the expense of

the lives and livelihoods of the indigenous peoples. The Canadian provinces of Manitoba, Saskatchewan and Alberta were created by land-hungry settlers following the same 'westering' urge that led to the formation of the US states of Kansas, Oklahoma and Oregon.

Another of Britain's colonies, Australia, was built on a similar impulse. Originally claimed by Britain as a penal colony in 1770, Australia began to grow as the descendants of convicts set out to farm the wide-open spaces of Victoria and Queensland. In the 1850s, the discovery of gold in Victoria attracted shiploads of prospectors, causing a dramatic rise in the Australian population. The rate of immigration in Australia was never on the scale of that in North America, but in the latter part of the 19th century, new arrivals came at an average of 40,000 per year. Similarly to immigrants to North America, Australian immigrants facilitated the peopling of the continent, allowing the British Empire to add to its colonial portfolio. The effect on the indigenous population was horrific: a combination of disease, loss of land and direct violence reduced the Australian Aboriginal population by an estimated 90 per cent between 1788 and 1900.

The extent to which immigrants became invested in their new communities occasionally became so strong over generations that it caused them to break away from the empire to which they belonged. The most obvious example were the colonies that gave rise to the United States, which declared independence from the British Empire in 1776, and went on to become an empire in its own right. But a more complicated example occurred in the British Cape Colony in South Africa, which was originally established by the Dutch East India Company in 1652. In 1806, the colony came under British rule, and the Boers (Dutch for 'farmer') who had been living there for generations began to resent British rule and the British settlers who came to the Cape in large numbers over the course of the 1820s. The region's harsh environment and regular droughts also made life in the Cape difficult, and the

Boers decided to head north to seek more fertile land where they could establish an independent colony. Over the course of the 1830s, as many as 12,000 *voortrekkers* (pioneers) left the settled coastal areas of southern Africa and headed inland to found the colonies of Transvaal and the Orange Free State, fighting the African Xhosa and Zulu peoples as they proceeded. The deeper they penetrated into the continent, the further the Boers departed from their European roots, until they came to see themselves as a distinct tribe of white-skinned Africans – the Afrikaners. The Cape Colony remained British, and in the eyes of Britain all its inhabitants – African, British or Afrikaner – were subjects of the Crown.

The Clash of Empires

At its peak in the early 20th century, the British Empire covered one-quarter of the world's land surface. Moreover,

the British Navy had long been the undisputed master of the world's seas, which meant that for most of the Victorian era nowhere was beyond the reach of British influence. Britain's position as the pre-eminent European empire was unassailable, but this inevitably brought Britain into conflict with other imperial nations.

In the 1870s, tension emerged between Britain and the Russian state, which had been steadily growing for some time. During the reign of Peter the Great (1682–1725), factory towns such as Ekaterinburg were founded beyond the Ural Mountains. Russian colonies and cities began to spring up ever further east, many of them sited to exploit Siberia's immense mineral wealth. Russia's eastward expansion did not concern the other imperial powers of the time, but when Russia annexed lands to the south in Central Asia at the start of the 19th century, it raised the alarm in Britain.

" It was a toss-up as to whether he got a job as a magistrate in Nyasaland or lecturer in English at Christchurch University in New Zealand. The Nyasaland job came through the letterbox first, and he was keen to be off. He went to the Colonial Office and asked them how he could get there, as he was rather vague about where it was. And they took out some maps and scratched their heads and said, 'Well, sir, we think you should take ship to Aden and then ask.' "

Kit Mullan on her father's first overseas appointment in 1901

Russia gained control of the Kazakh lands, and of Turkestan and the slave cities of Bukhara and Khiva, to protect its open southern borderlands, where Russian settlers were subject to repeated attacks by hostile Muslim tribesmen. But these successive incursions brought Russian troops ever closer to the northern border of British India, potentially posing a threat to the British Empire. The two countries came to the brink of war in 1884, when they competed for possession of Afghanistan, but conflict was averted by diplomacy.

The clash of empires, when it came in the 20th century, was not between Russia and Britain, but between the USSR, which evolved from the Russian Empire, and the United States – Britain's successor as the Anglo-Saxon superpower in the West following World War II. Migration was one of the tools that Soviet Russia used to consolidate its control over its possessions. After World War II, large numbers of ethnic Russians were settled in the Baltic states, and it was felt that their presence would act as a dampener on local nationalist feeling. Russians constituted a significant minority in all the Central Asian republics, and in the Slavic republics of Ukraine and Belorussia (modern Belarus). In the nominally independent countries of Eastern Europe – East Germany, Poland, Romania, Hungary, Czechoslovakia and others – the Russian presence bore a closer resemblance to the model adopted by the British in India: the local Russians functioned as a garrison to impose the imperial homeland's world view (in this case, Marxism-Leninism) on the local people.

The Communist ideology promoted by the USSR was in direct opposition to the principles of democracy and capitalism on which the United States had built its empire. This fundamental difference led to a power struggle over economic, military and technological advances that has come to be known as the Cold War. Although open hostility between the two world powers never materialised, tension remained high until the dissolution of the Soviet Union in the late 1980s.

The Fall of Empire

The dismantling of the European empires took place for the most part in the post-World War II period. Britain and other European empires became focused on rebuilding their own countries following the destruction brought about by war, and the idea that one country had the right to decide the fate of another was made unfashionable by the example of Nazi Germany. The dissolution of empires was itself the cause of a great deal of migration. Much of this migration was 'inward', involving a flow of people from former

Extent of Major World Empires, c. 1900

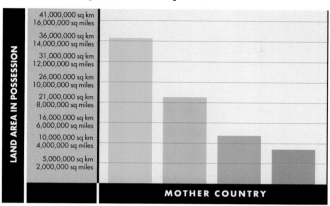

colonies towards the respective 'mother nation'. For France and Britain, this led to a transformation in the makeup of their societies: it made them multicultural. Algerians and other North Africans travelled to make homes in French cities, and Britain solved its post-war labour shortage by inviting West Indian migrants to work in its factories, hospitals and transportation systems. The British Nationality Act of 1948 reaffirmed the right of all 800 million citizens of the Commonwealth and Empire to settle in Britain if they wanted to. Among those who took up the invitation before the rules were changed in the late 1960s were almost 500,000 Asians with roots in the Indian subcontinent or East Africa – many of them refugees from persecution.

Russia's postcolonial migrations were more fraught than those of former European empires. When the USSR dissolved in 1991, the 15 Soviet Socialist Republics became 15 sovereign states, and many Russians suddenly found themselves living in the foreign countries of the 'near abroad'. The governments of some of these countries, notably the Baltic states of Lithuania, Latvia and Estonia, now dubbed their large Russian minorities *okkupanty*, or 'occupants' – the same word that had been used to refer to Nazis during the war. This was unfair to some Russians, who had lived peacefully in these states for two or three generations. But it was also true that most Russians were so unassimilated that they could not speak a word of the local languages. Many moved away rather than face what they saw as vindictive discrimination, and Russia was glad to take them back.

The golden age of empires came to an end in the 20th century, but its effects have left a mark on the modern world. In many places, cultural borders have become blurred, as traditions, languages and customs have flowed in and out of countries. They have been carried by migrants moving to a new colonial land, or returning to the embrace of the mother nation.

Left: At the end of the Victorian era, Britain's empire was by far the largest in the world. Russia's possessions, though they covered a gigantic swathe of Eurasia, amounted to roughly half as much land.

Britain

Russia

France

United States

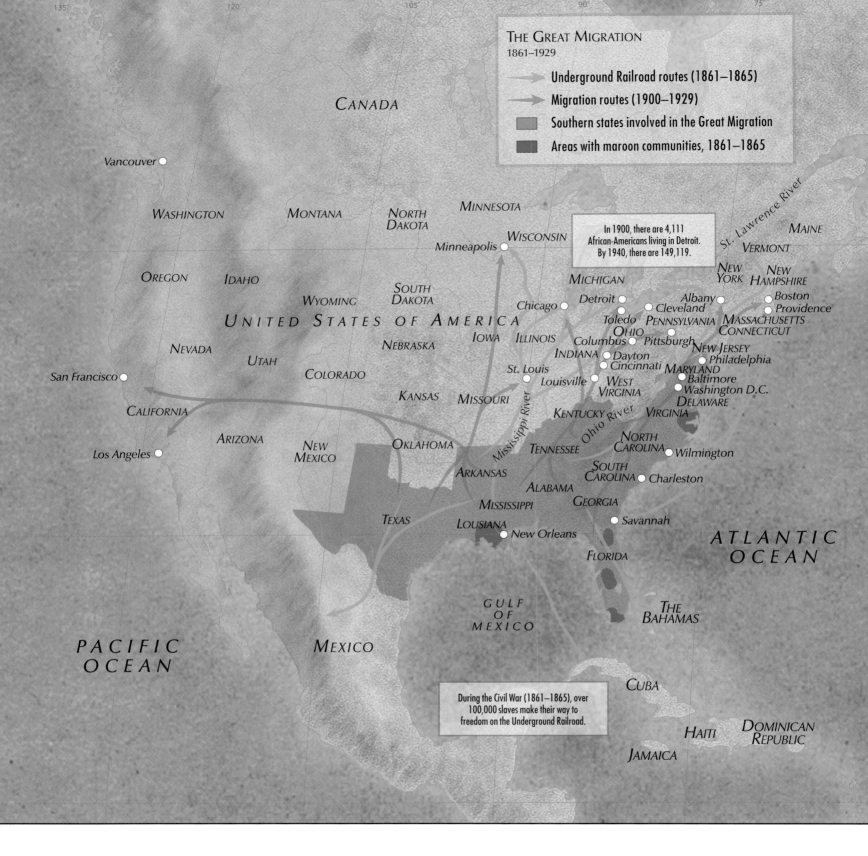

THE GREAT MIGRATION
1861–1929

→ Underground Railroad routes (1861–1865)
→ Migration routes (1900–1929)
▨ Southern states involved in the Great Migration
▨ Areas with maroon communities, 1861–1865

In 1900, there are 4,111 African-Americans living in Detroit. By 1940, there are 149,119.

During the Civil War (1861–1865), over 100,000 slaves make their way to freedom on the Underground Railroad.

CANADA

UNITED STATES OF AMERICA

VANCOUVER

WASHINGTON   MONTANA   NORTH DAKOTA   MINNESOTA

MINNEAPOLIS   WISCONSIN

OREGON   IDAHO   SOUTH DAKOTA   WYOMING   MICHIGAN   NEW YORK   VERMONT   MAINE   NEW HAMPSHIRE

Chicago   Detroit   Albany   Boston   Providence

Cleveland   PENNSYLVANIA   MASSACHUSETTS   CONNECTICUT

NEVADA   UTAH   COLORADO   NEBRASKA   IOWA   ILLINOIS   Toledo   OHIO   Pittsburgh   NEW JERSEY

Columbus   Dayton   Philadelphia

San Francisco   INDIANA   Cincinnati   MARYLAND   Baltimore

St. Louis   Louisville   WEST VIRGINIA   Washington D.C.

CALIFORNIA   KANSAS   MISSOURI   DELAWARE

Los Angeles   ARIZONA   NEW MEXICO   OKLAHOMA   KENTUCKY   Ohio River   VIRGINIA

Mississippi River   TENNESSEE   NORTH CAROLINA   Wilmington

ARKANSAS   SOUTH CAROLINA   Charleston

TEXAS   ALABAMA   GEORGIA   Savannah

MISSISSIPPI   ATLANTIC OCEAN

LOUSIANA   New Orleans

PACIFIC OCEAN   MEXICO   GULF OF MEXICO   FLORIDA   THE BAHAMAS

St. Lawrence River

CUBA

HAITI   DOMINICAN REPUBLIC

JAMAICA

THE JOURNEY TO FREEDOM

1847 Liberia becomes an independent republic.

1863 On New Year's Day, President Abraham Lincoln declares that all slaves in the rebel Confederate states are free.

1865 The Civil War comes to an end and the Thirteenth Amendment to the US Constitution abolishes slavery.

| C.E. | 1810 | 1820 | 1830 | 1840 | 1850 | 1860 | 1870 |

1822 Liberia is founded on the west coast of Africa by former US slaves.

1850 The Fugitive Slave Law is strengthened to deter runaways.

1861 Civil War breaks out in the United States between the northern Union states and the southern Confederate states.

1879 The 'Exodusters' leave for Kansas.

SEARCHING FOR FREEDOM LANDS

In the years between the American Revolution (1775–1783) and the American Civil War (1861–1865), the so-called 'Negroes' of the United States were subject to forced migrations that carried them deeper into the southern states, and deeper into bondage. The abolition of slavery in 1863 triggered yet another people movement, when the act of migration became an exercise in freedom for the former slaves of the American South.

Slavery was banned in the northern states of the United States in the late 18th century, but this did not mean that all northern slaves were freed. In 1793, the invention of the cotton gin had revolutionised the cotton industry in the South, vastly increasing the amount of cotton that could be processed in a day, and as a result, the demand for slave labour. In the North, the tobacco trade, for which the majority of slave labour had been used at the time, was in decline. Many slave owners in the tobacco trade made the decision to either change their line of business to cotton and move south with their human possessions, or offload their plantation slaves onto the cotton growers already established there. In either case, the result was a forced migration of thousands of African-American men and women.

The relocation of slaves to the South continued well into the 1830s. For those forced to undertake the journey, the move was every bit as traumatic and pitiless as the sea voyage into slavery that their African-born ancestors had endured generations before. Since that time, the paraphernalia of enslavement had not changed. Travelling slaves were chained together hand and foot, marching south in long columns and sleeping in the open, or else on the deck of the ships that carried them like cargo down the Mississippi River. Overseers made sure that the chains stayed on, day and night, until the goods arrived in the 'cotton kingdom'.

On the Run

While this tidal flux of enslaved African-Americans was heading south, a steady trickle of fugitive slaves was making its way north. In particular, slaves in the border states between the free North and the indentured South – including Maryland, Delaware, Missouri and Kentucky – were keenly aware that beyond the Ohio River there was a country where they could live as free men and women. Those with an eye to that opportunity tended to abscond in a moment of crisis: either when they learned that they were to be taken south, or when their families were broken up by the separate sale of husband, wife and children. In some places, runaway slaves found each other and came together to form outlaw bands, gathering in swampy areas and other inaccessible parts of the South, where they were beyond the reach of the law and unlikely to be discovered. These communes, known as 'maroon communities', usually consisted entirely of men, but there were some settled communities of men,

Above: To run away from a plantation in search of freedom was, for a slave, an individual and highly perilous act of migration. But for the slave owner, the runaway was just an irksome piece of lost property.

| 1880 | 1890 | 1900 | 1910 | 1920 | 1930 | 1940 | 1950 |

1895 The states of Mississippi, South Carolina and Louisiana adopt legislation to disenfranchise the African-American population. Other states follow suit.

1914 World War I begins. US industries begin to recruit workers from the African-American population.

1928 Oscar DePriest becomes the first African-American congressmen. He is elected to serve the congressional district of Illinois.

1941 Half of the African-American population of the United States consists of city-dwellers.

1909 The National Association for the Advancement of Colored People (NAACP) is founded.

1919 There are 75 lynchings of African-Americans in the course of the so-called 'Red Summer'. Race riots erupt in several cities in the North and the South.

Right: Frederick Douglass, born a slave in 1818, learned to write from white children. He escaped the 'peculiar institution' and went on to become a fine speaker and writer for the abolitionist cause. This poster advertises a song written in his honour.

women and children – all of them 'truant' slaves or their offspring. Most of these groups concentrated on their own survival, building homes, raising crops and livestock, and fortifying their communities against potential attacks from their former masters; but some engaged in guerrilla warfare with neighbouring plantations and provided a base to which other fugitive slaves could flee.

Many of the escaped slaves who made it across the Ohio River to freedom were helped on their way by the so-called Underground Railroad. This was the name given to the semisecret network of abolitionists and former slaves who provided shelter to runaways, concealed fugitives in ships bound for northern ports, or acted as guides on overland routes to free states. As many as 60,000 slaves may have escaped to the North with the help of the Railroad between 1830 and 1860. Most were shepherded to Chicago. From there, a great many were ferried across the border to Canada, where they were beyond the reach of their US owners, who might otherwise make legal attempts to have their property returned to them.

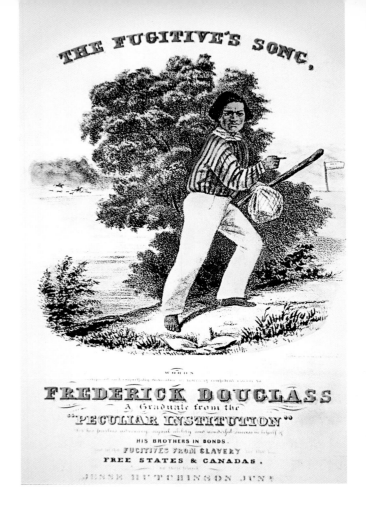

Civil War Brings Freedom to the South

The institution of slavery had become a contentious issue between the North and the South in the early 1800s. The conflict reached a head in 1861, when the 11 southern slave states declared their secession from the antislavery US federal government (the 'Union') to form the Confederate States of America. Civil war broke out, and the fighting went on for four years until the Union victory in 1865. The 1850s, the last decade before the US Civil War, was a time of increasing tension in the South. Many freed slaves took the opportunity to go north legally before war made it more difficult. Others took the more drastic step of leaving the United States altogether. In the 10 years before the war, 5,000 freed slaves returned to Africa and made a home in Liberia – a colony on the west coast that was founded by former slaves in 1822, and became an independent republic in 1847. About 3,000 African-Americans emigrated to Haiti between 1854 and 1865. These movements, though small, were significant because they represented a powerful response to the injustice of the slave system and the racial prejudice of white Americans: these former slaves chose to remove themselves en masse from the country in which they had been born enchained and go to a new land to live with people who had shared their experience of bondage.

The Union victory in the Civil War put an end to slavery in the United States. But although the four million slaves

in the southern states were now free, their lives were in many ways just as difficult as they had ever been. In the years of reconstruction following the war, economic and social discrimination against former slaves in the South made it hard for them to earn a living, and there was always the terrifying threat of mob violence. Lynchings involving despicable acts of torture became commonplace throughout the South, sometimes spiraling into wider attacks against entire African-American communities. Such terrorism became a fact of life, and remained a feature of relations between white and black Americans well into the 20th century – first in the South, but later in the North, too.

The Right to Flight

The Union victory, however, did mean that there was now no legal restriction on the right of African-Americans to leave the South. In fact, for many freed slaves the simple act of moving somewhere else was the touchstone of their newfound liberty. Following the Civil War, one former slave owner wrote ruefully to a relative that 'the negroes don't seem to feel free unless they leave their old homes, just to make it sure they can go when and where they choose'. One family in South Carolina offered to pay their African-American cook double the wages she had been offered elsewhere if she would stay with them, but the cook replied: 'No, Miss, I must go. If I stay here I will never know I am free.'

This psychological need of African-Americans to affirm their new status partly explains the mass migration of freed people out of the southern states in the 1870s. Tens of thousands made the decision to go north – or west into the still largely empty territories beyond the land inhabited by Native Americans – the 'Indian lands'. In 1879–1880 there was a more or less spontaneous exodus of 20,000 former slaves to Kansas, which had a more tolerant reputation than most other states at the time. The 'Exodusters', as they became known, hoped to live peacefully among their own people and farm free land provided by the government.

This mass migration was the Liberian solution to the race issue played out on home soil. Former slaves were choosing to get away from white Americans but not to leave America. Frederick Douglass (1818–1895), a former slave

The Great Migration

In the 19th century almost all African-Americans – both before and after emancipation, and whether they emigrated from the South or not – were rural workers. This pattern changed radically in the 20th century, when African-Americans began to abandon sharecropping to take jobs in factories. In a sense, this flight from rural hardship in search of better opportunities in the city echoed the story of the Industrial Revolution that had played out in England more than 100 years before, and provided Irish labour for America's growing cities in the 1840s. Now African-Americans, who for generations had been cut off by slavery from the normal economic and social influences that affect free migration, began to relocate to America's urban centres.

> " I am a young man and am disable, in a very great degree, to do hard manual labor. I was educated at Alcorn College and have been teaching a few years: but ah me the Superintendent under whom we poor colored teachers have to teach cares less for a colored man than he does for the vilest beast. I am compelled to teach 150 children without any assistance and receives only $27.00 a month, the white with 30 get $100. I am so sick I am so tired of such conditions that I sometime think that life is not worth while and most eminently believe with Patrick Henry 'Give me liberty or give me death.' If I was a strong able bodied man I would have gone from here long ago. "

Anonymous letter to the Chicago Defender, written from Lexington, Missouri, May 1917

and eloquent spokesman for the abolitionist movement, said approvingly that '[the African-American had] adopted a simple, lawful, and peaceable measure – emigration – the quiet withdrawal of his valuable bones and muscles from a condition of things which he considers no longer tolerable'. But at the same time, Douglass was concerned that the exodus did not help to solve racial tensions in the long term: 'It would make freedom and free institutions depend upon migration rather than protection; by flight rather than right. It leaves the whole question of equal rights on the soil of the South open and still to be settled.' Despite Douglass' misgivings, African-Americans continued to drain away from the South. The fact was, they could not be certain that the practice of slavery in the American South was never going to return. By the end of the 19th century, half the black population of the former Confederate states had left for the 'freedom lands'.

The mobility of African-Americans was particularly high during World War I (1914–1918). Immigration from Europe ceased for a time, and US industries that usually recruited labour from Ellis Island – the immigration landing depot in New York – now turned to the African-Americans of the South to fill vacancies. The rural workers of Tennessee and Louisiana were only too glad to accept the opportunity: wages were far better working in the automobile factories and on the railroads, and more urgently, the violence of resurgent lynch mobs and the Ku Klux Klan, a racist organisation advocating white supremacy, had made life in the South unbearable once again. 'There are about 12 or 15 of us with our famlys leaving the south', wrote one desperate man to a newspaper, asking for financial help to go north. 'We can hear of collored people leaving the south but we are not luckey enough to leave hear. Dr— came to be an agent to sind peples off and we has bin to

Opposite page: One practical thing that any free African-American could do to speed the abolition of slavery was to join the Union Army in the Civil War. The pride in the uniform is written all over the face of this soldier as he poses for posterity with his wife.

him so minnie times and has fail to get off until we don't know what to do … If we war able we wood sure leave this torminting place, but the job we as got and what we get it we do well to feed our family …'

Many did manage to find a way to the North. Between 1910 and 1920, the African-American population of Detroit increased from less than 6,000 to more than 40,000; the figures for Chicago in the same years are 44,000 and 110,000. The influx slowed during the 1920s, but took off again in the 1930s. A census conducted in 1940 showed that 90 per cent of non-white migrants in the North had come from the southern states. This was a massive population shift, and has become known as the Great Migration. The net result of this people movement was a new social phenomenon in American life: a 'black proletariat' that was vibrant, creative and self-aware.

Redistribution of the African-American population, 1910–1930

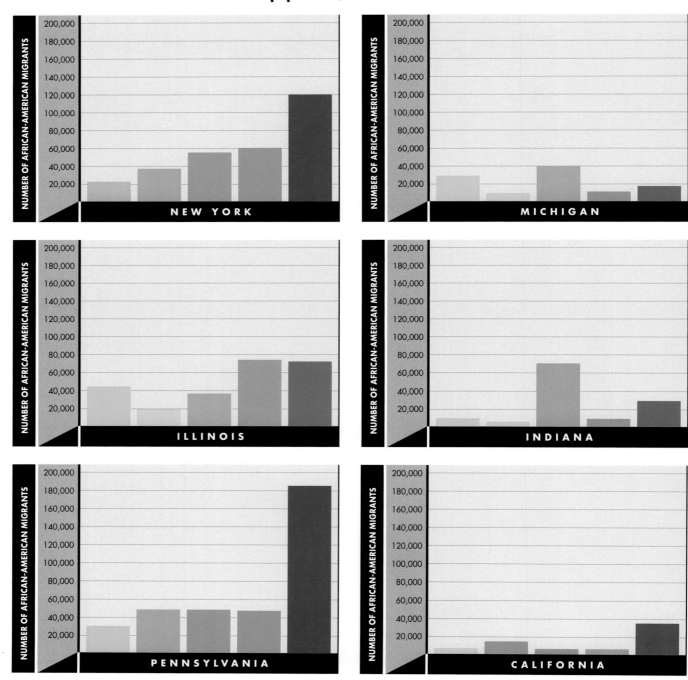

PRINCIPAL STATES OF ORIGIN

- Alabama
- Arkansas
- Florida
- Georgia
- Kentucky
- Louisiana
- Mississippi
- North Carolina
- Oklahoma
- South Carolina
- Tennessee
- Texas
- Virginia

OUR MANIFEST DESTINY

In 1845, American journalist John O'Sullivan, in an essay calling for the annexation of Texas to the United States, declared that it is 'our manifest destiny to overspread and to possess the whole of the continent which Providence has given us.' In so saying, he gave voice to what all Americans by then believed: the United States had a God-given right to ownership of the whole of North America – including British-owned Canada – from the Atlantic to the Pacific Ocean.

Above: In the dusty steppe of Nebraska, a family poses with the 'prairie schooner' in which they live and travel. The year was 1886, and by now families in search of a homestead were obliged to journey almost to the Pacific seaboard of the North American continent.

By the time O'Sullivan coined the resonant phrase 'manifest destiny', the gradual process of possession that it epitomised was well under way in the United States. The original 13 United States, when they came into being in 1776, occupied just a narrow coastal strip on the eastern seaboard of the North American continent. Up until the American Revolution (1775–1783), and for some decades afterwards, few European settlers had made homes in the lands that lay beyond the Appalachian Mountains, which run parallel to the coast and stretch from Atlanta in the south almost to the St. Lawrence River in the north. They formed the natural western boundary of the new republic, and were a formidable obstacle to the colonisation of the American interior. Beyond them lay the territory known as Kentucky. This, along with the valley of the Ohio River, and the southern shores of the Great Lakes, was the domain of the 'Six Nations' – a confederacy of Native American peoples.

Kentucky and the broader area west of the mountains, known as Trans-Appalachia, were regarded as uninhabitable wilderness, but that is not to say that the

region was unexplored by Europeans. These untamed lands were dotted with French forts, and there were a few adventurers who had undertaken to become acquainted with Trans-Appalachia and the people who lived there. The most prolific and gifted of these explorer-hunters was the American Daniel Boone (1734–1820). In the 1760s he spent two years as a frontiersman in the emptiness of Kentucky, living off elk and occasionally skirmishing with Native American peoples. He and other explorers discovered that the Appalachian wall had numerous gates in it: mountain passes such as the Cumberland Gap that were traversable by colonists and their wagons. Boone subsequently took his own family through the mountains and founded a fortified settlement – Boonesborough – on the Kentucky River in 1775. Farther south, a trickle of pioneers had begun to filter through the mountains' gaps and build settlements on the Cumberland and Watauga rivers. At the time, the land was occupied by the Cherokee people, and they were not pleased to see newcomers. But the Cherokee agreed to allow the colonists to live peacefully in exchange for $6,000 worth of blankets, guns and other goods.

SETTLING THE WEST

| C.E. 1760 | 1770 | 1780 | 1790 | 1800 | 1810 | 1820 |

1803 The "Louisiana Purchase" opens the West to settlers.

1821 The Santa Fe Trail is inaugurated.

1776 The original 13 United States declare independence from Britain.

CANADA

Columbia River

ROCKY

Missouri River

St. Lawrence River

Oregon City

OREGON
COUNTRY
1846

Snake River

The Oregon Trail
spans over half
the continent for
3,500 kilometres
(2,170 miles),
1841–1869.

LOUISIANA
PURCHASE
1803

SIX
NATIONS

The California Trail is used
by over 250,000 farmers and
gold-seekers to reach the
California gold-fields, 1840–1860.

M
O
U
N
T
A
I
N
S

Ohio River

ORIGINAL THIRTEEN STATES

Appalachian Mountains

Sacramento

MEXICAN
CESSION
1848

Colorado River

Independence

St. Louis

UNITED
STATES
1783

ATLANTIC
OCEAN

Santa Fe

The Santa Fe Trail is
a vital commercial
and military highway,
1821–1880.

Mississippi River

GADSEN
PURCHASE
1853

Rio Grande

TEXAS
ANNEXATION
1845

EXPANSION OF THE UNITED STATES
1776–1853

PACIFIC
OCEAN

FLORIDA
CESSIONS
1810–1819

━━━━ Oregon Trail

━━━━ Santa Fe Trail

━━━━ California Trail

- - - - Lewis and Clark Expedition

MEXICO

GULF
OF
MEXICO

The Louisiana Purchase

With or without the acquiescence of the Native Americans, white settlers continued to spread farther west, towards the banks of the Mississippi River and the territory of Louisiana that lay beyond it. The French had acquired Louisiana from Spain in 1800, along with its trading colony of New Orleans. The territory was far larger than the present-day state of Louisiana, extending north to the Canadian border in an immense swathe. Louisiana encompassed everything (with the exception of Texas, which at the time was part of Mexico) that lay between the Mississippi River and the peaks of the Rocky Mountains.

Napoleon, the ambitious new ruler of France, had been planning to make Louisiana the core of a French Empire in the New World, but his commitments to war in Europe had rendered this scheme unfeasible. He now reasoned that the United States was bound to wrest the territory from his control sooner or later, and that he would do better to sell

1832 The settlement of the Oregon Territory via the Oregon Trail begins.

1849 The Gold Rush brings 80,000 prospectors to California, and hastens its incorporation as a US state.

1867 The United States buys Alaska from Russia for $7.2 million; Canada becomes a self-governing dominion of the British Empire.

1880s Drought and severe winters devastate cattle herds in the western US states.

1830	1840	1850	1860	1870	1880	1890	1900

1841 The first wagon train leaves the East on the six-month journey to California.

1847 The Mormons leave Illinois en masse for the Great Salt Lake.

1862 The Homestead Act encourages the ongoing colonisation of the Great Plains. Conflict with Native Americans steadily intensifies.

1876 Sioux braves annihilate General Custer and his 266 men at the Little Bighorn.

1886 The surrender of the Apache chief Geronimo marks the end of the Indian Wars.

1890 A US Census announces that the frontier has closed.

Above: The Native American peoples of the prairies were understandably suspicious of the white newcomers from the east. The settlers, for their part, showed scant regard for the land rights of the people whose territory they occupied.

" Our fuel for cooking was dry buffalo droppings. We usually cooked our meat by boiling it in our camp kettles. It was rather hard fare. The men would almost quarrel for any part of the animal that had any tallow, even the caul. I was a little surprised that I stood this change of life about as well as the mountaineers, and as to a camp life I rather enjoyed its ways. I had for bed purposes, the half of a buffalo robe, an old cloak with a large cape, and a blanket. I spread the robe on the ground, wrapped the blanket about my feet and the cloak around me, throwing the cape loosely over my head to break off the moonshine, and a saddle for my pillow. We had tents, but it never raining and but little dew, we did not use them. And oh! I always slept most profoundly. "

From the memoir of John Ball, who travelled the Oregon Trail in 1832

that beyond it Mexico laid claim to Texas and to the Pacific southwest up to the 42nd parallel, while Britain saw itself as the sole proprietor of the Oregon Territory, that is, all the land west of the Rocky Mountains and north of the 42nd parallel as far as Canada. To assess the worth of his impulse buy, President Jefferson sent a small expeditionary force into Louisiana in 1804. The expedition, led by William Clark and Meriwether Lewis, was one of the great feats of exploration. The group penetrated as far as the Pacific Ocean, and reported back two years later that the land was good.

Life on the Prairies

The Lewis and Clark Expedition opened up the West for colonisation. Trappers were the first to venture into Louisiana, blazing a trail from Missouri to Santa Fe in Mexican-owned Texas, collecting animal pelts to sell on in the fur trade. More permanent settlers followed in their wake, utilising the rich prairie lands for farming. As the number of Americans in Texas (known as Texians) grew, they became dissatisfied with Mexican rule and began to agitate for membership in the United States. In March of 1836, the Texians declared independence and raised arms against the Mexican government. In April of the same year, after the Texians defeated Mexican forces at the Battle of San Jacinto, the Republic of Texas was formed. In 1845, Texas was annexed by the United States and an even greater number of migrants began to head into the western US

Homesteaders, determined would-be farmers and their families, trundled west in their 'prairie schooners' along routes mapped out by early traders and missionaries (the Oregon, Sante Fe and California Trails). Their covered wagons carried the family together with seeds, tools, provisions and bedding – everything they would need to start a new life from scratch on the lonely, windswept plain. The wagon trail was a journey out of the settled east and into the legend of the American West. Even at the time, these tough, optimistic migrants knew they were involved in something extraordinary. 'No other race of men with the means at their command would undertake so great a journey', wrote Jesse Applegate, who travelled the northerly Oregon Trail in 1843. 'None save these could successfully perform it, with no previous preparation, relying only on the fertility of their own invention to devise the means to overcome each danger and difficulty as it arose. They have undertaken to perform with slow-moving oxen a journey of two thousand miles. The way lies over trackless wastes, wide and deep rivers, ragged and lofty mountains, and is beset with hostile savages.'

it while he could. The profits could then be used to fund his planned invasion of Britain. In 1802, Napoleon offered to hand over the whole of Louisiana to the United States for the bargain price of $15 million. The offer astonished President Thomas Jefferson. It was the biggest real-estate deal in history, and Jefferson had serious doubts about whether the constitution allowed for the extension of the country's borders by such means. In the end it was decided that it was too good an opportunity to let pass. A contract between the two nations was signed in 1803: at the stroke of a pen the United States more than doubled in size.

Aside from the dubious legality of the Louisiana Purchase, as it became known, the deal itself was something of a gamble. It was not known whether the unexplored central slice of North America was good for farming, or for any other useful commercial activity. The exact boundaries of the territory were also undefined – all that was known was

Above: The Mormons were the most determined and indefatigable of the settlers to go west. Once they arrived in the empty spaces of Utah, they happily endured penury and hardship in order to be able to practise their faith freely.

Life was hardly less tough for the homesteaders once they arrived at their destination. The loamy earth, though rich once it was planted, was heavy and difficult to plow. That it was workable at all was due largely to the recent invention of the revolving plow, which cut deep into the earth as it turned it. The first settlers discovered that only certain hardy crops would grow – a species of wheat imported from the Russian steppe proved successful – but crop failure was an ever-present danger. There was no wood to be found on the plains, so the same hard earth used for planting had to be cut and dried to make bricks with which to build a house, known as a 'soddy'. The absence of wood also meant that the only fuel for the stove was buffalo dung.

As well as these hardships, settlers were under the constant threat of attack by dispossessed and increasingly desperate Native American peoples. Other nomads roaming the American plains were also a danger: the mercenary cowboys. The interests of these hired horsemen were directly opposed to those of the homesteaders, who wanted to fence in the plains and keep everybody – cattle drivers and Native Americans alike – off their precious land.

The US government was ultimately on the side of the homesteaders. In 1862, in the middle of the Civil War, a remarkable law was passed. The Homestead Act decreed that anyone who agreed to produce a crop within five years was entitled to 160 acres of free land in the Midwest. Thousands jumped at the chance of a life of independence, despite the backbreaking work it entailed. The Act also stated that the children of these pioneers could have 160 acres of land once they were old enough to work it, and as long as they were prepared to go farther west to claim it. In this way, the 'westering' process proceeded from one generation to the next, turning tough country into bountiful wheat fields that stretched to the horizon and far beyond.

Emigration Canyon

Most of the Americans who headed west hoped and expected that the land they occupied would eventually be formed into a US state and join the Union. A notable exception was the Mormons, who in 1846–1847 travelled to what would become Utah. Members of the Mormon Church of Latter Day Saints in Ohio were persecuted for their heretical beliefs and, after the founder of the Church, Joseph Smith Jr., was lynched in 1844, the Mormon elders decided to lead their community west and set up a commune on the Salt Lake in Oregon Territory, beyond the borders of the United States.

This mass exodus was organised with admirable efficiency by Brigham Young, the new leader of the Church.

He researched the route, making sure that posts were set up along the way by advance parties, and enforced sensible procedures to make overnighting safe, such as the practice of forming rings of wagons to afford protection. Once the new country had been reached, Young apportioned land with scrupulous fairness. He also organised evangelical missions to Europe, so that there would be a great enough influx of new believers to Salt Lake to keep the community viable.

At the end of the Mormon Trail there was a high pass that led through a ring of mountains to give trekkers their first view of their New Jerusalem by the Great Salt Lake. This pass was given the inspired name Emigration Canyon. Not all American migrants can, like Brigham Young's Mormons, point to a time or place where the act of emigration was made complete. But almost everyone in the United States is someone, or is descended from someone, who left home to start a life in a new place, passing through their own Emigration Canyon along the way.

Left: The Mormons who migrated west, like the Irish Catholics who went to New York, built impressive churches as a sign that they had come to stay. This white temple, a modern take on European Gothic, is in San Diego, California.

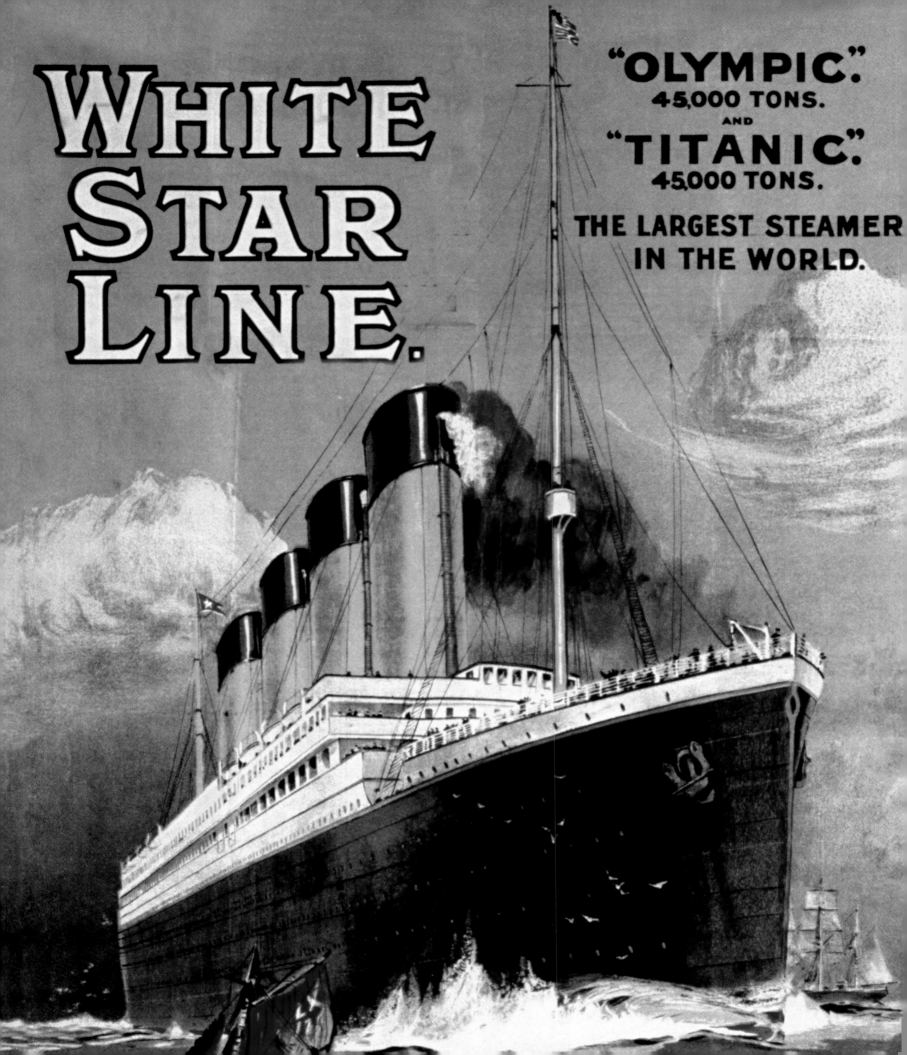

THE NEW WORLD

M igration is central to the 19th-century American experience – not only for American immigrants, but also for the American-born citizens who, more or less willingly, welcomed successive waves of newcomers to their growing nation. The mass of immigrants that flooded into the United States between the end of the Napoleonic Wars in 1815 and the beginning of World War I in 1914 was made up of many different nationalities, each with its own cultural traditions and religious beliefs. Many of the first 19th-century immigrants, primarily from Britain or Germany, assimilated quickly to their new home, and their arrival went almost unnoticed. It was not until the dramatic advent of the Irish-Catholic refugees, fleeing the potato famine in Ireland in the 1840s, that US immigration became a visible, and therefore political, issue. The Irish, too, eventually made an American life for themselves, as did all successive waves of immigrants: the dispossessed Jews of the Russian Empire, the impoverished Italian peasants and the resourceful Chinese from the Pearl River delta – as well as many others. The ancestral roots of most Americans lie in a distant land, and this has left its mark on the culture and the topography of the United States.

Left: The White Star Line was one of several shipping companies that carried European migrants to the New World. Popular routes ran from Liverpool, England, to New York, Boston and Philadelphia.

WHITE STAR LINE.

"OLYMPIC." 45000 TONS
TITANIC. 45000 TONS
THE LARGEST STEAMERS IN THE WORLD

HUDDLED MASSES YEARNING TO BE FREE

Below: The Statue of Liberty, made in France and shipped to New York in 1885, was for millions of immigrants the first sight and the preeminent symbol of the United States.

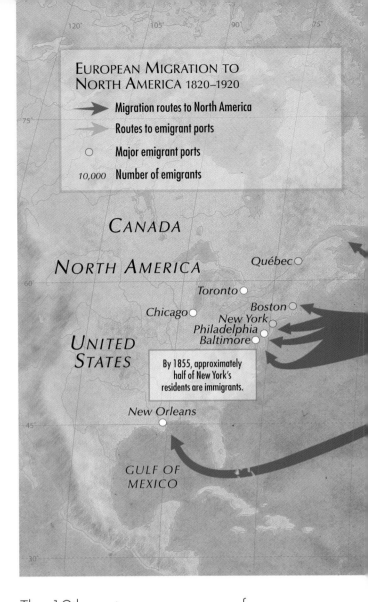

EUROPEAN MIGRATION TO NORTH AMERICA 1820–1920

→ Migration routes to North America

→ Routes to emigrant ports

○ Major emigrant ports

10,000 Number of emigrants

CANADA

NORTH AMERICA

Québec ○

Toronto ○

Chicago ○

Boston ○

New York ○

Philadelphia ○

Baltimore ○

UNITED STATES

By 1855, approximately half of New York's residents are immigrants.

New Orleans ○

GULF OF MEXICO

The 19th century was an era of mass migration to North America. Immigrants arrived from across Europe, drawn by the promise of freedom and a brighter future. The first half of the century saw an influx of settlers from Britain, Germany, Scandinavia and Ireland. At the end of the century, a second wave of immigrants came from Italy, Poland and Russia. Together, these incomers would transform North American society.

EUROPEAN MIGRATION TO NORTH AMERICA

1730s Scotch-Irish and German immigrants colonise the American colonial borderlands.

1775 War breaks out in the American colonies and Britain suspends emigration.

1815 The end of the Napoleonic Wars ushers in a century of mass migration to North America.

C.E.	1700	1710	1720	1730	1740	1750	1760	1770	1780	1790	1800	1810	1820

1727 Pennsylvania requires all alien immigrants to swear allegiance to the British monarch.

1803 The Passenger Act passed in Britain places a limit on the number of people that can be carried in emigrant ships.

1825 Packet ships of the Black Ball Line, employed to carry mail, goods and passengers, begin regular service from Liverpool to New York.

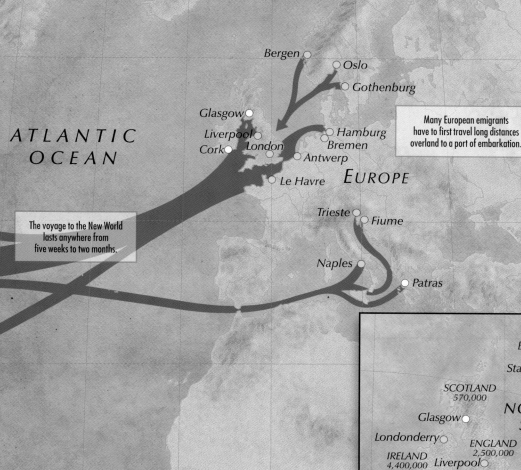

Many European emigrants have to first travel long distances overland to a port of embarkation.

The voyage to the New World lasts anywhere from five weeks to two months.

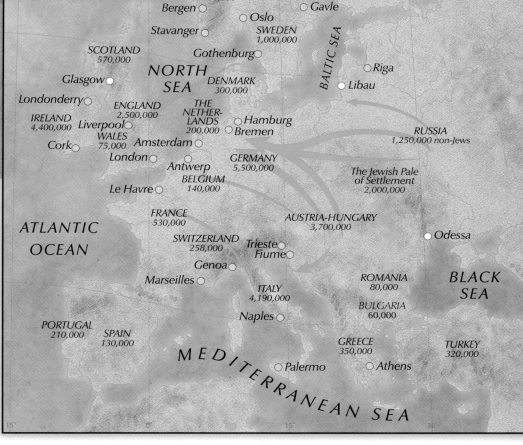

The founders of the United States understood from the beginning that their country was the creation of immigrants, and that its future depended on a steady flow of newcomers. Benjamin Franklin (1706–90) was one of the first to put America's policy into words when he extended a frank but eloquent invitation to the people of the Old World. 'The only encouragements we hold out to strangers are: a good climate, fertile soil, wholesome air and water, plenty of provisions, good pay for labor, kind neighbors, good laws, a free government, and a hearty welcome.'

This impressive list of attributes may not have been entirely accurate, but it corresponded quite closely to the idealised image of the United States that was current

1848 Revolution in Germany and elsewhere in Europe calls for liberal reform. The American Passenger Act regulates a minimum amount of space for each emigrant on board ships.

1852 The British Passenger Act is revised, but proves all but unenforceable at sea.

1886 The dedication of the Statue of Liberty takes place.

1904 The volume of immigrants reaches 1 million a year, and remains so until the outbreak of World War I.

1921 and 1924 The US Congress places quotas on immigrants according to their nationality. The system remains in force until 1965.

| 1830 | 1840 | 1850 | 1860 | 1870 | 1880 | 1890 | 1900 | 1910 | 1920 | 1930 | 1940 | 1950 | 1960 |

1855 Castle Garden opens in New York as the first Emigrant Landing Depot in the world.

1860s Steamships begin to replace sailing ships on trans-Atlantic routes. Passage to North America is reduced from three months to two weeks.

1892 Ellis Island opens as a purpose-built centre for processing immigrants, replacing Castle Garden.

1914 World War I begins in Europe, drastically reducing immigration to North America.

1954 Ellis Island is closed down.

in Europe throughout the 19th century – one that had a magnetic effect on immigrants. America was the land of promise. The exact nature of this promise no doubt took a different form in the mind of every potential immigrant, but on the whole it was the prospect of good pay and free government – and the better life that comes with these things – that prompted millions of people to leave their homes and venture across the Atlantic Ocean to the New World.

During the Napoleonic Wars (1799–1815) in Europe, marauding armies and blockading navies made travel within and out of the continent close to impossible. When the conflict ended, however, Europeans began to flood US shores, and went on to do so for the next 40 years. In the 1820s, the first decade in which US authorities kept immigration records, 151,000 people came to settle in the country. In the following decade the figure was almost 600,000, and from there it rose exponentially: to 1.7 million in the 1840s, and to 2.3 million in the 1850s. More than one-half of these immigrants were from Britain or Ireland, and about one-third were from German states. The British and

German immigrants were for the most part farmers who were barely able to subsist on their tiny holdings in their home countries. Many of them realised that they were doomed to poverty unless they took steps to change their circumstances. In Ireland, the overwhelming disaster of the potato blight in the late 1840s, which destroyed the country's agricultural mainstay for five consecutive years, turned Ireland into a land of hunger and prompted many to leave. Men often made the voyage first and their wives and children followed months or years later, once the paterfamilias had scrimped together enough money to pay for their family's passage.

The Voyage

In 1817, as the rate of immigration in the United States was just beginning to rise, US Secretary of State John Quincy Adams (1767–1848) restated Franklin's open-door policy in rather brusque terms. He said that America invited none to come, but would not keep out those who had the courage to cross the Atlantic. This was a tacit admission that the journey to the United States was a daunting undertaking in itself. For most emigrants it was nothing less than a form of seaborne purgatory. 'Before the emigrant has been a week at sea he is an altered man,' wrote one Irish philanthropist who made the voyage in the 1840s to see what his fellow countrymen were enduring. 'Hundreds of poor people huddled together without light, without air, wallowing in filth and breathing a fetid atmosphere, sick in body, dispirited in heart, the fevered patients lying in sleeping places so narrow as almost to deny them the power of indulging the natural restlessness of the disease.'

The level of overcrowding in steerage was extremely high, and passengers were provided with few toilet facilities, no privacy, and poor food. Conditions on board naturally led to outbreaks of diseases such as cholera, and the long, empty days of these westward voyages were punctuated by burials at sea, with children often being the first victims. The appalling conditions were largely due to the greed of the shipping lines. Most of the vessels on which emigrants travelled were freighters, and their main role was to bring raw materials to Europe from the United States. To fund the return voyage, shipping companies hastily converted the vessels to passenger ships at Liverpool, England, to carry emigrants to the New World. The shipping lines viewed these emigrants as merely another type of cargo, and a troublesome one at that. Shipping operators did not pay the slightest heed to English legislation, which set minimum standards of care on passenger vessels. Indeed the ships' officers often behaved abominably towards passengers – making them pay for food and water that was supposed to be free, and abusing and striking them as though they were convicted criminals rather than paying customers.

The ordeal did not end when emigrants reached their destination, which for the vast majority during these boom years was New York. On the quayside, shiploads of tired and debilitated men and women were met by gangs of 'runners'. Ostensibly, runners offered their services to new arrivals to help them find lodgings, but in fact their sole aim was to rob and swindle. Scams ranged from the straightforward theft of a suitcase to relatively complex stings that involved selling forged tickets to inland destinations such as Chicago. Runners worked in rival gangs and were sometimes in cahoots with ships' captains, who would arrange to 'sell' the pick of his passengers to a particular gang.

Each to His Own
The fraudulent reception that new arrivals received in New York was a far cry from Franklin's promise of 'kind neighbors … and a hearty welcome', but immigrants

soon became streetwise. Most took refuge among the familiar accents and attitudes of their own countrymen. Newcomers of the same nationality tended to congregate in certain parts of the city and recreate as much as they could a semblance of the 'old country'. In New York, even before the potato famine drove Irish citizens overseas in the tens of thousands, there was a distinctly Irish community on the Lower East Side. North of this neighbourhood in the 1850s was a district known as *Kleindeutschland* (Little Germany), where 65,000 Germans lived an entirely German life, speaking their native tongue, reading German newspapers and drinking lager in convincingly authentic beer cellars.

The tendency to cling to one's own kind existed at a regional as well as a national level. German Bavarians stuck with other Bavarians, and Irish Kerrymen with other Kerrymen. In 1920, 200 families from the Italian town of Cinisi were living on the same street in New York. Although these transplanted communities have now dispersed, the New York tradition of ethnic enclaves lives on. Brighton Beach and Coney Island, for example, were colonised by Russian immigrants in the early 1990s. Today, shop signs are still in Russian, and the restaurants still serve Russian food. Brighton Beach, or *Braiton* as the Russians call it, is

Origin of Immigrants in the US, 1854–1907

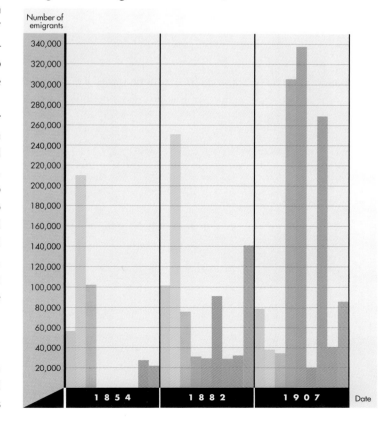

Left: At the start of the 19th century, barely 1 in 100 US citizens had been born abroad. By 1850, the proportion of foreign-born citizens was about 1 in 10.

also a good example of how the émigré urge to recreate the abandoned homeland can manifest as a nostalgic exaggeration of the 'old country'. Most of the Russian immigrants that settled in Brighton Beach left Russia when communism collapsed in the early 1990s and restrictions on emigration were lifted. As a result, *Braiton* resembles the 1980s Moscow that immigrants remember from their childhood, and is much more Soviet in character than any corner of present-day Moscow.

As well as patriotism, both regional and national, other factors affected the settlement patterns of immigrants in the United States. Some made their homes where their individual skills were most in demand: Welsh miners travelled to the coalfields of Pennsylvania; Cornishmen from England, used to digging for tin, to the copper mines of Michigan; and English potters from the Staffordshire Potteries to Trenton, New Jersey, where the clay was ideal for pottery making. Other emigrants were drawn to America by the promise of being able to follow their religious or philosophical beliefs free from persecution. This promise is a long-standing US tradition that reaches back to the Pilgrim Fathers themselves – the early settlers

in the first colonies in North America who travelled to the New World in the 15th century, fleeing religious persecution in their homelands and hoping to find enough space to build undisturbed their own private New Jerusalem. In the 19th century other sects followed in their footsteps, such as the German Inspirationists, who ultimately settled in Amana, Iowa, and the Doukhobors, a clean-living sect of Russian Christians that fled persecution by the Russian Orthodox Church and made a home in Canada.

Another group of ideological immigrants were the European intellectuals who fled their home countries when the revolutions of 1848, which called for liberal reform across Europe, were put down. Unlike many other migrants, these exiles were generally wealthy and well educated. Unsurprisingly, then, quite a few of these immigrants went on to lead impressive careers in the United States, editing newspapers and becoming active in local and national politics. During the American Civil War, Forty-Eighters, as the German exiles were known, sided with the Union because of their objection to Confederate

Below: *Clutching their belongings and holding their emigration documents in their teeth, a shipload of newly arrived Italian immigrants heads confidently for the inspection hall on Ellis Island, c. 1900.*

slavery, and many went on to hold prominent positions within the US government.

A New Generation of Immigrants

By 1855, roughly half of the inhabitants of New York were immigrants. In the city there were loud murmurings against the immigrant population, who were over-represented in the jails and the hospitals, but in the country at large immigrants were still very much in demand. The white, native-born population of the United States stood at about 20 million people – not nearly enough to fill the wide open spaces in the west. From 1860 onwards new waves of incomers flooded into the country, this time from southern and eastern Europe. In Italy, peasants were forced out of their homes by an unsustainable system of land distribution, a practice that also catalysed the Irish emigrations of the 1840s. Farms, which were subdivided between the offspring of tenants or owners, had become too small to be viable. Added to this, the market for Italian citrus fruit and grapes collapsed in the 1880s. Many southern Italian farmers were reduced to penury and fled to America in response.

In that same decade, oppressive legal restrictions were beginning to make life intolerable for Jews in Russia: Jews were not permitted to study at university or live outside the notorious 'Pale of Settlement', the 15 westernmost provinces of the Russian Empire (modern-day Lithuania, Belarus, Poland, Moldova, Ukraine and parts of western Russia). They were also prevented from worshipping openly. All this may have been borne in silence but for the outbursts of anti-Semitic violence – the pogroms – that were unleashed on Jewish communities. Each pogrom prompted a new surge of westward migration. A proportion of these exiles settled in Western Europe, but most crossed the Atlantic to New York, where they displaced the Irish in the slums of the Lower East Side.

In the late 19th century, the passage to the United States was more comfortable and less dangerous than it had been for earlier immigrants. Steam ships designed for carrying passengers had become the norm. They were cleaner and faster, and the transport network was far more extensive. It was now possible for an Irish emigrant to board a ship at an Irish port rather than having to first travel to Liverpool in England, and Russians could sail from local ports rather than having to make a long, arduous journey across half a continent to Hamburg in Germany.

In New York, city authorities had outwitted quayside crooks by ensuring that all immigrants landed at a reception centre on Castle Garden Island, off the southern tip of Manhattan. Here immigrants had to undergo the small indignity of a medical inspection, but they could buy inland tickets and book lodgings without the fear of being robbed or conned. In 1892, after the care of immigrants became the responsibility of federal authorities, a new centre built on Ellis Island became the 'gateway to America' for the next generation of immigrants. Although it was often criticised for its prison-like atmosphere, the Ellis Island centre provided a much more secure welcome to the United States than that experienced by previous generations of incomers.

Appropriately, both Castle Garden and Ellis Island command a view of the Statue of Liberty. Presented to the United States by France in 1885, the Statue of Liberty today symbolises the promise of betterment that drew so many emigrants to America's shores. On its pedestal is inscribed an open invitation to the world's nations, one that acts as a reminder of the United States' immigrant heritage: 'Give me your tired, your poor, your huddled masses yearning to be free. The wretched refuse of your teeming shore, send these, the homeless, tempest-tossed, to me: I lift my lamp beside the golden door.'

Below: More than 12 million migrants passed through Ellis Island between 1892 and 1954. For many of them, the perfunctory medical inspection was the worst part of the ordeal.

FAREWELL, DEAR ERIN, FARE THEE WELL ...

Between 1740 and 1860 almost two million Irish men and women migrated to the United States – one of the largest influxes of people the country had ever seen. Driven out of their homeland by poverty and hunger, migrants sought refuge and fortune in the New World. This mass migration had a significant effect on the Irish mindset, influencing popular culture and traditions, and considerably decreased Ireland's population.

Although the potato famine in Ireland (1845–1849) sparked a dramatic rise in the number of Irish immigrants to the United States, Irish immigration to North America in fact began decades before. As many as 250,000 Irishmen settled in America in the 50 years or so before the United States declared independence in 1776. Most of these immigrants were Ulster Protestants from northern Ireland – Presbyterian descendants of Scots who had come to Ireland in the course of the 17th century when Protestant Irish landlords, keen to attract settlers of their own religion, offered them generous terms on land leases. When the leases expired in the early 1700s, however, the landlords took the opportunity to increase the rent. The second- and third-generation Scottish Ulstermen who had inherited the land decided to cut their losses and leave.

Most of these Ulster Protestants settled in Pennsylvania, where they were drawn by another attractive offer of land. In the mid-18th century, Pennsylvania was still very much frontier territory and the state authorities needed people to bolster America's border with the wilderness. Life there was hard, and attacks by Native American peoples were commonplace. However, the 'Scotch-Irish', as they became known, seemed tough enough to deal with these challenges: they were born frontiersmen.

The steady outflow of Irish emigrants from Ulster continued in the 19th century, when it was joined by a burgeoning number of emigrants from the Catholic south. At first, at least one-half of these wayfarers made their way to settle not in the United States, but in England. In the early 19th century, London and Liverpool exerted as strong a magnetic pull on the Catholic Irish as the United States did. England was closer to home and was familiar to many Irish workers who were used to spending part of the year picking crops in English fields, or 'scarring the face of England' as navvies on the canals and railways. In these years, there was such a large population of Irish Roman Catholics in Wolverhampton, for example, that the town became known as 'Little Rome' and Gaelic could be heard everywhere in the slum district called Caribee Island.

Famine Strikes Ireland

This migration pattern changed decisively in the autumn of 1845 when potato blight struck throughout Ireland, turning the entire countryside into a vast wasteland of rot and putrefaction. The effect on the country was devastating. The Irish peasantry depended entirely on potatoes for their survival as they produced more food per acre than any other crop. Given the large size of the average family and the tiny dimensions of the average family plot, potatoes were the only crop that gave tenant farmers any hope of feeding their dependents. Even then

IRISH MIGRATION TO THE UNITED STATES

1771 A downturn in the Ulster linen trade sends a new wave of Scotch-Irish to America.

1798 An unsuccessful Irish rebellion against the British takes place. Some of the rebel leaders take refuge in the United States.

C.E.	1700	1710	1720	1730	1740	1750	1760	1770	1780	1790

1720 Protestant Ulstermen begin to leave Ireland for America.

1770 450,000 Irish settle in America between 1717 and 1770.

1776 The War of Independence leads to the founding of the United States of America.

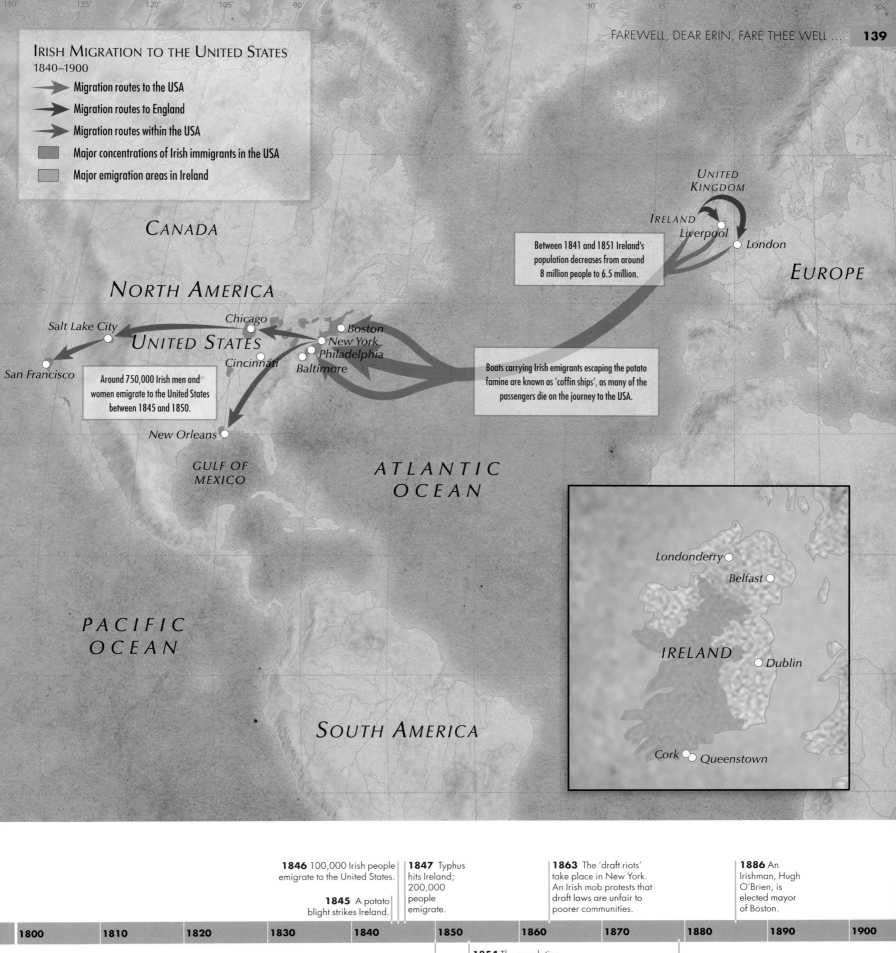

IRISH MIGRATION TO THE UNITED STATES
1840–1900

→ Migration routes to the USA

→ Migration routes to England

→ Migration routes within the USA

▬ Major concentrations of Irish immigrants in the USA

▬ Major emigration areas in Ireland

CANADA

NORTH AMERICA

Salt Lake City

UNITED STATES

Chicago

Boston
New York
Philadelphia
Baltimore

Cincinnati

San Francisco

Around 750,000 Irish men and women emigrate to the United States between 1845 and 1850.

New Orleans

GULF OF MEXICO

Between 1841 and 1851 Ireland's population decreases from around 8 million people to 6.5 million.

UNITED KINGDOM

IRELAND
Liverpool
London

EUROPE

Boats carrying Irish emigrants escaping the potato famine are known as 'coffin ships', as many of the passengers die on the journey to the USA.

ATLANTIC OCEAN

PACIFIC OCEAN

SOUTH AMERICA

Londonderry
Belfast

IRELAND

Dublin

Cork Queenstown

1846 100,000 Irish people emigrate to the United States.

1845 A potato blight strikes Ireland.

1847 Typhus hits Ireland; 200,000 people emigrate.

1863 The 'draft riots' take place in New York. An Irish mob protests that draft laws are unfair to poorer communities.

1886 An Irishman, Hugh O'Brien, is elected mayor of Boston.

| 1800 | 1810 | 1820 | 1830 | 1840 | 1850 | 1860 | 1870 | 1880 | 1890 | 1900 |

1850 The populations of New York, Baltimore, Philadelphia and Boston are each one-quarter Irish.

1854 The population of Ireland is reduced by one-quarter because of the effects of the famine and emigration.

1879 A new famine strikes Ireland.

farmers could barely earn a living. When the potato harvest failed in 1845, and again in the subsequent four years, famine took hold of the country.

The British authorities were slow to react to the crisis in Ireland. Their failure to deal with the catastrophe was down to ineptitude rather than callousness – it is unlikely that any government at that time, however good their intentions, could have coped with a human disaster on the scale of that which was unfolding in rural Ireland. The mass of hungry Irish, however, felt that they had been abandoned. Over 500,000 Irish men, women and children starved to death, and those who survived the famine were left with a deep resentment that would

EJECTMENT OF IRISH TENANTRY.

THE EJECTMENT.

Above: Up to 500,000 people were evicted from their homes between 1847 and 1854, as Irish landlords sought to rid impoverished farmers and labourers from their land.

linger on in the Irish psyche for years. In the short term, particularly the 20 years following the famine, the vast majority of Irish emigrants turned away from England and instead looked to 'the shores of Americay', as one Irish song of the time put it, hoping for a better life.

A further incentive to emigrate came in 1847 when the British government, in an attempt to alleviate the worst of the poverty caused by the famine, invoked the Poor Laws. This legal manoeuvre obliged landlords to feed the people who lived on their property. In Ireland, however, the landowners' wealth came from the rent paid to them by their tenants. With the stroke of a pen, Irish tenants had been transformed from a lucrative asset into a huge liability. Suddenly landowners, who constituted about 1 per cent of the population, were

responsible for feeding destitute millions out of their own funds.

Faced with this obligation, many landowners found it was cheaper to offer their tenants the price of a passage to the United States. Thousands accepted, and some earned an extra five shillings by tearing down their own hovels before they departed. Those who were unwilling to leave were forced out, and as often as not watched as their home was torn down by 'destructives' – employees of the landlord. The process of 'shoveling out', as it was known, allowed the landowners to consolidate their holdings, and gave penniless tenants some hope of a brighter future in a new country. At the time, though, mere survival seemed enough. 'All we want is to get out of Ireland,' declared one emigrant. 'We must be better anywhere than here.'

A Settled Habit

The famine ended in 1850, but the westward flow of the Irish did not end with it. Once begun, migration to the United States seemed to gain a momentum of its own: between 50,000 and 100,000 Irish people went to the United States almost every year between the end of the famine and the start of World War I, and Ireland became the only country in modern history to see its population decline – from 8 million in 1846 to 4.5 million in 1901 – as a direct result of emigration.

There were many reasons for the continual rise in Ireland's emigration rates. The memory of the potato famine convinced many, certainly, that life in Ireland was

Population of Ireland, 1841–1901

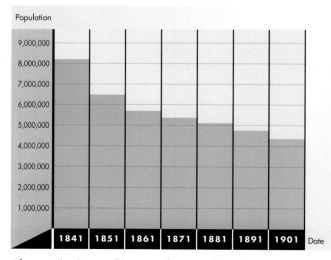

Above: The disaster of the potato famine and forced evictions led to a steady reduction in Ireland's population.

Left: St Patrick's Cathedral, on 50th Street and 5th Avenue, was built between 1858 and 1878 to serve the many thousands of Catholics who came to New York City from Ireland and Italy.

too precarious – 'the only place in Ireland that a man can make his fortune is America,' ran one rueful joke. But there was a more fundamental economic cause. The rural Irish practice of subdividing a farm between the children of the tenant or owner was in decline – and came to an end completely during the famine years. Plots were becoming so small as to be unviable, so instead the farm was left to the eldest son in its entirety. The younger children – of which there may have easily been six or seven – were left with no possible means of making a living. Ireland was still a largely rural country with no established industries, so going to a city to work in a factory was not an option as it was in England. Moving abroad seemed the only answer, and Irish children grew up with the idea that their future was in America. 'Emigration is a settled habit,' wrote one Irishman. 'And as a nation we are strangely wedded to our habits.'

The United States was the obvious destination because, as so many Irish people had moved there during the famine, most families already had a friend or relative living there. Moreover, wages in America were four times higher than in Ireland. Irish men and women made the hazardous, unpleasant crossing to New York knowing that when they arrived they would receive help from their own kith and kin, and that there was money to be made if they worked hard. Once established, newcomers often sent home money or a prepaid ticket to the United States along with a letter extolling the many wonders and advantages of the New Ireland. In

this manner, Irish emigrants tempted another – a wife, brother or sister – to follow in their footsteps. 'My dear father,' wrote one young woman after her arrival in New York in 1850. 'I must only say that this is a good place and a good country. For if one place doesn't suit a man he can go to another and can very easy please himself. Any man or woman without a family are fools that would not venture and come to this plentiful country, where no man or woman ever hungered or ever will …'

Back in Ireland, entire villages would often gather together to hear a letter from America read aloud, or translated into Gaelic. Most correspondence was upbeat and optimistic, full of tales of minor triumphs and successes, and so constituted an unwitting but constant source of positive, pro-American propaganda. The public reading of American letters became a form of entertainment – a piece of popular drama that persuaded many young people to quit Ireland and try their own luck in the United States. The money orders that letters home often contained provided the most convincing argument in favour of emigration, as well as the means for emigrating. Millions of dollars flowed from the United States to Ireland in letters home, fuelling the Irish perception that America was a land of plenty where, if you worked hard enough, you might find yourself with money to spare. This vision soon found expression in certain Irish turns of phrase. For example, in Donegal it became a cliché to say that something obtained with little or no effort was 'like money from America.' Elsewhere in Ireland, affluent families were said to 'have America at home'.

The surge in emigration was also naturally reflected in the popular culture of the time, and countless ballads were written on the subject. These songs were often printed on cheap paper and sold for a penny. Most of them dwelled in tearful fashion on the heartbreak of leaving 'the shamrock shore'. One stanza, from a song called 'The Emigrant's Farewell to Donegall', is typically maudlin, but nevertheless realistically reflects the poor conditions that prompted many Irish to emigrate:

> *Farewell, dear Erin, fare thee well,*
> *that once was called the Isle of Saints,*
> *For here no longer I can dwell,*
> *I'm going to cross the stormy sea.*
> *For to live here I can't endure,*
> *there's nothing but slavery,*
> *My heart's oppressed, I can find no rest,*
> *I will try the land of liberty.*

No Tsar in America

On 15 May 1882, Tsar Alexander III of Russia introduced the May Laws, which banned Jews from settling in many major cities in Eastern Europe and restricted their rights to work and education. This policy of discrimination prompted a surge of Jewish migration to the United States, the sheer scale of which eclipses everything in the peripatetic record of the Jews, in the immigration records of the United States, and indeed in the entire history of migration.

Above: Anti-Semitism was endemic in the Russian Empire well into the 20th century. These Jewish refugees are fleeing their homes at the outbreak of World War I in 1914.

The arrival of Jews in the United States is often said to have occurred in three distinct stages. In the decades before the War of Independence (1775–83), a small number of Spanish Jews made their home in the Americas. In the years between 1820 and 1880, a steady flow of German-speaking Jews emigrated from the then disunited German states. The biggest influx, however, arrived between 1881 and 1920, when an immense wave of persecuted and dispossessed Jews fled Russia, Romania and other Eastern European lands. The reality of Jewish migration to the New World, however, is slightly more complicated.

America's First Jewish Communities

Jews were among the first Europeans to have a presence in the New World. The surnames of some members of Christopher Columbus's crew, who sailed to America in 1492, provide evidence that the crew may have included Marranos – Spanish Jews who had converted to Christianity, either willingly or by force. There was also a strong Jewish community in Brazil by the mid-1600s. Many of these Jews had first travelled to the Netherlands from Spain and Portugal after the Dutch won independence from Spain in 1561. Dutch cities became a safe haven for many Jewish traders and bankers who had been expelled from Spain and Portugal a century before. Some of these well-to-do Jews invested heavily in the Dutch West India Company, which had a trade monopoly in the West Indies, and within 100 years the Dutch colony of Recife on the Brazilian coast had a freely professing Jewish community with its own synagogue and a rabbi imported from Amsterdam. This was the first Jewish congregation on the American continent.

The Jewish community in Brazil, however, was short-lived. In 1654, the Portuguese conquered Recife, and the Jews residing there were told to leave, or stay and await the arrival of the Inquisition. Most returned directly to the Netherlands, but 23 Jews took to the sea and sailed north. In September 1654 they landed at the Dutch outpost of New Amsterdam on the Hudson River. In 1664, the British

JEWISH
MIGRATION
TO THE
UNITED STATES

1790 George Washington addresses a letter to the Jews of Newport, Rhode Island.

1827 Russian Jews are obliged to serve 31 years in the Russian army from the age of 12.

C.E.	1750	1760	1770	1780	1790	1800	1810	1820	1830

1775 There are around 2,000 Jews living in the North American British colonies.

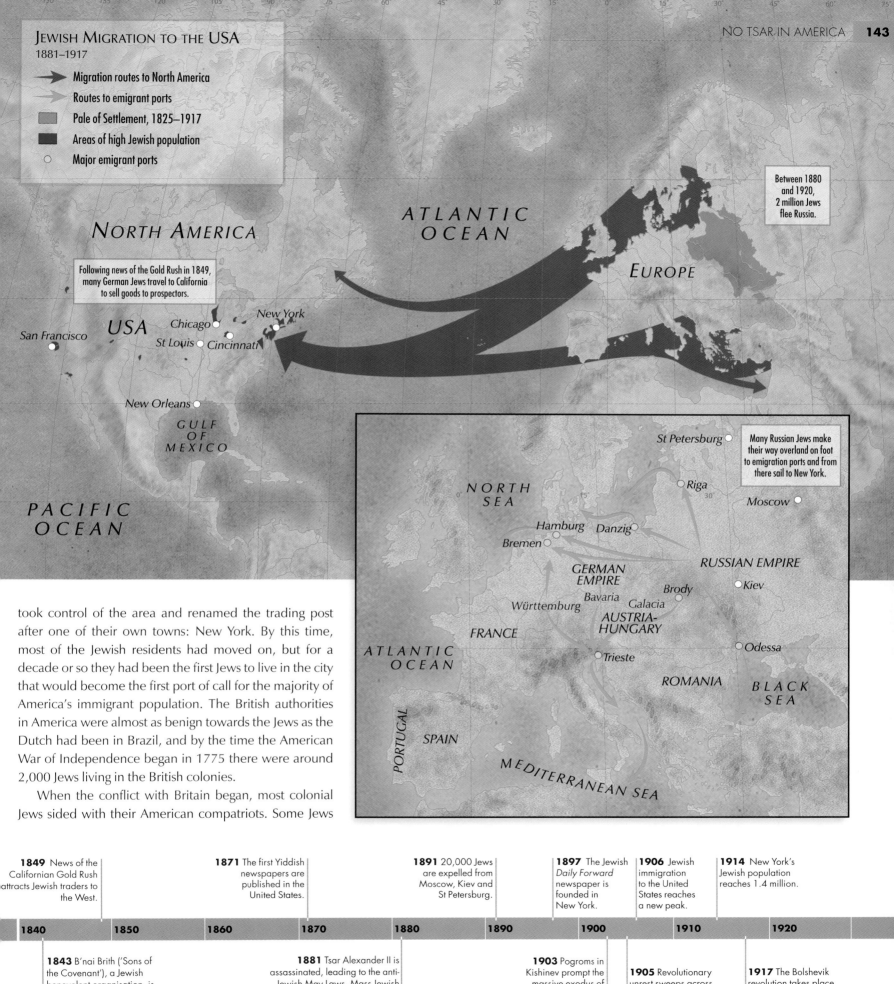

JEWISH MIGRATION TO THE USA
1881–1917

→ Migration routes to North America

→ Routes to emigrant ports

▢ Pale of Settlement, 1825–1917

▪ Areas of high Jewish population

○ Major emigrant ports

NORTH AMERICA

ATLANTIC OCEAN

EUROPE

Between 1880 and 1920, 2 million Jews flee Russia.

Following news of the Gold Rush in 1849, many German Jews travel to California to sell goods to prospectors.

San Francisco

USA

Chicago

St Louis • Cincinnati

New York

PACIFIC OCEAN

New Orleans

GULF OF MEXICO

Many Russian Jews make their way overland on foot to emigration ports and from there sail to New York.

NORTH SEA

St Petersburg

Riga

Moscow

Hamburg Danzig

Bremen

GERMAN EMPIRE

RUSSIAN EMPIRE

Kiev

Württemburg Bavaria

Brody

Galacia

FRANCE

AUSTRIA-HUNGARY

ATLANTIC OCEAN

Trieste

Odessa

PORTUGAL

SPAIN

ROMANIA

BLACK SEA

MEDITERRANEAN SEA

took control of the area and renamed the trading post after one of their own towns: New York. By this time, most of the Jewish residents had moved on, but for a decade or so they had been the first Jews to live in the city that would become the first port of call for the majority of America's immigrant population. The British authorities in America were almost as benign towards the Jews as the Dutch had been in Brazil, and by the time the American War of Independence began in 1775 there were around 2,000 Jews living in the British colonies.

When the conflict with Britain began, most colonial Jews sided with their American compatriots. Some Jews

1849 News of the Californian Gold Rush attracts Jewish traders to the West.

1871 The first Yiddish newspapers are published in the United States.

1891 20,000 Jews are expelled from Moscow, Kiev and St Petersburg.

1897 The Jewish *Daily Forward* newspaper is founded in New York.

1906 Jewish immigration to the United States reaches a new peak.

1914 New York's Jewish population reaches 1.4 million.

1840	1850	1860	1870	1880	1890	1900	1910	1920

1843 B'nai Brith ('Sons of the Covenant'), a Jewish benevolent organisation, is founded in New York.

1881 Tsar Alexander II is assassinated, leading to the anti-Jewish May Laws. Mass Jewish emigration from Russia begins.

1903 Pogroms in Kishinev prompt the massive exodus of Moldovian Jews.

1905 Revolutionary unrest sweeps across Russia.

1917 The Bolshevik revolution takes place in Russia.

physically fought against the British, while others backed the Revolution financially. In 1790, George Washington wrote a letter to the congregation of the Touro Synagogue in Newport, Rhode Island, acknowledging their contribution to the American cause, and stressing their position as free and equal citizens of the United States: 'All possesses alike liberty of conscience and immunity of citizenship. It is now no more that toleration is spoken of, as if it was by the indulgence of one class of people, that another enjoyed the exercise of their inherent natural rights. For happily the government of the United States … gives to bigotry no sanction, to persecution no assistance … [and] requires only that those who live under its protection demean

Above: On Hester Street c. 1900, in the busy heart of New York's Jewish quarter, the haberdashers and ironmongers were as likely to advertise their wares in Yiddish as in English.

themselves as good citizens.' Washington's assurance of equality and tolerance towards the Jews was somewhat idealistic. There was plenty of petty prejudice against the Jews in the United States – immigrants from the Old World had brought this kind of bigotry with them – but there was almost no institutional discrimination and no outright persecution. Jewish immigrants had the same rights and freedoms as every other US citizen. This alone was enough to make the United States seem like a promised land to many European Jews.

The Arrival of German Jews

At the start of the 19th century, the turmoil created by the Napoleonic Wars (1799–1815) made emigration to the New World all but impossible. But in the aftermath of the conflict, thousands of Germans made the decision to leave the war-torn principalities of middle Europe and head

west. Among them were many Jews, predominantly from southern German lands such as Bavaria and Württemburg, where the restrictions placed on Jews were intolerable. In Bavaria, for example, Jewish communities were obliged to maintain a list, called the *Matrikel*, of all their families. The purpose of this list was to restrict the number of Jewish households in any given area. A Jewish man could set up home and marry only when a place became free following the death of an old married Jewish couple. 'The register makes it little short of impossible for young Israelites to set up home in Bavaria,' reported one German-Jewish newspaper at the time. 'Often their head is adorned with grey hair before they receive the permission to set up house and can therefore think of marriage.' By emigrating to the United States young Jewish men could avoid the *Matrikel*, make some money and then return to Europe to marry. Once married, the newlyweds would travel together to their US home.

Many of these Jews – *Dorfjuden*, or village Jews, as they were called – made a living in the United States as peddlers, fulfilling a need in America's burgeoning economy. Jewish traders went west in the wake of pioneering settlers and supplied frontiersmen with the tools and provisions they needed to hew a living out of the untamed country. Clothing proved to be the most lucrative item. Many began selling garments out of a handcart, and then graduated to a wagon and then a shop as business grew. One or two of these *Dorfjuden* went on to make a fortune out of the clothing trade: Macy's and Bloomingdale's are two retailing giants that have their roots in the thrift and industry of Jewish peddlers.

By 1880, German Jews had spread across the United States. There were 5,000 Jews in New Orleans, and 16,000 in San Francisco – many of them were traders, or the family of traders, who had gone west following news of the California Gold Rush in 1849 to sell picks, sieves and dry goods to prospectors. In some places the Jewish population was large enough to influence the toponymy of the region: Solomonville, Arizona, is named after its Jewish founder, Isadore Elkan Solomon; Goldtree, California, is an anglicisation of the Jewish name of its first citizen, Morris Goldbaum; and Jewtown, Georgia, is rather less equivocal about its provenance. In all, the Jewish population of the United States in 1880 was about 250,000 out of 50 million.

German Jews and their offspring also had a cultural impact on the United States. Throughout the 19th century the Jewish faith that was brought over from the Old World evolved into a new form of worship better suited to the established middle-class status of the American Jews. The synagogues of Reform Judaism, as this new branch was called, resembled Baptist churches or Methodist chapels. The curtained area reserved for women found in traditional synagogues was abolished in favour of family pews, sermons were delivered in English, and mixed choirs took the place of Hebrew prayers and plangent singing of the cantor. Some congregations even took to holding services on Sundays rather than on the Jewish Sabbath. Second- and third-generation German Jews described themselves as being 'of the Jewish persuasion', as if being Jewish were entirely a matter of conviction and personal choice. By 1880, US Jews were happily and almost entirely assimilated. The following year, however, an event occurred in the Russian capital that would turn the settled world of US Jewry upside down.

become so impoverished that approximately one-third depended to some degree on Jewish welfare organisations.

The discrimination experienced by Russian Jews came to a head in the early 1880s. On 13 March 1881, a terrorist assassinated Tsar Alexander II (r. 1855–1881) in St Petersburg. Some of the revolutionaries involved in the assassination were Jewish, and as a consequence the entire Jewish population were made scapegoats for the death of the tsar. In 1882, the new tsar, Alexander III (r. 1881–1894), introduced the May Laws, which placed strict quotas on the number of Jews allowed into secondary and higher education, and many professions. This assassination also triggered outbreaks of violence against Jews – pogroms that were tacitly encouraged by the Russian government. Konstantin Pobedonostsev, procurator of the Holy Synod of the Russian Orthodox Church and close adviser of

> ' No expensive steamship fares need be paid in order to visit this ghetto. Step off a car at the corner of Hester Street and the Bowery some Friday morning and walk east. The pavements along both sides of Hester Street are lined by a continuous double row of pushcarts filled with eatables of every kind agreeable to the palate of the Russian Jew. Here is a cart laden with grapes and pears, and the fruit merchant, a short, dark-complexioned fellow, clad as to the outer garments in an old cap, a dark-blue sweater, and a nondescript pair of dirty-hued trousers, is shrieking at the top of his voice: "Gutes frucht! Gutes frucht! Metziehs! ['bargains' in Yiddish]. Drei pennies die whole lot!" '
> *New York Times*, 1897

Mass Exodus Begins

The Jewish population in Russia was largely confined to the Pale of Settlement, a western border region of Imperial Russia created in 1791 by Catherine the Great (r. 1762–1796). Russian society at the time was divided into nobles, serfs and clergy, but industrial progress led to the emergence of a middle class, which was quickly being filled by Jews who did not belong to any traditional social sector. By confining the Jewish population to the Pale, the imperial powers hoped to rid Russia of Jewish business competition and ensure the growth of a non-Jewish middle class. More than 90 per cent of Russian Jews were forced to live in the Pale, which made up only 4 per cent of Imperial Russia. The concentration of Jews in the Pale made them easy targets for discrimination: they paid double taxes and were forbidden to lease land. As the Jewish population grew, the restrictions placed on professions and trade increased economic competition within the community, causing the poverty rate to rise. At the end of the 19th century, the Pale population had

Alexander III, made a chilling prediction: 'One-third of the Jews [in Russia] will convert, one-third will die, and one-third will flee the country.' The flight of Jews out of Russia began almost immediately, and continued more or less steadily until the Bolshevik Revolution of 1917 closed the gates on Russian emigration.

Pogroms occurred spasmodically throughout the reign of Tsar Alexander III, and continued during the rule of his son, Nicholas II (r. 1894–1917). Each outburst of murderous violence strengthened the resolve of thousands of Jews to desert their homeland. 'I am very anxious to leave Russia,' wrote one young Jew in his diary. 'Do I not rise daily with the fear lest the mob attack me? Do I not pray that my sisters may escape the clutches of the drunkards lest they be raped? Do I not pray that my brothers do not die of hunger? Be thou cursed forever, my wicked homeland.' Most prospective emigrants were walkers – *fusgeyer* – who made their way to the border of the Russian Empire and crossed illegally into the Austro-Hungarian Empire. The border town of Brody was

periodically filled to overflowing with Jewish refugees, nearly all of them intending to go to the United States because, as one emigrant put it, 'there is no tsar in America'.

Most of the Russian Jews made their way overland to Hamburg or Bremen, and from there sailed to New York. The number of Jewish immigrants arriving in the United States rose exponentially as the political situation in Russia deteriorated: 37,000 Jews arrived in 1900; 77,500 in 1904; 92,400 in 1905; and 125,000 in 1906. Americans were awed and concerned by the enormity of this Jewish invasion. 'The thoroughly acclimated American Jew stands apart from the seething mass of Jewish immigrants,' wrote one journalist in 1894. 'He has no religious, social or intellectual sympathies with them. He is closer to the Christian sentiment around him than to the Judaism of these miserable darkened Hebrews.'

Surprisingly this opinion, dripping with snobbish distaste and a species of anti-Semitism, was printed in the *Hebrew Standard*, New York's leading Jewish newspaper. The German Jews in America were deeply worried that this new wave of Jewish immigrants, often viewed as shaggy, needy Russian peasants, would undo all the good work of assimilation that had been achieved by the previous two generations of German Jews, and that they would make all US Jews the target of resentment and anti-Semitism.

Despite the brewing animosity, most established US Jews recognised that these 'miserable darkened Hebrews' were their ethnic and spiritual brothers and sisters, and that it was their duty to offer them a helping hand. German-Jewish aid agencies began to develop, and did much useful charitable work for Galician, Russian, Polish and Romanian Jews. Most of this work, which included setting up soup kitchens and providing clothing, took place in Manhattan's Lower East Side, the traditional staging area of immigrants in New York. The Irish who had been occupying the area for much of the 19th century began to move out to make way for the teeming mass of Eastern European Jews. By 1892, they were crammed into the tenements at a density of 1,000 people per acre, prompting the writer Arnold Bennet to say that the doors and windows of this vast slum seemed to 'sweat humanity'. At the time, Calcutta and Bombay were the only places on Earth more densely populated.

The vast majority of the Lower East Side Jews made a living by making clothes. They favoured this business partly because it was a traditional job in the old country – Kravets and Portnoi, two common Jewish surnames, are respectively the Ukrainian and Russian words for 'tailor'. But many Jewish families took up the trade because it was

labour to which the whole family could contribute. Even small children would sit amid piles of shirts in crowded apartments and cut loose threads with tiny pairs of scissors. The fact that Jewish families worked in their own homes meant that they could observe the Sabbath, although even those who worked in clothing factories were often employed by German-Jewish entrepreneurs who were sympathetic to the demands of religious observance. Also, because tailoring was paid as piecework, hard toil was guaranteed to translate into increased earnings, allowing workers more control over their betterment.

And betterment is what most of the Eastern European Jews found. Many moved on and up out of the Lower East Side within a generation. This is remarkable considering the vast numbers of incomers. In 1880, almost 6 million of the world's 7.7 million Jews (75 per cent) were in Eastern Europe, and only 3 per cent were in the United States. By 1920, 2 million Jews had left Russia, and 23 per cent of the world's Jews were in the United States. Pobedonostsev's prediction that one-third of the Jews in Russia would leave had come true.

In the 1930s, another 100,000 persecuted Jews came to the United States – this time from Germany. Their arrival was the last westward Jewish emigration before World War II began and the tragedy of the Holocaust descended on Europe. In its wake, the Jewish vision of a promised land moved away from the United States and back to its ancient nexus: the biblical land of Canaan, soon to be the sovereign state of Israel.

Above: A wedding at the synagogue on Eldridge Street in New York. The building was completed in 1887.

Opposite page: Most Jewish salesmen started with a pushcart, and hoped to work their way up from there. The market on the Lower East Side in New York was a hub for small-time entrepreneurs.

ALL THE LITTLE ITALYS

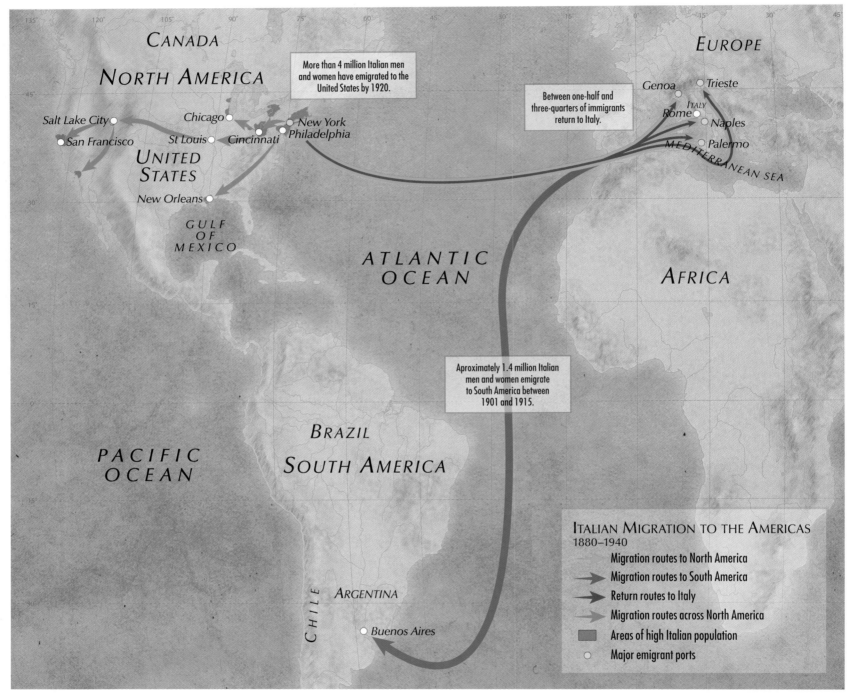

More than 4 million Italian men and women have emigrated to the United States by 1920.

Between one-half and three-quarters of immigrants return to Italy.

Aproximately 1.4 million Italian men and women emigrate to South America between 1901 and 1915.

CANADA

NORTH AMERICA

Salt Lake City
San Francisco
Chicago
St Louis   Cincinnati
New York
Philadelphia
New Orleans
UNITED STATES

GULF OF MEXICO

ATLANTIC OCEAN

PACIFIC OCEAN

BRAZIL
SOUTH AMERICA

CHILE   ARGENTINA
Buenos Aires

EUROPE

Genoa   Trieste
ITALY
Rome   Naples
Palermo
MEDITERRANEAN SEA

AFRICA

ITALIAN MIGRATION TO THE AMERICAS
1880–1940

— Migration routes to North America
→ Migration routes to South America
→ Return routes to Italy
→ Migration routes across North America
▊ Areas of high Italian population
○ Major emigrant ports

ITALIAN MIGRATION TO THE UNITED STATES

1861 The unification of Italy takes place.

1870s The Italian population of the United States reaches 250,000.

C.E.	1800	1810	1820	1830	1840	1850	1860	1870

1820s Small-scale immigration from northern Italy to the United States begins.

Italians, led by the Genoese adventurer Christopher Columbus, were among the first Europeans to set foot on North and South America. Italian migrants, however, who crossed the Atlantic in droves in the 19th and early 20th centuries, were relative latecomers to the United States. Although the period of their migration partly overlapped that of the Eastern European Jews, and they settled in many of the same places, the Italian migration experience was vastly different from that of Jewish refugees from tsardom. The motivation behind Italian immigration, in fact, bears closer resemblance to that of the Irish men and women who ventured to the United States almost half a century before.

The vast majority of Italian immigrants in the United States, like their Irish counterparts, came from poor, rural areas, primarily from southern Italy. However, this mass migration from the south was preceded by a steady trickle of incomers from the more affluent north in the mid-19th century. Most of these first Italian immigrants came from Liguria, a coastal region that borders with France. There was an established tradition of migrant work in this part of Italy and labourers and fruit pickers often sought seasonal employment in neighbouring countries (just as the Irish did in England before the 1840s). The small number of Italians who decided to travel to the United States was merely continuing this tradition in a new, more far-off land.

Rather than labourers, however, most of the immigrants from Liguria were lower-middle-class artisans and small businessmen in search of new markets. They were restaurateurs and saloonkeepers, dry-goods merchants and barbers. Some were even brave enough, and wealthy enough, to speculate in real estate. These professions demanded a city-dwelling clientele, and Italian businesses and communities soon became part of the urban landscape, not only in New York, but also in other big towns such as Philadelphia and Chicago. In the 1860s, for example, Chicago held its first Columbus Day parade, an event organised largely by Italian-Americans to honour the first and most famous Italian-American of them all: Christopher Columbus. Chicago's Italian community also had a newspaper, *L'Unione Italiana*, and a mutual benefit society called the *Società di Unione e Fratellanza*. But although Italians had a visible presence in the United States in mid-19th-century society, it was not a dominant one. Even by 1880, less than 2,000 of Chicago's 500,000 inhabitants were Italian, and in New York

Above: At the start of the 20th century, Italian immigrants took over the clothing business from the Jews. This family is manufacturing neckties in their tenement on Division Street, New York, 1890.

1880s Crop failures and political strife in Italy spur mass emigration from the south of the country.	**1890** 90 per cent of labourers in New York's Department of Public Works are Italian immigrants.	**1920** Italian emigration to the United States, after reaching 4 million in 40 years, begins to taper off.		**1933** Italian Air Force Marshall Balbo leads a mass demonstration from Rome to Chicago, marking the height of pro-Mussolini feeling in the United States.

1880	1890	1900	1910	1920	1930	1940	1950	1960

1881 The first Italian parish in Chicago, the Church of the Assumption, is established.	**1890** Eleven Sicilians are lynched in New Orleans, after being acquitted of murder.	**1922** Mussolini comes to power in Italy, to the approval of most Italian-Americans.	**1933** Italian-Jewish lawyer Fiorello La Guardia is elected mayor of New York.	**1941** The United States and Italy are at war.	**1944–1945** Many young Italian-Americans fight in World War II on Italian soil.

City, which had a population of 1.9 million, there were only about 12,000 foreign-born Italians.

Emigration from southern Italy to the United States started to increase in the 1880s. It began slowly and grew steadily. It was not sparked by a sudden catastrophe equivalent to the potato famine in Ireland or the terrifying pogroms in Russia. Instead it resulted from the dawning knowledge among the poorest rural folk, the *contadini*, that life was not going to get better. The system of land tenure was as unfair and feudal in Italy as anything in pre-famine Ireland. Added to this was the growing sense that unification of the country, which occurred in 1861, had not, as expected, led to the abolition of such injustice or brought any material benefit to the poor south. Disappointment and a loss of hope sent the first *contadini* emigrants westward.

About 100,000 Italians left their homeland each year in the mid-1880s, but about one-half of these emigrants were destined for Argentina or Brazil rather than the United States. South America was an attractive destination because its climate was similar to that of the Mediterranean, its Hispanic culture was less alien than that of the English-speaking, Anglo-Saxon United States, and it had a familiarly strong Catholic tradition.

The Turning of the Tides

At the end of the 1880s, a series of unrelated economic and political events changed the nature of Italian emigration. First, US fruit growers in Florida began to undercut Italian imports: homegrown US lemons and oranges became cheaper than the produce of southern Italy, and thousands of Italians who depended on the export market to North America for their livelihoods were ruined. Almost at the same time, the French government put a prohibitive tax on the import of Italian wines. Vintners and grape-pickers in Italy depended on foreign buyers for their income as completely as lemon-growers did, and many of them were also forced out of business. With no way of making a decent living in their homeland, orchard owners and armies of fruit pickers and packers began to look outside of Italy for better opportunities.

At this point, Italian emigration to the New World was still divided fairly evenly between North and South America. But in the early 1890s civil war broke out in Brazil, which naturally made it a less attractive destination. In the wake of the war, cholera took hold of Brazil, and the Italian government stepped in and forbade its citizens

to settle there. In Argentina, meanwhile, there was endless civil strife throughout the 1890s. Strikes, attempted coups and a border dispute with Chile that came close to all-out war convinced prospective Italian immigrants that it was not a good place in which to start a new life. Consequently, the flow of immigration shifted northwards to the United States, which was in any case closer to Italy, and therefore cheaper to reach. By 1900, 100,000 Italians were arriving in the United States each year – and in the next 10 years they were joined by 2 million more.

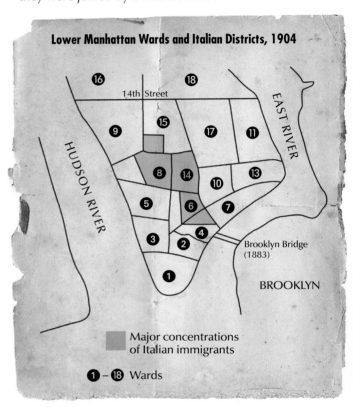

Above: At its height, Little Italy was concentrated in three or four wards in Lower Manhattan, with Mulberry Street at its centre.

The Pull of *Campanalismo*

At first, the bulk of Italian emigrants were young, unskilled men. Although they were country folk in their native land, when they arrived in the United States they instantly became part of the urban proletariat. Italian immigrants were dockworkers and labourers in New York, and in Chicago the legions of young southern Italian navvies vastly outnumbered older, north Italian tradesmen. There were not interested in creating rural farming communities. These young men knew little about agriculture – they were farm labourers rather than farmers – but more that, they had come to America to escape the poverty and vagaries of a rustic life.

Once they arrived in the United States, Italian immigrants went through many of the same experiences as the Irish that had arrived before them. They were filtered through Ellis Island Immigration Depot and dumped on the streets of New York to fend for themselves. Some had kinfolk to seek out, and the spirit of *campanalismo* – the attachment to people born within sight or sound of the same bell tower – was a strong social force among Italian immigrants. People from the same village in Italy regrouped in one street in New York, or even in a single tenement building. On one side of Mott Street, for example, lived Italians from Napoli, and on the other were emigrants from Basilicata; Hester Street was the home of people from Apulia, as well as European Jews; Elizabeth Street and Prince Street were little Sicilys; and west of Broadway

was the territory of northern Italians – the Ligurians and Piedmontese. It was as if a map of Italy had been broken up, jumbled in a hat and put back together again in Lower Manhattan.

This arrangement lasted well into the 20th century, which is surprising because the actual population of Italian New York, and of Italian America in general, was highly fluid. Most Italian immigrants who travelled to the United States did so with the intention of making money and then returning to Italy – an objective that set them apart from other European immigrants in the country. The Irish did not go home in large numbers because they felt the sea journey was too dreadful to face and because, for many, their homes had been torn down when they left. Similarly, there was no desire or possibility of return to Russia for the

Above: The living conditions of many Italian immigrants were appalling. This family occupied a shack on Jersey Street, and were fortunate to at least have an open yard with some sunshine and fresh air.

Right-hand page:

The Feast of San Gennaro, held each year in New York, celebrates Naples' patron saint. At one time, each local Italian community marked the saint's day of the village from which they had come.

Below: Women line up at an Italian bank on Mulberry Bend. Many Italian immigrants came to the United States with the aim of making money and then returning to the old country.

persecuted, exiled Jews. Italians, however, kept the way back to Italy open. Between one-half and three-quarters of Italian immigrants were 'birds of passage' – they stayed in the United States for a matter of years, and then returned home. 'We brought to America only our brains and our arms,' said one *ritornato* (returnee). 'Our hearts stayed there in the little house in the beautiful fields of our Italy.'

Nostalgia and Patriotism

Given the dire conditions of the Italian ghettos in New York, it is not surprising that many immigrants held on to an idealised view of their homeland. The degree of overcrowding in the Italian tenements was staggering, and it was exacerbated by the universal Italian practice of taking lodgers, turning an already confined space into an impossibly populous ant hill. An 1879 report on living conditions in the Italian enclave of Jersey Street contained this vivid description: 'Opposite the door stood a stove upon which meat was being cooked; to the right stood a bedstead roughly constructed out of

boards, and in the left-hand corner a similar one. The small room contains another. These board bunks were covered with three or four blankets, and each would accommodate four men. There was no other furniture in the room, which was so dark that we could only see by waiting till the eyes became accustomed to the light. There was scarcely standing room for the heaps of bags and rags, and opposite them stood a large pile of bones, mostly having meat on them, in various stages of decomposition. The smell could be likened only to that of an exhumed body. There were nine men in the room at the time of our visit, but a larger number occupy the room.'

Despite the obvious squalor, the report concluded that: 'Jersey Street at first looks like a pestilence-breeding, law-breaking colony. However, no more peaceable, thrifty, orderly neighbors could be found than those Italians.' Although the tenements were crowded, everybody earned their keep. Lodgers took turns to sleep when they were not at work, and the rags and bones that filled the room were not mere detritus: they were the raw material of the rag picker's trade. There was money to be made from sorting rubbish, and it fell to the Italians, as the poorest of the poor, to do it.

Nostalgia for the old country was not confined to those who intended to return to Italy. Even those who had made permanent homes in the United States took pride in the achievements of their native homeland. In the 1920s, this patriotism led many Italian-Americans to become eager supporters of Benito Mussolini's regime. Here was a man who, it seemed, had put Italy back on the map, and he was anti-Communist to boot. The clamorous Italian-American press was warmly supportive of Mussolini, and a few misguided young Americans of Italian descent went to Italy to join the Fascist Army. Italian-American enthusiasm began to dissipate once formal treaties were established between Mussolini's Italy and Adolf Hitler's Germany – and it evaporated entirely after the attack on Pearl Harbor in 1941 brought the United States into World War II against the Axis Powers.

In 1944 and 1945, many young Italian-Americans found themselves on Italian soil, fighting in a landscape their grandfathers might have known, against men who, under other circumstances, would have been their fellow countrymen. Back home in the United States they may have described themselves as Sicilians or Neapolitans, but while fighting in World War II their identity had become clear. They were certain that as Italian-Americans they were Americans first and Italians second. That was the uncompromising promise the United States demanded from all its newcomers; and most were more than happy to pay that price.

SOJOURNERS ON THE GOLDEN MOUNTAIN

CHINESE MIGRATION TO THE UNITED STATES
1849–1882

→ Migration route to North America

→ Migration routes throughout the USA

▬ Major concentrations of Chinese immigrants

▬ Major emigration areas in China

····· Transcontinental Railroad

CHINA

Over half of the Chinese immigrants in the United States are from Taishan.

Guangdong
Pearl River Delta
Guangzhou ○
Taishan ○ ○ ○ Hong Kong
Macau

SOUTH CHINA SEA

PHILIPPINES

Immigration into the United States was a predominantly east-coast phenomenon. About 90 per cent of the people who settled in America in the 19th and early 20th centuries were Europeans who journeyed across the Atlantic. But one group of immigrants who went on to have a significant impact on the makeup of the United States travelled across the Pacific Ocean to America's west coast. They were the Chinese, and their acceptance as full citizens of their adopted land was harder won than that of any other migrant group.

Chinese adventurers were first drawn to the western seaboard of North America when gold was discovered in the Sierra Nevada mountains of central California in 1848. These immigrants were among the many thousands of men who rushed to the United States from all over the world to make their fortunes. In the early part of that year, before the Gold Rush began, there were a mere 50 ethnic Chinese living in the state of California. Four years later there were 25,000 – nearly all of them 'Forty-Niners': miners and prospectors who arrived in California in 1849 hoping for a life-changing gold strike. For the Chinese peasants of Guangzhou in southern China in particular, the concepts of 'gold' and 'America' were closely intertwined: the Cantonese word for California – *jinshan* – translates as 'golden mountain'.

CHINESE MIGRATION TO THE UNITED STATES

1839 The First Opium War begins between Britain and China over trade and diplomacy issues.

1848 Gold is discovered in California.

1860s The 'Six Companies' are formed to represent Chinese interests and regulate Chinese society in San Francisco.

1863 Work begins on the Transcontinental Railroad.

1882 The Exclusion Act is passed, prohibiting Chinese labourers from entering the United States.

C.E.	1820	1830	1840	1850	1860	1870	1880	1890

1842 The Port of Guangzhou (Canton) is opened for trade. Hong Kong cedes to Britain.

1852 20,000 Chinese migrate to California – almost all are men.

1854 The California Supreme Court rules that a white man charged with murder cannot be convicted on the testimony of a Chinese witness.

1870s The unemployment rate in California rises.

1892 The Exclusion Act of 1882 is renewed, and its provisions are tightened.

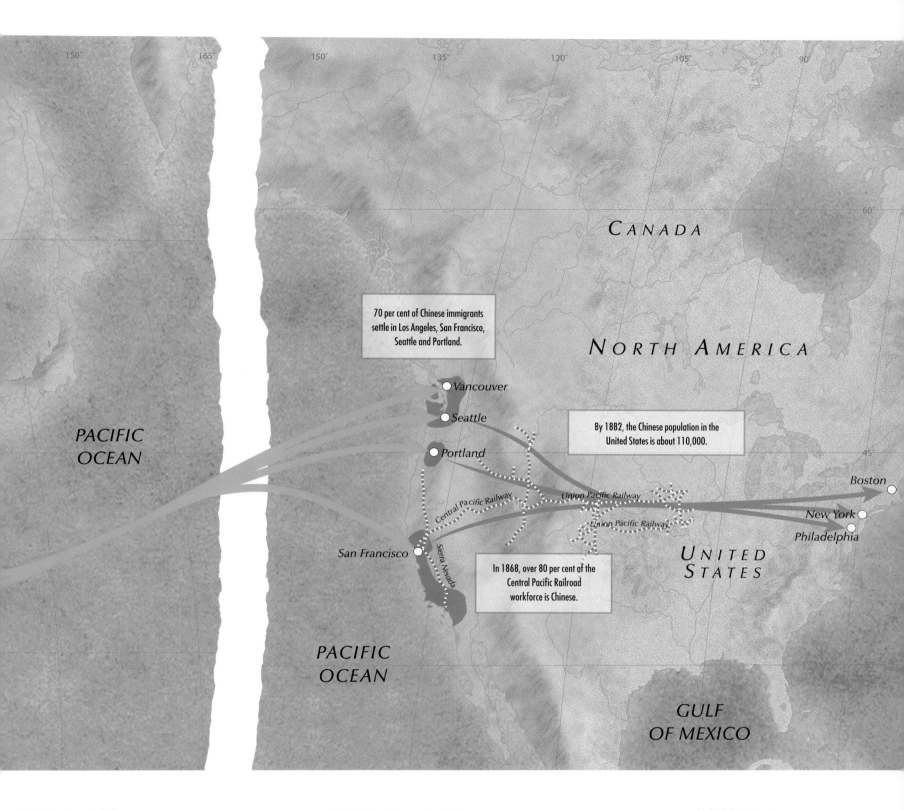

70 per cent of Chinese immigrants settle in Los Angeles, San Francisco, Seattle and Portland.

By 1882, the Chinese population in the United States is about 110,000.

In 1868, over 80 per cent of the Central Pacific Railroad workforce is Chinese.

CANADA

NORTH AMERICA

UNITED STATES

PACIFIC OCEAN

PACIFIC OCEAN

GULF OF MEXICO

Vancouver

Seattle

Portland

San Francisco

Sierra Nevada

Central Pacific Railway

Union Pacific Railway

Union Pacific Railway

Boston

New York

Philadelphia

1900 The Boxer Rebellion occurs in China, in which the Chinese rebel against foreign influence in trade, politics, religion and technology.

1930s Restrictions against Chinese immigrants begin to ease. In 1930, Congress allows the admission of Chinese wives married to American citizens before 1924.

1965 Discriminatory immigration quotas are abolished.

| 1900 | 1910 | 1920 | 1930 | 1940 | 1950 | 1960 | 1970 | 1980 |

1906 The San Francisco earthquake and fire destroys birth records. Chinatown is rebuilt in a Chinese style on the same ground.

1943 The Exclusion Act is repealed.

1945–1950 Almost 8,000 Chinese women come to America as GI brides following World War II.

The Gold Mountain Guests

It was from Guangzhou (Canton) that almost all of the Chinese immigrants in the United States came. More narrowly than that, they almost all hailed from Taishan county on the west bank of the Pearl River, the region then known as the 'Four Districts'. At the time, Taishan, which was about 80 square kilometres (30 square miles), was fraught with ethnic conflict, overpopulation, economic downturn and crop failure – an amalgam of all the individual woes that had driven Europeans from their homes over the course of the past half-century. When the chance to dig for American gold came along, the men of Taishan (almost all of the Chinese immigrants were men) leaped at the chance. The port of Hong Kong was barely 80 kilometres (50 miles) away, and Macau was closer still – they could be on board ship and en route to a fortune in a matter of days.

Although open to the Pacific Ocean, Taishan was cut off from neighbouring areas by mountains, and what's more, the dialect spoken in adjacent provinces was unintelligible to the Taishan people. While ships could bring news of the Gold Rush from abroad, it did not spread beyond the physical and linguistic boundaries of this enclave. The relative segregation of Taishan from the rest of China explains one of the most striking and unusual features of Chinese emigration to the United States: the remarkably small size of the catchment area. A comparable situation would be if the first British settlers in North America had come exclusively from Chorley in Lancashire, for example, during the reign of Queen Victoria, bringing with them a distinct accent and dialect, their local food and their old Lancashire traditions. How strangely skewed would the US view of England then have been? This, however, is precisely what happened with the first wave of Chinese immigration. In the United States (and in Britain, too) Chinese meant Cantonese – and the immense diversity of Chinese culture and ethnology has remained almost a closed book to the West right up to the present day.

Prospectors from Taishan were referred to in their home province as 'sojourners' or 'Gold Mountain guests'. To an even greater extent than the Italians then congregating in New York, Chinese immigrants hoped to make a fortune and return home to a restful retirement. This was a dream that few achieved. Golden Mountain failed dismally to live up to its name. Mining was hard work and often not profitable even if a prospector did strike gold. The racist attitudes of 'native Americans' (which at the time meant white Americans) also put Chinese prospectors at a disadvantage. They were elbowed out of the most promising areas, and forced to try their luck at old or worked-out claims.

Left: *Many Chinese people came to the United States to make their fortunes as gold miners, but ended up earning a living as tinkers or shopkeepers. This street vendor purveys goods from home to his countrymen in San Francisco's Chinatown, c. 1900.*

A City of Men

By the mid-1850s, 'gold fever' had subsided, and the Chinese immigrant population sought other ways of making a living. A few followed their gold lust to Australia when gold was discovered in Victoria – 'New Gold Mountain' as it was called in Cantonese – in 1857. Many stayed in California but turned to other forms of mining: digging for quicksilver, borax or coal was no less back-breaking and was never going to make a man rich overnight, but at least it was steady work. A high proportion of Chinese turned to unskilled labour – just as the Irish and Italians had done in the eastern United States. There was an almost endless demand in the increasingly mighty US industries for manual workers, and immigrants were always the first in line. Chinese immigrants constituted the majority of the workforce on projects such as the Central Pacific Railroad, part of the great Transcontinental Railroad, which was completed in 1859. Workers moved east as they laid the track, and many chose to settle inland in the towns and cities of the Midwest.

The mobility of the Chinese immigrant community was in part due to the fact that it was almost exclusively male. The gold mining opportunities that had brought Chinese immigrants to the United States was considered to be too hard work for women, and in any case the patriarchal system in China meant that families were more interested in sending their sons than their daughters to the United States to earn a fortune. Throughout the 1880s in California there were more than 20 Chinese men for every Chinese woman. In Victoria, Australia, the differential was greater still: in 1857 there were 25,421 Chinese men and only three Chinese women. Single men, and men who had left their wives and families at home, were free to seek work wherever it was available.

The Chinese who remained near the western seaboard of the United States found themselves in a bizarre kind of bachelor society. Chinese ghettos emerged in many major cities, and the pre-eminent 'Chinatown' in San Francisco was a city of men. There were precious few married couples, and hardly any children. No 'native Americans' lived in Chinatown, and few ever went there except to seek out the diversions that an all-male enclave provided: specifically brothels, gambling houses and opium dens. Although many immigrant groups congregated in the same area, the isolation of the Chinese was unique. By way of comparison, in none of the Little Italys in America did ethnic Italians ever constitute more than half of the local population.

The Rise of Anti-Chinese Sentiment

Like immigrants everywhere, the Chinese in the American West were subject to petty discrimination and occasional acts of racial violence. Such incidents increased when the Californian economy slumped in the 1870s and the perception arose that the Chinese were 'taking American jobs'. In Denver in 1880, a veritable pogrom was unleashed on the Chinese quarter of the city, resulting in the destruction of Chinese businesses, the looting of Chinese homes and the lynching of a Chinese man. At Rock Springs in Wyoming in 1885, a posse of white track-layers attacked their Chinese coworkers, killing 28 of them. The general anti-Chinese feeling was both reflected in and fuelled by newspapers across the country. The *New York Tribune* went so far as to suggest that Chinese immigration represented a threat to the existence of the republic, saying that unless it was stopped 'the youngest home of the nations must in its early manhood follow the path and meet the doom of Babylon, Nineveh and Rome'.

Such views, however pompously expressed, helped to sway the federal government to take action against Chinese immigration. In 1882 the Exclusion Act was passed. It banned the immigration of Chinese labourers, and barred the Chinese already in the United States from qualifying for US citizenship. This was the first time in US history that legal restrictions had been placed on immigration – and on the immigration of a specific national group. It was the unedifying low-point in the United States' usually generous attitude to outsiders wishing to make a life in a new land.

Paper Sons and American Citizens

Chinese immigrants did their best to evade the exclusion laws. The most ingenious and notorious method was to invoke the Fourteenth Amendment, which grants the right of citizenship to anyone born in the United States and their foreign-born children. The only criteria necessary to assure citizenship was for another Chinese person to swear that you had been born in the United States, and many were happy to tell that white lie as a favour – or for a price. In this regard, the Chinese community of California was the accidental beneficiary of the San Francisco earthquake of 1906, which destroyed any records of births in the Chinese community, rendering many claims to citizenship unimputable. Although the authorities knew what was going on, the constitution was sacred and so they could do nothing to stop it. One judge remarked that 'if the story told in the courts were true, every Chinese woman in the United States twenty-five years ago must have had at least 500 children'.

Left: Chinese workers on the Transcontinental Railroad. Chinese immigrants often performed the toughest jobs. In 1880, Chinese migrants constituted 25 per cent of California's workforce.

A refinement of this loophole was the scam known as the 'paper son'. A Chinese with pre-exclusion citizenship would return to Guangzhou for a number of years, and each year register the birth of a fictitious child. Twenty years later, he could sell the registration documents to a would-be immigrant and bring him over to the United States, claiming that the young man was his own flesh and blood. So long as this 'paper son' could pass an immigration officer's interrogation about his 'family' – paper sons were all carefully coached for this ordeal – he could enter the country with all the longed-for rights and benefits of an American citizen, namely the right to stay and work in the United States.

The exclusion laws remained in force until 1943, when they were repealed by the Magnuson Act. This repeal, which restored to Chinese people the right to naturalisation, was in part a recognition of the contribution that Chinese-Americans were making to the war effort during World War II (notably, their role in the US Merchant Marine). It was also intended to encourage Chinese nationalists to continue the fight against Japan in the Far East. But the annual national quota for Chinese immigrants set out by the Magnuson Act remained minuscule: a mere 105 individuals per year. Illegal immigration continued, and was so widespread that in the 1950s an amnesty was declared for those illegal migrants who would come forward and register: 20,000 took up the offer. Avoiding the restrictions set out by the Magnuson Act altogether, almost 8,000 Chinese women came to America in the five years after World War II as GI brides: for the first time in the history of Chinese migration to the United States, women were the overwhelming majority of new Chinese arrivals. Discriminatory quotas were finally abolished in 1965, and Chinese America has been steadily replenished by newcomers ever since.

THE MODERN WORLD

T he second half of the 20th century witnessed vast people movements around the globe. In the years leading up to World War II, countless Soviet citizens, accused of being "enemies of the people", were arrested and deported to Gulag labour camps in Siberia and other parts of the USSR During the war years, this practice was employed to relocate entire ethnic groups and to dispel any growing nationalist, anti-Soviet feelings in annexed areas. In the 1940s, Europe's Jewish population was removed to camps even more terrible than those in the Soviet Union. Millions perished in Nazi death camps. For those who survived, the creation of the independent State of Israel in 1948 meant that there was at last a Jewish homeland in which to take refuge. India was also granted independence in the late 1940s, leading to a dramatic and traumatic exchange of populations between it and the new state of Pakistan. In the closing decades of the 20th century, a large proportion of global migration was voluntary. Inexpensive travel, open borders and economic equality between nations combined to make migration easier and more desirable than at any other time in human history.

Left: Jamaican immigrants arrive at Victoria Station in London in 1956. They, like many of the migrants of the second half of the 20th century, were voluntary economic migrants, invited by the host country to rectify a labour shortage.

THE GULAG NATION

Russia has a longstanding tradition of using forced migration as a form of criminal punishment. But during the 20th century, Russia's practice of criminal transportation grew into an immense and relentless operation. Millions of people were uprooted from their homes and forcibly relocated to Gulag labour camps.

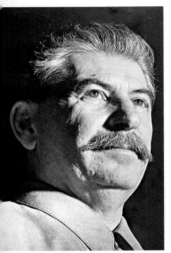

Above: Joseph Stalin's paranoid personality was the primary cause of the purges and the mass deportations. He saw enemies everywhere: in his family, in his entourage, in the Communist Party and in the country at large.

From the 14th to the 18th century, the tsars of the Russian Empire banished political prisoners and common criminals from Western Russia or Russian-held territories to Siberia. Stretching from the Ural Mountains in the west to the Pacific Ocean in the east, Siberia was an empty wasteland, and its inhospitable climate and impossibly distant location provided an ideal setting for "internal exile". Russia's practice of removing convicts from its central populations was not unique: Britain, for example, exiled their criminal population to Australia in the late 1700s. The Russian authorities' attitude to Siberian exile resembled the 19th-century British system of transportation in other ways, too. For both empires, sending undesirables to remote regions was a way to add new territory to the colonial portfolio. Inhabited land was claimed for the crown – regardless of whether the people who scraped a living from the unforgiving earth had wanted to go there or not.

When Russia's tsarist regime fell following the revolution of 1917, the Bolsheviks took control, evolving into the political party that would run the world's first communist state: the Communist Party of the Soviet Union (CPSU). Anyone suspected of opposing the party's policies was seen as an "enemy of the people". To deal with such enemies, the CPSU took the established tsarist tradition of internal exile and turned the business of arresting and deporting supposed "criminals" into a mighty industrial process. Untold numbers were gathered up and sent east to work in forests or mines – fed into a prison system that churned out slave labour to be deployed wherever the regime saw fit. The government department responsible for such prisons

was called the Glavnoe Upravlenie Lagere (Main Camp Administration), which became known by the acronym GULAG. Over time, the word Gulag came to denote the prison system in general – its geography, culture, mores and hierarchies. It has been estimated that the total number of people to go through the Gulag system between its official founding in 1929 and Stalin's death in 1953 was just short of 29 million.

What makes this huge figure all the more astounding is that the deportations occurred in secret, or at least in silence. Although Soviet citizens knew that the government's secret police, the NVKD, were making mass arrests of innocent people, they also knew that to speak a word in protest would result in being instantly arrested themselves. Outside the Soviet Union, the huge upheaval of the purges went practically unnoticed; they were overshadowed by the equally gargantuan but more visible processes of collectivisation and industrialisation. Very few outside observers ever suspected that industrial showcase projects such as the White Sea–Baltic Canal and the magnificent Moscow metro system had been built not by happy socialist workers but by miserable prisoners, cowed members of the Gulag nation.

Life in the Gulag

Prisoners of the Gulag lived in camps or clusters of camps that were dotted all over the Soviet Union like islands in a huge ocean. It was this cartographical analogy, and the insularity of the system itself, that led the Russian writer and dissident Alexander Solzhenitsyn to speak of the "Gulag

PEOPLING THE GULAG

1917 The October Revolution brings the Bolsheviks to power.

1936–1938 The Great Terror is at its height, during which millions are shot or consigned to the Gulag.

1940–1945 The mass deportation of "enemy nationalities" takes place.

C.E. 1900   1910   1920   1930   1940

1918 The "Red Terror", a campaign of mass arrests and deportations, is unleashed on enemies of the Bolshevik regime. The first labour camp is set up on Solovetsky Island.

1930 The Gulag is officially established. Collectivisation of agriculture is accompanied by the liquidation of *kulaks*, or well-off peasants.

1939 The Gulag population, including colonies, is more than 1.6 million.

1941 Germany invades Russia. Many Gulag prisoners are released and sent to the front.

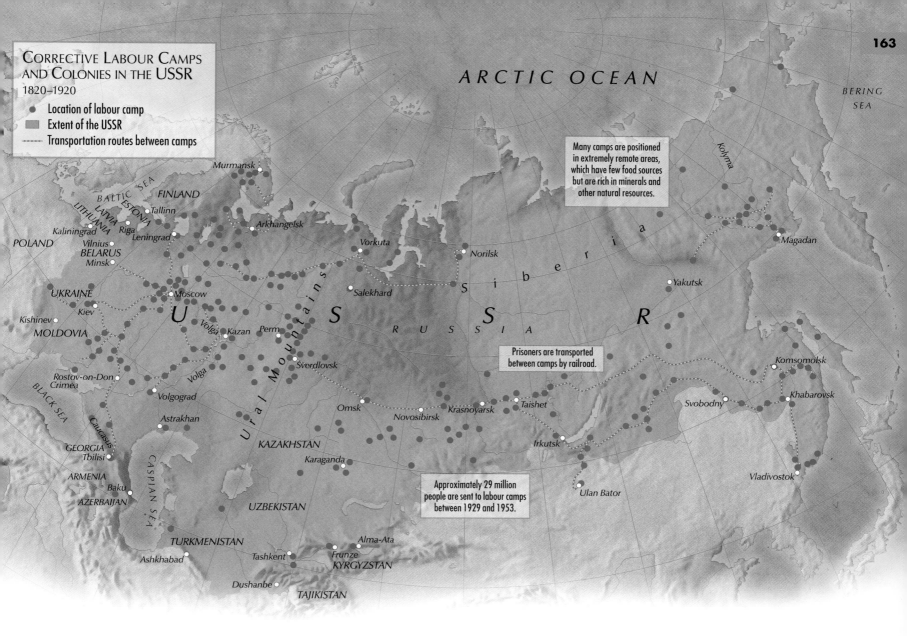

CORRECTIVE LABOUR CAMPS
AND COLONIES IN THE USSR
1820–1920

- Location of labour camp
- Extent of the USSR
- Transportation routes between camps

ARCTIC OCEAN

BERING SEA

Many camps are positioned in extremely remote areas, which have few food sources but are rich in minerals and other natural resources.

Prisoners are transported between camps by railroad.

Approximately 29 million people are sent to labour camps between 1929 and 1953.

Murmansk, Kolyma, Magadan, FINLAND, BALTIC SEA, LATVIA, ESTONIA, LITHUANIA, Tallinn, Arkhangelsk, Vorkuta, Norilsk, Kaliningrad, Riga, Leningrad, POLAND, Vilnius, BELARUS, Minsk, Salekhard, Yakutsk, UKRAINE, Moscow, Kiev, U S S R, Kishinev, Volga, Kazan, Perm, Siberia, MOLDOVA, Sverdlovsk, RUSSIA, Komsomolsk, Rostov-on-Don, Volga, Crimea, Omsk, Krasnoyarsk, Taishet, Volgograd, Novosibirsk, Irkutsk, Svobodny, Khabarovsk, Astrakhan, Ural Mountains, KAZAKHSTAN, Karaganda, Vladivostok, GEORGIA, Tbilisi, CASPIAN SEA, Ulan Bator, ARMENIA, Baku, AZERBAIJAN, UZBEKISTAN, TURKMENISTAN, Alma-Ata, Ashkhabad, Tashkent, Frunze, KYRGYZSTAN, Dushanbe, TAJIKISTAN, BLACK SEA, Caucasus

Archipelago". In his book of the same name, published in 1973, Solzhenitsyn, who was sentenced to eight years in a labour camp in 1945 for criticising Stalin in private correspondence with a friend, describes the Gulag's geography, history, people and culture. "Scattered from the Bering Strait almost to the Bosphorus are thousands of islands of the spellbound Archipelago", he wrote. "They are invisible, but they exist. And the invisible slaves of the Archipelago have to be transported from island to island …

Great ports exist for this purpose – transit prisons; and smaller ports – camp transit ports. Sealed steel ships also exist: railroad cars".

The ships and ports of the Gulag Archipelago were at their busiest in the late 1930s, when the Soviet government, led by the grotesquely paranoid Stalin, was gripped by a mass obsession about "spies" and "wreckers" during a period known as "the Great Terror". In 1937 and 1938, the entire Soviet nation lived in dread of a nighttime knock at

1956 De-Stalinisation under Nikita Khrushchev, Stalin's successor, entails the release and rehabilitation of Gulag inmates.

1991 The Soviet Union ceases to exist.

1950   1960   1970   1980   1990   2000

1953 Joseph Stalin dies.

1960 The Gulag is officially liquidated – but the prison population remains large throughout the last decades of Soviet power.

Right: This photo of apparently cheerful and well-fed prisoners taking a shower is a piece of Soviet propaganda. For most Gulag inmates, the years of imprisonment were unremittingly cold, hungry and miserable.

was gripped by depression and loneliness. I was unable to cry; I had forgotten how to, and that was what made the ache in my heart so unbearable."

Displaced Nations

It was not only individuals such as Grankina who underwent the trauma of dislocation and the removal from everything they knew. During World War II, ethnic groups and even entire nationalities in areas occupied by Soviet troops were arrested en masse and interned or resettled far from their homelands. This was done in an attempt to undermine any local nationalist feeling that could potentially give rise to an anti-Soviet rebellion and threaten the state. The process of deportation began as soon as the war got underway. When the USSR annexed eastern Poland under the terms of the German-Soviet Nonaggression Pact in 1939, hundreds of thousands of Poles were channelled into the prisons of the Soviet secret police and then transported east to the far reaches of the USSR Arrests of Polish nationals were made wholesale, according to social background first and foremost. Thus, the principle that in the previous 10 years had condemned countless Russian *kulaks* (well-off peasants), engineers, army officers and intellectuals now swallowed up tens of thousands of Polish landowners, businesspeople, police officers and government officials.

The Poles were merely the first nationality to be subjected to the CPSU's experiment in what was later termed "ethnic cleansing": the targeted population changed according to Russia's shifting fortunes in the war at large. In 1940, in what became known as the "Winter War", Soviet forces under Stalin invaded Finland to claim land they believed should fall within the USSR's boundaries, and ethnic Finns and other Scandinavians were forcibly resettled away from the disputed border. In 1941 and 1942, Soviet citizens of "enemy nationality" came under suspicion. These "enemies" included yet more Finns, as well as Romanians and Germans living within the USSR The chief victims of this particular purge, however, were the descendants of Germans who had settled on the River Volga by the invitation of Catherine the Great (r. 1762–1796) almost 200 years before. The "Volga Germans" no longer spoke German and were to most intents and purposes entirely assimilated Russians. But they had preserved some German customs – many bore obviously Teutonic surnames, and crucially their passports gave their nationality as German at a time when in the USSR the word was synonymous with "fascist" and "murderer". As German Nazis advanced into the Soviet Union towards Volga, Stalin feared that the Volga

the door, which could only mean arrest. For many, arrest and interrogation were followed by summary execution. For the rest, it was the beginning of years of enforced wandering on the trade routes of the Gulag.

The experience of one Gulag prisoner, Nadezhda Grankina, was tragically typical. Grankina was arrested in 1937 and sentenced to 10 years of penal servitude for being the daughter of a priest and because, in her youth, she had read some speeches by Leon Trotsky, an influential politician expelled from the Communist Party by Stalin in the 1920s. Over the course of her sentence, Grankina went on a fitful journey that took her the width of Russia, from the west to the notorious camp complex at Kolyma in the far east. "From March 1938 they began to convoy people out of the prisons to the labour camps where they had been assigned", she wrote in her memoirs. "The journey across the country is difficult even in normal conditions. We were shunted around for a month, often without water in the July heat, with almost no hot food, in closed wagons. We had no bedding, and no personal belongings. We slept on the bare boards. At night if the train had stopped, we would be awakened by the sound of someone hammering the walls or running along the roof. The guards were checking that the wagons were secure. The farther we went, the more I

Germans would collaborate with them against the state. In 1941 he ordered a 24-hour relocation of Volga Germans, and well over one million were dispatched to the frozen wilds of the Russian far east.

The mass deportations continued even after it became clear that World War II was going to be won by the Allies. In 1943 and 1944, as German forces withdrew from the southern reaches of Russia, the NKVD turned their attention to the tribal people of the North Caucasus – the Chechens, Ingush and Karachai, among others. Certainly, many people within these nationalities were at best indifferent to Soviet power, and some had even collaborated with the Nazis in the hope that they might topple Stalin's tyranny. But in the eyes of the government, the treasonous acts of the few proved the guilt of all. There was a mass purge and deportation of Caucasian peoples: 390,000 Chechens, 90,000 Ingushetians and 70,000 Karachai, plus many more from other small nationalities, were herded into trains and sent on the long journey to the barren steppe of Kazakhstan and Uzbekistan. Among the banished were women and children, who were deemed as guilty as the rest of their people. Many thousands did not survive the journey or – if they did – perished during their first winter in exile. The homelands of these peoples were erased from Soviet maps and all mention of them was deleted from textbooks and encyclopedias. Even their cemeteries were obliterated, as if the dead were as guilty of treason as the living.

The deported peoples were not kept behind barbed wire in prison camps. Instead they were confined to "exile settlements", which they were forbidden to leave, and where they were obliged to work under the loose scrutiny of the security police. This enforced colonisation was applied to other categories of politically suspect citizens as well. Entire communities made up of former prisoners who had served out their terms, but yet were not allowed to return to live in the cities of European Russia, were herded together in "labour settlements". These prisoners were known somewhat euphemistically as "free settlers", and they too were obliged to do useful work. Their settlements were often associated with nearby camps – so freed prisoners could find themselves doing similar work to their jailed neighbours. In effect, they were indentured colonists, unwilling or unresisting pioneers in a harsh land.

The Legacy of the Gulag

In a sense the mass dislocation of Soviet people in the Stalin era achieved everything it set out to achieve. Large numbers of citizens were resettled in the sparsely populated areas of the Soviet east and Central Asia. They were more or less compelled to remain there and provide very cheap labour for the state – both while they were inmates of the Gulag and after their release. Political dissent was disrupted, and then utterly crushed during Stalin's rule and in the decades that followed. Although the state continued to maintain the Gulag system after Stalin's death in 1953, the grip of the camp authorities steadily weakened and the release of political prisoners soon became widespread. By the end of the 1950s, virtually all Gulag labour camps had been dissolved, and the system was officially liquidated in 1960. It was only then that peoples such as the Crimean Tatars – 180,000 of whom were deported in 1944 – were restored their rights, allowed to return to their homes and recognised once more as an ethnic group. Although now free, many former prisoners found it hard to return to their home cities, and colonies around former camps continued to exist. For some, it was too much of a struggle to reestablish their lives and regain their national and cultural rights after years of isolation and degradation. Although the Gulag had by then dwindled away almost to nothing, it nevertheless remained a vast and profoundly tragic success.

Above: Alexander Solzhenitsyn was a young army officer when he was arrested and sent on a journey through the Gulag system. In the 1970s, after his history of the camps was published in the West, he was expelled from the USSR and thus became a forced migrant for a second time.

"
My partner, Nikolai, had been an administrator in a factory before his arrest, and had spent most of his career making up numbers and filing false reports. He taught me how to make our norm in only four or five hours a day. Our job was to cut down trees, clean off the branches, cut the logs into segments of equal length, and stack them for hauling. Nikolai's mission was to find stacks left over from last year, of which there were plenty. 'All we need to do,' Nikolai explained, 'is cut off the end of the logs so they look freshly cut.' We put our signatures on the fresh ends and buried the scraps we'd sawn off. I felt happy and proud that I had learnt to cheat efficiently. "

Janusz Bardach on working in a labour camp in the 1940s

A LAND OF MILK AND HONEY

For nearly two millennia, from the destruction of the Temple in Jerusalem in 70 B.C.E. until the rise of Zionism at the turn of the 20th century, Jewish communities spread throughout the world. Through persecutions, pogroms and holocaust they preserved their rich culture and their ancient religion and held on to the hope that, one day, they would return to the Promised Land. In 1948, the State of Israel was officially declared.

Below: An elderly Jew tills the soil of Palestine. His name was Alter Baruch, and he emigrated from Minsk, in the tsarist empire. At this time the prospect of a homeland for Jews in the Bible lands was still a distant dream.

NORTH SEA

DENMARK

SWEL

BAL

IRELAND

UNITED KINGDOM 14,000

NETHERLANDS 3,600

EAST GERMANY

BELGIUM 3,500

WEST GERMANY 12,000

AUST 4,0C

FRANCE 27,000

SWITZERLAND 2,00

ITALY 3,700

SPAIN

MEDITERRANEA

TUNISIA 56,000

MOROCCO 260,000

ALGERIA 15,000

JEWISH MIGRATION TO ISRAEL, 1945–1975

→ Jewish migration routes
000 Number of Jews emigrating to Israel
● Major Nazi death camps

In the late 19th century, there were 10,000 or so Jews living in the old Bible lands of Palestine – mostly in Jerusalem itself. Some members of this community were native born, but many were immigrants from Eastern Europe. In 1878 a small group of families living in Jerusalem decided to leave their urban existence and begin a new life in the Palestinian countryside. They

JEWISH MIGRATION TO ISRAEL

1880–1914 60,000 Jews emigrate to Turkish-ruled Palestine, mostly from Russia, Galacia, Romania and Poland.

1920 The Palestine Mandate is granted to Britain by the League of Nations.

1933–1939 European Jews flee Nazi persecution.

C.E. | 1870 | 1880 | 1890 | 1900 | 1910 | 1920 | 1930

1917 In the Balfour Declaration, Britain promises to facilitate a "Jewish National Home" in Palestine.

1920–1929 Frequent attacks occur on Jewish settlers in Palestine.

1936 A Royal Commission recommends the partition of Palestine as two states.

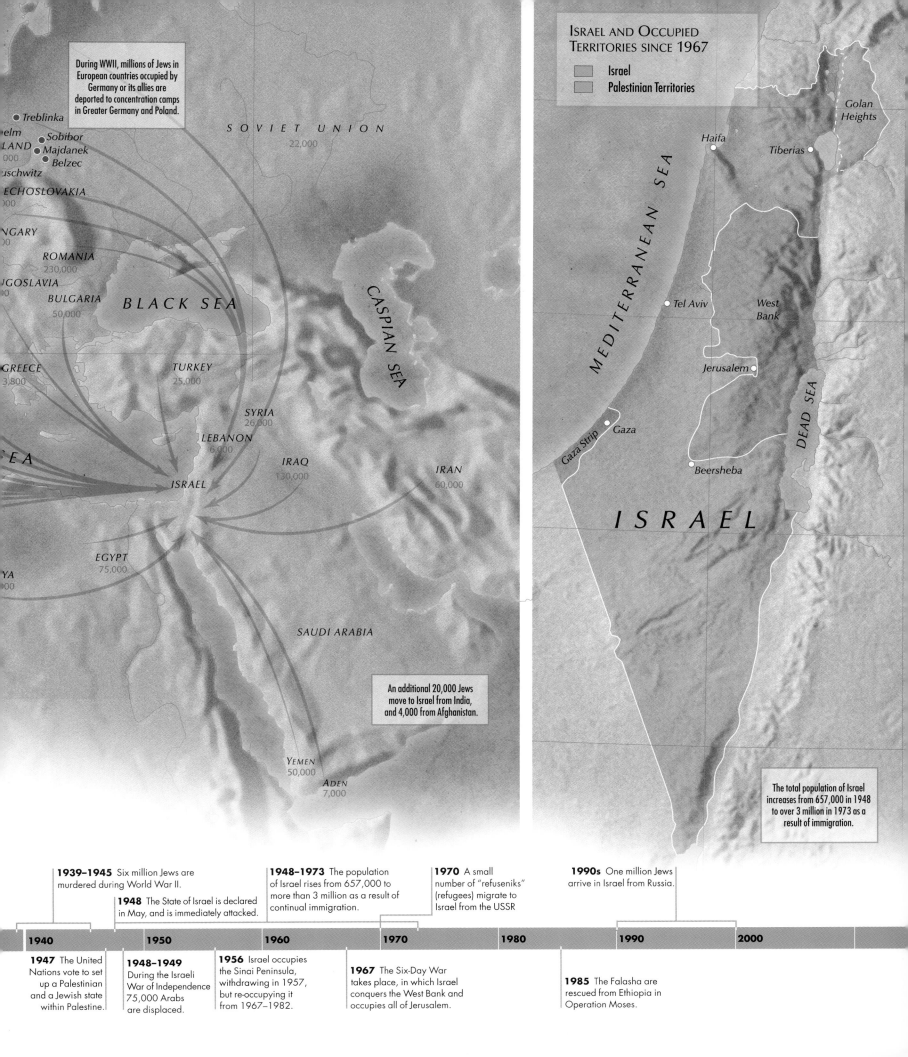

During WWII, millions of Jews in European countries occupied by Germany or its allies are deported to concentration camps in Greater Germany and Poland.

ISRAEL AND OCCUPIED TERRITORIES SINCE 1967
- Israel
- Palestinian Territories

SOVIET UNION
22,000

Treblinka
Sobibor
Majdanek
Belzec
...elm
...LAND
uschwitz
ECHOSLOVAKIA
NGARY
ROMANIA 230,000
GOSLAVIA
BULGARIA 50,000
BLACK SEA
GREECE 3,800
...EA

Golan Heights
Haifa
Tiberias
MEDITERRANEAN SEA
TURKEY 25,000
SYRIA 26,000
LEBANON 6,000
IRAQ 130,000
IRAN 60,000
CASPIAN SEA
Tel Aviv
West Bank
ISRAEL
Jerusalem
Gaza Strip
Gaza
DEAD SEA
Beersheba

SAUDI ARABIA
EGYPT 75,000
...YA
...000
I S R A E L

An additional 20,000 Jews move to Israel from India, and 4,000 from Afghanistan.

YEMEN 50,000
ADEN 7,000

The total population of Israel increases from 657,000 in 1948 to over 3 million in 1973 as a result of immigration.

1939–1945 Six million Jews are murdered during World War II.

1948 The State of Israel is declared in May, and is immediately attacked.

1948–1973 The population of Israel rises from 657,000 to more than 3 million as a result of continual immigration.

1970 A small number of "refuseniks" (refugees) migrate to Israel from the USSR

1990s One million Jews arrive in Israel from Russia.

| 1940 | 1950 | 1960 | 1970 | 1980 | 1990 | 2000 |

1947 The United Nations vote to set up a Palestinian and a Jewish state within Palestine.

1948–1949 During the Israeli War of Independence 75,000 Arabs are displaced.

1956 Israel occupies the Sinai Peninsula, withdrawing in 1957, but re-occupying it from 1967–1982.

1967 The Six-Day War takes place, in which Israel conquers the West Bank and occupies all of Jerusalem.

1985 The Falasha are rescued from Ethiopia in Operation Moses.

declared that their aim was "to settle the land of Israel by tilling the earth and getting our daily bread from it." It was to be a kind of agricultural commune, "a plot of land which we shall cultivate and on which we shall live according to the precepts of the Bible. Thus do we intend to put a new life into our families, labouring on this land is good for body and soul alike".

The new life envisioned by this community – coming a lifetime before the foundation of the Jewish state, and more than 20 years before the Zionist movement came into being – could be said to represent the aim of the Jewish people as a whole. In essence, they wished to live freely and work honestly, and so create "the land flowing with milk and honey" that God has promised to Moses in the Old Testament. The band of Jews from Jerusalem founded their commune and called it Petah Tikva – "Gateway of Hope". It was the first Jewish colony in Palestine.

aid of the wealthy Jewish banker and philanthropist Baron Edmond de Rothschild (1845–1934).

The wave of refugees from tsarist persecution, now known in Jewish history as the First Aliyah, set a precedent for Jewish migration to the Old Testament lands. The Hebrew word *aliyah* literally means "ascent", and it is no coincidence that the same word denotes the act of going up to read from the Torah in synagogue. The physical and geographical business of immigration is bound up in Jewish thought with the spiritual act of prayer. For many Jews – whether they are religious or not – there has always been something sacred about "coming home" to the land of Israel.

The Second Aliyah

The subsequent history of Jewish immigration to Palestine is the story of successive *aliyahs*. In the 10 years before World War I, 40,000 Jews emigrated to Palestine. This

> " The life of the settlers was very hard. The way from the village to the fields was long and passed through Arab lands; the Arabs often put up roadblocks to prevent passage. The baking of bread was a heartbreaking job and a whole day was needed to bake enough for one family. There were no ovens and no dry wood for making fire, so a primitive oven modelled on the Arab one was set up, and cattle dung or thorny bushes used for fuel. The staple food was boiled beans and corn. The workers in the fields drank the swamp water after sieving it through their handkerchiefs to get rid of insects, frogs' eggs and leeches. "
>
> *A Jewish settler in the Gateway of Hope, 1880s*

The First Aliyah

At first, Petah Tikva was a small, local experiment, and cultivation of the land did not take hold on a sustainable scale until the 1880s, when Jews began to migrate to Palestine in their thousands. The impetus for this people movement was the same as that which prompted many thousands of Jews to travel to North America in the late 19th century: the vicious pogroms against Jews – who were blamed for the assassination of Russia's Tsar Alexander II in 1881 – in the Pale of Settlement. As many as 30,000 Jews, from Russia, Poland and Romania, settled in Palestine between 1881 and 1891. Many of them set up agricultural communes, but most struggled to survive. The incomers were inexperienced at farming, and the plots were located in what was a malarial swamp, so settlers were forced to evacuate when the disease spread. Many of their farms and vineyards had to be rescued from ruin by the financial

Second Aliyah, like the first, came mostly from Russia and had been driven out of the country by successive pogroms and growing anti-Semitism. Many of the individuals who made up this group were socialists or communists who had taken part in the failed Russian Revolution of 1905, and they brought their left-wing ideas with them to Palestine, establishing some of the pillars that would go on to support the future Israeli state. In 1909, the first kibbutz (a communal farming settlement) was set up under strict socialist guidelines by incomers of the Second Aliyah. They also helped create a Jewish polity by founding political parties, trade unions and newspapers.

The Second Aliyah is also largely credited with reviving Hebrew, which, during the early 20th century, ceased to be just a liturgical language and instead became the normal language of discourse among Jews in Palestine. To make this possible, a committee of linguists worked to coin new

words from ancient Hebrew roots, or back-form them from Aramaic or Greek stems. Their work led to the publication of the first Hebrew dictionary, but the consequences of their efforts were much greater than this: in effect, they breathed life back into a dead language. This is a unique event in the history of philology, and it was crucial in shaping the character of the future Israeli state. All Jewish immigrants were bound together by a language that was rooted in their common heritage.

Successive Aliyahs

The 40,000 immigrants who made up the Third Aliyah came mostly from Eastern Europe between 1919 and 1923, and included many agronomists and professional farmers who applied their expertise to Jewish agriculture, which at last began to prosper. The Fourth Aliyah included about 82,000 people who arrived between 1924 and 1929 (23,000 subsequently left Palestine for the United States and elsewhere). The group largely consisted of middle-class Jews from Poland and Hungary who were forced out of their countries by anti-Semitic legislation. Unlike earlier waves, the relative wealth of the Fourth Aliyah meant that families could travel together. They brought their knowledge of commerce with them and, like previous aliyahs, applied their particular know-how to their new communities. As a result, towns saw a great deal of urban development as homes and factories were built to accommodate the Polish

Jews, their families and their businesses. Between 1929 and 1939, 250,000 immigrants, many of them German Jews fleeing Nazi persecution, arrived in Palestine, making up the Fifth Aliyah. Many of these individuals were well-off professionals such as doctors, industrialists and academics. This aliyah also included a large number of artists and architects who introduced Bauhaus architecture to Tel Aviv.

Immigration During World War II

In the 1930s, Palestine had no status as a country, but was instead governed by Britain under a mandate from the League of Nations. The Palestinian Arab population saw the Jewish settlers in the region as foreign intruders and, although British troops tried to maintain order between the two communities, it became increasingly difficult to keep the peace. As Jewish agencies continued to purchase land for an increasing number of settlers, many Arab tenants were evicted from their homes to make way for the Jews of the kibbutzim. This led to Arab resentment of the growing Jewish community, and violent attacks against Jews became widespread. In 1939, the British government placed strict limits on Jewish immigration to Palestine with a view to halting it altogether by 1944. Warships were dispatched to guard the ports and enforce the ban, but Jewish aid organisations did their best to evade these restrictions – with a great deal of success. Throughout World War II, Jewish escapees and refugees from Germany and German-

occupied countries were smuggled into Palestine under the nose of the British Royal Navy, or travelled overland across the border from Syria or Iraq. In all, 110,000 people arrived, but this number was just a fraction of the total who were in need of asylum: the Jews who did not escape faced an unimaginable horror.

During World War II, approximately six million European Jews were murdered in the Holocaust by the Nazis. To

Above: Ethiopian Jews, known as Falashas, gather outside the Israeli Embassy in Addis Ababa, hoping for a new life. In May 1991, more than 14,000 Falashas were airlifted out of Ethiopia.

facilitate the mass genocide, an efficient system was set in place in all German-occupied territories. When a country came under Nazi control, all resident Jews were carefully registered and documented. They were later summoned to collection points, from where they were sent to concentration camps in Greater Germany, or to sealed ghettoes, most of which were in Eastern Europe. Many Jews died there of disease, starvation or ill treatment. Most of the surviving populations of the camps and ghettoes were

later siphoned off and dispatched to extermination camps – such as Auschwitz, Sobibór and Treblinka. The whole undertaking constituted a horrific form of deportation, in which millions of Jewish men, women and children underwent a forced migration to Nazi death camps.

The State of Israel is Formed

In 1947, the British, weary from war in Europe, decided to withdraw from the Palestine Mandate. Violence from Arab groups against Jewish communities had continued throughout the war years, and Jewish immigration from Europe had remained uncontrollable. The United Nations approved a Partition Plan that divided Palestine into two states, one for Jews (Israel) and one for Arabs (Palestine). In 1948, British forces withdrew, the Mandate came to an end, and on May 14 the Jewish State of Israel came into being.

The birth of Israel, however, was not a peaceful one. Palestinian Arabs rejected the partition set out by the United Nations, and other Arab nations in the Middle East did not want a Jewish state in their midst. Immediately upon Israel's declaration of independence, the new country was attacked by a coalition of Arab countries that included Egypt, Syria, Lebanon, Iraq, Transjordan and Saudi Arabia, setting in motion the 1948–1949 War of Independence. The war ended in the total defeat of the Arab armies, leaving Israel in control of large sections of Arab territory, which it was loath to relinquish. In these newly acquired territories, and in Israel proper, Arabs who had lived in Palestine for generations were forcibly expelled by the Israelis, who feared that their potentially hostile presence constituted a security risk to their state. More than 700,000, or two-thirds of Palestinian Arabs, flooded into the surrounding Arab countries. The Palestinians call this exodus the *Nakba* (Arabic for "disaster" or "catastrophe").

It is estimated that by 2002 there were more than 4 million Palestinian refugees, most of them living in refugee camps in neighbouring countries. One third live in the West Bank and Gaza, nearly a third live in Jordan, 17 per cent in Syria and Lebanon, and approximately 15 per cent in other Arab or Western countries. The plight of the Palestinian refugees is one of the world's most longlasting and politically sensitive problems, and, as long as negotiations that will allow them to return to their former lands within Israeli territory remain unresolved, their future remains bleak.

The years immediately following the War of Independence also saw a mass exodus of Jews from North Africa and countries such as Yemen, Iran and Iraq. The total number of people involved in this Arab aliyah was approximately 700,000. Every new influx of refugees to Israel, once it was absorbed, made the state stronger and more viable, while Palestine's refugees, now in their third generation, remain a problem for their host countries.

The Right to Return

In 1950, Israel enacted the Law of Return, which guaranteed the right of Jews, and those with Jewish parents and grandparents, to immigrate to Israel and become an Israeli citizen immediately upon arrival. It was a highly symbolic piece of legislation: an open invitation to the Jews of the world to come and take part in the grand project of creating a Jewish homeland. The use of the emotive word "return" reflects the view that all Jews have a reserved place in the State of Israel, because a Jew is by definition a member of one of the ancient tribes of Israel.

One of the most spectacular "homecomings" in the history of Israel was the rescue of the Falasha – Ethiopian Jews who converted to Christianity and then returned to Judaism. Their form of Judaism is very ancient, and it is unclear how they had come to practise the faith, but rabbinical judgments made it clear that these Africans were as Jewish as any European Jews. In 1985, as war and famine raged in their home country, Israel organised an airlift, codenamed Operation Moses, to save the lives of their brethren. The Falasha in Israel now number around 100,000.

By far the largest postwar aliyah has come from Russia. More than two million Jews resided in the Soviet Union in the late 20th century, during the last decades of its existence. The majority of them were entirely secular – most had never seen a Hebrew Bible and did not adhere to Jewish practices – but they were nevertheless keenly aware of their Jewishness. Soviet citizens at the time had their nationalities inscribed in their passports, and "Jewish" was one of the options. Being Jewish inevitably meant that you were a target for institutional discrimination – for example, some institutes of higher education were closed to Jews – but many politically active, anti-Soviet Jews insisted on their nationality because it meant that they might be granted permission to leave the USSR, where the regime opposed emigration to Israel.

A small number of determined Russian Jews did manage to leave the Soviet Union in the 1970s. In the 1980s, it was more common to apply to leave for Israel but to "change one's mind" once one was outside the Soviet Union and head for the United States. The political and religious situation in Israel was still tense, and the United States provided an attractive alternative destination. During the 1990s, amid the political and social chaos that followed the collapse of the Soviet regime, there was a marked rise in anti-Semitic violence and rhetoric. This recalled the pogroms against the Jews of the 1880s and 1900s, and stimulated a huge surge in emigration to Israel. The Russian government no longer opposed emigration in principle, with the result that more than one million Russian Jews went to Israel in a single decade.

The Russian immigrants have profoundly changed the character of Israeli society, and pose questions for politicians and social planners. Unlike previous waves of immigrants in Israel, Russian Jews have shown themselves to be disinclined to assimilate and learn Hebrew: they are very happy to keep their Russian culture and language, and there are enough of them to create the Russian-only communities that make that possible. They have their own political party, their own newspapers and they watch Russian television by satellite.

Alarmingly for religious Israelis, many of the Russian immigrants are not Jewish by strict rabbinical standards, since their Jewish nationality in Russia tended to be predicated on their father's nationality (and so a Jewish surname) rather than on their mother's – which is how Jewishness is passed down according to the law of Moses. There are also many spouses of Russian Jews who are not Jewish in any sense at all. How this admixture will affect Israeli society in the future remains to be seen: perhaps even this huge aliyah will eventually adapt or be absorbed. In the meanwhile, the rueful Israeli proverb seems to apply: "Israel loves immigration, but does not always like immigrants".

Below: The first years of Israeli statehood saw a massive influx of Jews to the new country. Some of these were the remnants of European Jewry; others were young idealists from countries unaffected by the Holocaust, such as Britain and the United States; still others were refugees from North Africa and the Middle East.

Population Growth in Israel, 1940–1960

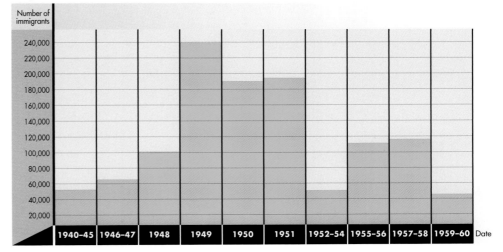

INCOMPATIBLE GODS

Redrawing a region's political borders can have a dramatic effect on the equilibrium of established populations. Settled communities can suddenly become foreigners in a land where they have spent all their lives, and marginalised minorities can find that civil power has unexpectedly fallen into their hands. Throughout the 20th century, many countries saw their borders redrawn, but nowhere was the breaking of nations so bloody or so turbulent as in India in 1947, when British rule came to a close.

The roots of the bloodshed, and of the terrible migration that it provoked, lay in the early years of the century. It was then that Indian politicians and activists, among them Mahatma Gandhi (1869–1948), began to express their discontent with British overlordship of their country. The two main political parties in India at the time were the Indian National Congress, which was dominated by Hindus, and the All India Muslim League. In 1915 these two parties formed an alliance with a view to demanding a national legislative assembly. Although the British recognised that growing nationalism within India was placing the country on the path to independence, they continued to resist the process throughout the 1920s and 1930s in an attempt to hold on to the commercial assets to which dominion over India gave them access.

The Quit India Movement

When World War II broke out in 1939, the British, who needed India's economic resources to fight the Axis Powers in Europe, unilaterally entered India into the war without consulting the country's representatives. The Congress party tapped into the outrage that this disregard for Indian civil rights triggered, and in 1942, under the guidance of Mahatma Gandhi, passed a resolution demanding complete independence from Britain. Known as the Quit India Movement, the draft proposed that if Britain did not

meet the party's demands, mass civil disobedience would ensue. In response, the British imprisoned all of Congress's leaders, including Gandhi, and banned the party. Nevertheless, large-scale demonstrations and protests were held throughout India, and the British attempted to regain control over the public by levying fines, dropping air bombs and publicly flogging resisters. This only created further sympathy for the cause among the Indian population, but without the direct leadership of Congress, there was a sense that the movement had failed, and when the war ended in 1945 Britain was still in control of the country.

The failure or success of the Quit India Movement is a debated question, but the fact remains that it motivated a population of millions to express that independence was a non-negotiable goal, and following World War II the British Empire was indeed less willing to continue its rule over the country. The war in Europe had drained much of the empire's economic, political and military energy, and the British were perhaps more concerned with rebuilding their own nation. In early 1946, the British openly adopted a political dialogue with the Indian National Congress for the eventual transfer of power.

Independence and Partition

As independence became imminent, a struggle arose between Congress and the All India Muslim League. The

THE PARTITION OF INDIA

1906 The All India Muslim League is founded.

1933 The name Pakistan, meaning "pure country", is coined.

1943 Muslim-majority provinces come under the control of the Muslim League.

1942 Congress is outlawed by the British. Mass disturbances occur throughout India.

C.E.	1900	1905	1910	1915	1920	1925	1930	1935	1940

1919 Mahatma Gandhi begins his civil disobedience movement.

1940 The Indian National Congress demands complete independence for India. Mohammad Ali Jinnah, leader of the Muslim League, calls for a separate Muslim state.

1945 Congress leaders are released from prison by the British.

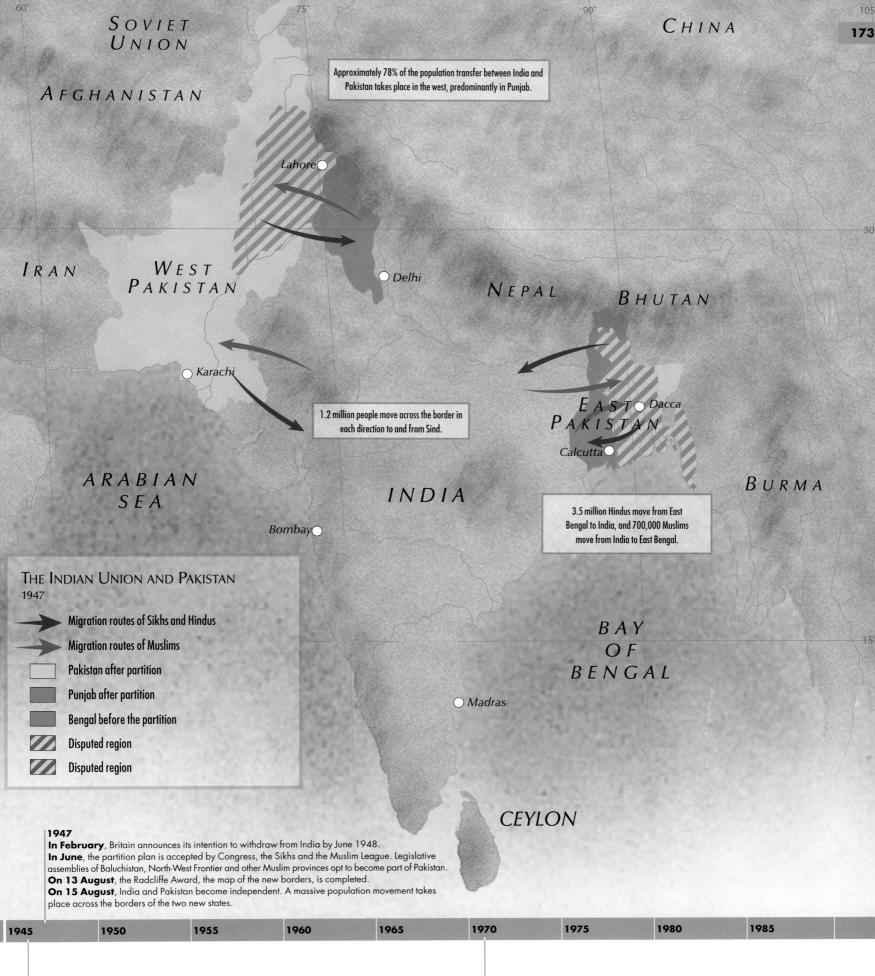

SOVIET
UNION

CHINA

AFGHANISTAN

Approximately 78% of the population transfer between India and
Pakistan takes place in the west, predominantly in Punjab.

Lahore

IRAN

WEST
PAKISTAN

Delhi

NEPAL

BHUTAN

Karachi

EAST
PAKISTAN

Dacca

1.2 million people move across the border in
each direction to and from Sind.

Calcutta

ARABIAN
SEA

INDIA

BURMA

3.5 million Hindus move from East
Bengal to India, and 700,000 Muslims
move from India to East Bengal.

Bombay

THE INDIAN UNION AND PAKISTAN
1947

Migration routes of Sikhs and Hindus

Migration routes of Muslims

Pakistan after partition

Punjab after partition

Bengal before the partition

Disputed region

Disputed region

BAY
OF
BENGAL

Madras

CEYLON

1947
In February, Britain announces its intention to withdraw from India by June 1948.
In June, the partition plan is accepted by Congress, the Sikhs and the Muslim League. Legislative
assemblies of Baluchistan, North-West Frontier and other Muslim provinces opt to become part of Pakistan.
On 13 August, the Radcliffe Award, the map of the new borders, is completed.
On 15 August, India and Pakistan become independent. A massive population movement takes
place across the borders of the two new states.

| 1945 | 1950 | 1955 | 1960 | 1965 | 1970 | 1975 | 1980 | 1985 |

1946 Hindu–Muslim riots take place in
Calcutta in August. Thousands are killed.

1971 East Pakistan breaks away to become
the independent state of Bangladesh.

Muslim League, then led by Mohammad Ali Jinnah (1876–1948), felt that Muslims would be disadvantaged in the new independent India because most of the population was Hindu. They began to campaign for an independent Muslim state in the parts of India where they constituted the majority. That meant separating off two corners of the country – made up of Baluchistan, Sind, the western half of Punjab and the North-West Frontier Province in the west, and half of Bengal in the east. While this proposal appeased Indian Muslims, it agitated Hindus, who believed that nationalist leaders were slighting the Hindu population in favour of the Muslim minorities. As fear and suspicion intensified on both sides, the British agreed that a political partition of territories was necessary to avoid a full-scale civil war. Independence would entail dividing the state into two new countries: Hindu India and Muslim Pakistan. The borders were determined by a British government-commissioned report known as the Radcliffe Award after the London-based lawyer, Sir Cyril Radcliffe, who wrote it. His deadline was the day set for independence: midnight on August 14, 1947.

As the appointed day of partition approached, Hindus and Muslims in the Punjab began to commit appalling atrocities against their neighbours. Mobs rampaged through villages, destroying property and murdering indiscriminately. Women were often the primary targets of aggression. On the Pakistani side of the border, instances of rape and abduction were commonplace, as were cases of women being mutilated and forcibly branded or tattooed with symbols of Islam. Many Hindu women committed suicide rather than face even the risk of such violation, as well as to avoid the equally alarming prospect of being forced to "convert" to Islam. It was also not unusual for Hindu men to kill their own wives and daughters for the same preemptive reasons – or else in order to put an end to their shame if they had already been assaulted. Indeed many observers described the violence that erupted between Hindus and Muslims in 1946 and 1947 as "a war on each other's women", underlining the terrible fact that women and children are often disproportionately victimised during wars and the inevitable flight of refugees from war zones.

In November 1946, as the first outbreaks of communal violence took place, Jawaharlal Nehru (1889–1964), the leader of Congress at the time, remarked that "murder stalks the streets and the most amazing cruelties are indulged in both by the individual and the mob. It is

extraordinary how our peaceful population has become militant and bloodthirsty. Riot is not the word for it – it is just sadistic desire to kill." On independence, Nehru became prime minister of the new India, although he remained powerless to bring an end to the disorder. He could not prevent Muslims in Pakistan attacking Hindus, and he could not hold back Hindus in India from doing the same to Muslims. Part of the problem was that the army and the police force were as partisan and factionalised as the population at large. Police officers and soldiers joined in the killing, and were responsible for some of the worst excesses of torture and mass murder. For the most part, however, the violence was enacted by civilians who had conceived a seemingly sudden and overwhelming hatred

for people with whom they had lived peaceably side-by-side for generations, their religions notwithstanding.

A third people, the Sikhs, were also involved in the conflict surrounding the independence and partition of India. The Indian Sikh population had a strong military tradition, and many had served honourably in the British Army in both World War I and World War II. Sikh neighbourhoods were established throughout Punjab, and the new border between the Hindu and Muslim states inevitably divided their community. The Sikhs were angry that they, unlike the Muslims and Hindus, had not been granted an independent homeland in the division of India. They were also alarmed that many of their people now found themselves living inside the new state of Pakistan, for

Above: Despite the bloodshed, people celebrate on the streets on the first Independence Day, August 15, 1947, and Indians have celebrated on this day ever since.

Below: As
independence
approached, rioting
between Hindus and
Muslims broke out in
some Indian cities. Many
people took this as their
cue to gather up their
belongings and escape.

their relations with Muslims had deteriorated rapidly in the lead up to independence. Attacks on Sikhs in West Punjab began to occur in 1947. Muslim mobs set fire to the uncut beards of Sikh men and, in Lahore, three dozen Sikhs were stabbed in one night, their bodies left on the street. Radical Sikhs responded to such outrages by setting up *jathas*, or militia units. It was claimed that these units were for self-defence, but innocent Muslims were often made the victims of revenge attacks. The Sikh leader Master Tara Singh (1885–1967) encouraged such violence, declaring: "Our motherland is calling for blood and we shall satiate the thirst of our motherland … Finish the Muslim League."

Population Exchange

The direct consequence of the violence that took hold of the Punjab Province was a two-way migration across the new Pakistan–India border. Millions and millions of people fled as the hostility increased. It has been estimated that nearly nine million Sikhs and Hindus came to India from Pakistani territory. About five million crossed over from West Pakistan, and the remaining four million arrived from East Pakistan (the future Bangladesh). On the other side of the border, six million Muslims escaped Hindu violence by crossing from India into Pakistan. This enormous dual exodus occurred within the space of a few months. Before

> " We realised it was time to leave. The *zamindars* [landowners] began to say, well, it is easy for you shopkeepers – all you have to do is take your weighing scales and your stones and go off, but what about us, we have land here. How can we take that away? We can't carry land on our heads. Shopkeepers can take up anywhere. And people kept telling themselves these kinds of things saying: no, it won't happen, kings may change but when does the public ever leave its place and go? "

Rajinder Singh, on his decision to leave his home in soon-to-be Pakistan

independence, there had been talk among the political parties of a "population exchange" once the borders came into force, but it was dismissed as irrelevant. This vast and impromptu departure had not been expected.

The journey between India and Pakistan was terrifying for all who undertook it. People snaked towards the borders in long columns called *kafilas*. Some travelled in buses or on bullock-carts, but most went on foot. The largest of the *kafilas* was estimated to comprise 400,000 people, and took eight days to pass any given position on the road. The *kafilas'* large numbers, however, did not guarantee safety, and marauders constantly attacked the columns. Sometimes the members of one *kafila* would attack a *kafila* of equally desperate people travelling in the opposite direction, and many women on the fringes or the tail ends of columns were abducted. Trains heading for the Pakistan border were shot at and sometimes derailed by explosives – a technique employed by the Sikh *jathas*. In some instances, entire trainloads of refugees were slaughtered.

The testimony of Mohammad Gill, a Muslim refugee who was 12 years old when he walked 160 kilometres (100 miles) from a holding camp in India to Pakistan, gives some idea of the hardships endured: "The day arrived when the refugees were to walk to the new holy land. There were all kinds of fears in the minds of the people. The overwhelming fear was: would we be safe on the road? We walked all day under the blazing sun. I went a little off the road looking for drinking water. I came to a well in which dead bodies had been dumped, and it was choked with them. In the evening, we stopped for the night. People were calling for relatives who got separated from them during the day's trudge. This was a nightly event. On the second day I heard some people shouting at someone. We discovered that a young mother was trying

to bury her infant baby alive whom she couldn't carry. People reproved her harshly for the inhuman act that she was about to commit. But her problem was also real; she found it hard to carry the baby every day while walking twenty to twenty-five miles. We were on the road for four days; on the fifth, we crossed into Pakistan. The sense of fear which had gripped my heart for the last month and a half faded away. My elder brother was employed in Lahore and we found shelter in his house."

Experiences like Gill's were shared by millions of refugees, and they have left a lasting mark on the societies of both India and Pakistan. The Urdu poet Ismat Chughtai has written eloquently on the deep spiritual cleft wrought by Partition: "It was not only that the country was split in two", he says. "Bodies and minds were also divided. Those whose bodies were whole had hearts that were splintered. Families were torn apart. One brother was allotted to Pakistan, the other to Hindustan. The bonds of relationship were in tatters, and in the end many souls remained behind in Hindustan while their bodies started off for Pakistan."

Division of Religious Populations in India, 1947

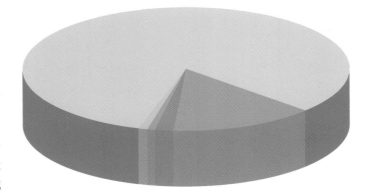

Below: As a result of partition, about 7.25 million Muslims moved from India to the new state of Pakistan, and roughly the same number of Hindus and Sikhs made the reverse journey from Pakistan to India. But India still has the second largest Muslim population in the world – after Indonesia.

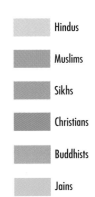

Hindus

Muslims

Sikhs

Christians

Buddhists

Jains

WORLD IN FLUX

The patterns of human migration since the end of World War II are complex, but there are nevertheless discernible trends in the teeming flow. The booming postwar economy provided opportunities for many workers looking to make a better life for themselves in a new land, while others were driven out of their countries by ongoing war and conflict. Together, these people movements have altered the face of the modern world, bringing to the fore vibrant and multicultural societies.

NORTH AMERICA

Throughout history, the causes of human migration have been varied. Sometimes, a particular region simply becomes too small to support a growing population, which then naturally spreads to other, less crowded areas: the age-old phenomenon of overcrowding leading to colonisation. In other instances, migration is brought about by a specific trigger, such as war, famine or natural disaster, which can drive entire populations out of one place and into another. In general, the more severe the trigger, the larger and swifter the flow of population. Voluntary migrations have also taken place, whereby people choose to uproot themselves and seek out a better life elsewhere.

Borders, transport systems, nation states, immigration laws and other governmental institutions today constitute the machinery of human migration. In cases of illegal immigration, however, these mechanisms are evaded, and borders, such as that between Mexico and the United States, become "porous", as those avoiding the normal channels of immigration seep across a frontier. In modern times, governments are making great efforts to find ways of rendering their borders as strong as possible, so that they are not inundated with newcomers and so they can regulate and monitor the demographic makeup of their countries.

The Postwar Peak

World War II produced tidal waves of displaced persons, mostly in and around Germany. At the war's conclusion, Poland was allotted a large slice of former German territory in the west to compensate for the land it had lost to the Soviet Union in the east. Poland's borders were, in effect, suddenly moved to the west. This geographical shift forced the migration of millions of ethnic Germans westwards out of the newly acquired Polish territory and into the shattered remains of Germany. Over the next 15 years, these *Heimatvertriebene* ("those expelled from the homeland") were joined in Germany by three million German refugees who drifted back from the various places they had been carried to by the tide of war. These millions of

IMMIGRATION IN THE MODERN WORLD

1945 At the end of World War II there are millions of displaced persons (DPs) spread throughout Europe.

1962 Britain restricts immigration from Commonwealth countries. By this time, 600,000 Indians and Pakistanis have already settled in the United Kingdom.

1960s 623,000 Britons emigrate to Australia, mostly by means of assisted passage.

C.E.	1940	1945	1950	1955	1960	1965	1970

1947 The first West Indians arrive in Britain. Partition and "population exchange" take place in the Indian subcontinent.

1948 The State of Israel is formed and the free immigration of Jews begins.

1955 Germany signs its first *gastarbeiter* agreement with Italy. Further agreements follow with Spain and Greece in 1960, Turkey in 1961 and 1964, Morocco in 1963, Portugal in 1964, and Yugoslavia in 1968.

1973–1974 All Western European countries put a stop to recruiting migrant workers in the wake of the oil crisis.

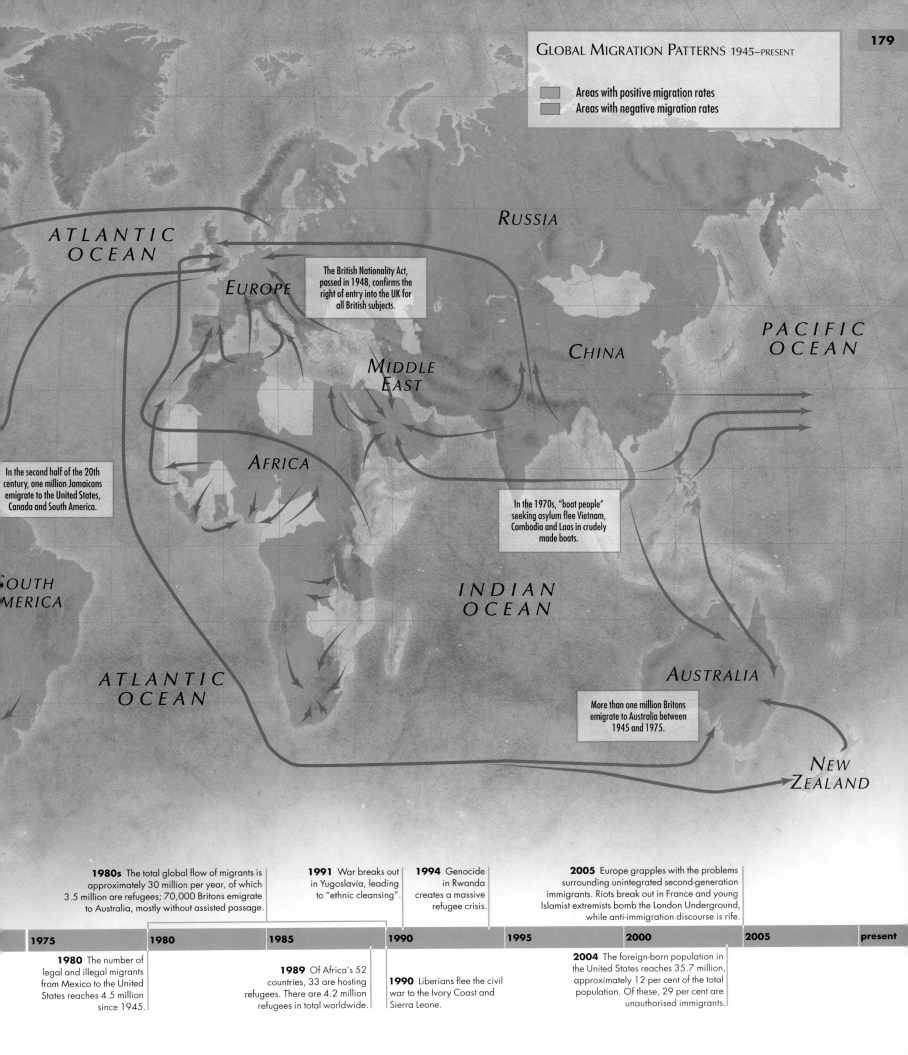

GLOBAL MIGRATION PATTERNS 1945–PRESENT

Areas with positive migration rates
Areas with negative migration rates

RUSSIA

ATLANTIC
OCEAN

ATLANTIC
OCEAN

EUROPE

The British Nationality Act,
passed in 1948, confirms the
right of entry into the UK for
all British subjects.

MIDDLE
EAST

CHINA

PACIFIC
OCEAN

AFRICA

In the second half of the 20th
century, one million Jamaicans
emigrate to the United States,
Canada and South America.

In the 1970s, "boat people"
seeking asylum flee Vietnam,
Cambodia and Laos in crudely
made boats.

SOUTH
AMERICA

INDIAN
OCEAN

ATLANTIC
OCEAN

AUSTRALIA

More than one million Britons
emigrate to Australia between
1945 and 1975.

NEW
ZEALAND

1980s The total global flow of migrants is
approximately 30 million per year, of which
3.5 million are refugees; 70,000 Britons emigrate
to Australia, mostly without assisted passage.

1991 War breaks out
in Yugoslavia, leading
to "ethnic cleansing".

1994 Genocide
in Rwanda
creates a massive
refugee crisis.

2005 Europe grapples with the problems
surrounding unintegrated second-generation
immigrants. Riots break out in France and young
Islamist extremists bomb the London Underground,
while anti-immigration discourse is rife.

| 1975 | 1980 | 1985 | 1990 | 1995 | 2000 | 2005 | present |

1980 The number of
legal and illegal migrants
from Mexico to the United
States reaches 4.5 million
since 1945.

1989 Of Africa's 52
countries, 33 are hosting
refugees. There are 4.2 million
refugees in total worldwide.

1990 Liberians flee the civil
war to the Ivory Coast and
Sierra Leone.

2004 The foreign-born population in
the United States reaches 35.7 million,
approximately 12 per cent of the total
population. Of these, 29 per cent are
unauthorised immigrants.

migrants were absorbed into the two German states that had emerged from the wreckage of Nazism: the Federal Republic of Germany in the west, and the communist German Democratic Republic in the east.

The pooling of the German population in two new countries was the largest migratory process to result directly from World War II. It occurred in the same years as two other great migrations that came as an indirect result of the global conflict, namely the partition of India and the creation of a Jewish state in Israel. It could be said that never before or since in human history have so many people been on the move as in the years following World War II. In terms of the sheer volume of human traffic, the late 1940s constitute a spectacular peak in the long history of human migration.

A Multicultural Europe

After the turmoil of the war and its aftermath, there was a period of about 30 years during which peaceful, economically driven migration was the norm. People travelled abroad in large numbers to make new homes for themselves and their families. First, millions of labour migrants travelled from the fringes of Europe to work in more industrially advanced countries, such as Sweden, the renascent Germany and others. Second, "colonial" people of the former prewar empires went to live in the "mother country" – North Africans migrated to France, Afro-Caribbeans to Britain, and Indonesians to the Netherlands. Third, the governments of the British dominions of Canada, Australia and New Zealand, perceiving a need to "populate or perish", opened the floodgates to immigration from Britain and later from other European countries. These population movements all had one thing in common: they were deliberately engineered to satisfy the people-hunger of the receiving country. Germany, Australia, Britain and France all had a similar problem: there was not enough labour to facilitate their booming postwar economies. Immigration from countries that were poorer, or where opportunities were fewer, was seen as the universal solution to the dearth of workers.

Britain was the first European country to throw open its doors to foreign migrants. On June 22, 1948, a former German pleasure steamer named *Empire Windrush* arrived in London's docks carrying 492 migrants from Jamaica. These people were the pioneers of a new wave of immigration. By 1951, there were 218,000 people of colonial origin living in Britain; by 1961, the figure had risen to more than half a million. Many of the first West

Indian immigrants were housed in wartime bomb shelters in Clapham in south London. They registered to work at the nearest labour exchange, which was in Brixton. Many immigrants settled in the area once they had employment, and in time changed the character of that gray suburb forever: it became the capital of Caribbean culture in Britain.

The need for new workers had waned in Britain by the early 1960s, but this did not halt the flow of migrants from the West Indies (nor from Africa and the Indian sub-continent). Many of the earlier migrants were young men, who had wives in their home countries or returned there to marry. Wives and children travelling to join their family in the motherland dramatically increased the number of incomers in Britain. By 1981, 1.5 million people in Britain – just under 8 per cent of the population – were immigrants from the "New Commonwealth", or were the children of first-generation immigrants. This naturally altered the nature of the British public, and not just in south London. The United Kingdom became a multicultural society, but not all Britons were happy to broaden their definition of British to include people of different ethnic backgrounds. Racism directed at black and Asian people became a fact of British life for immigrants and their British-born children. Many of their grandchildren are still grappling with discrimination today.

"We got off the boat at Tilbury and caught the train for Victoria, and what struck me as really weird was to see that the train driver was white. I expected him to be black. I also expected all the porters to be black – because that's how it was in Jamaica. I'd never seen a white person work in my life. When I looked at the people, comparing them with the passengers coming off the boat – we had all kinds of floral dresses, bright clothes – the English people seemed drab and shabby. Of course I didn't know about rationing and things of that sort."

Vincent Reid, who came to Britain from the West Indies in 1948, aged 13

Similar societal changes took place in mainland Europe, particularly in West Germany. In the late 1950s, the West German government set up offices throughout southern Europe to recruit labourers for German industry. Workers, with the agreement and cooperation of their home countries, were invited to emigrate to West Germany from Italy, Greece, Turkey, Portugal, Yugoslavia and elsewhere. These incomers were known as *gastarbeiter* – "guest workers" – and it was expected that, like good guests, they would not outstay their welcome. The idea was that the migrants would work hard in Germany for a year or two, and then take their savings home before they became a burden on Germany's social infrastructure. In the event, many chose to stay, and the German government chose not to try to expel them. The migrant *gastarbeiter* became established ethnic minorities – not by governmental design, as was the case in Britain, but by accident. In Germany, as in Britain, social strife was seen as an inevitable consequence of this new multiculturalism. The very word *gastarbeiter* acquired disparaging overtones, and was exported to other languages with these connotations. In right-wing circles throughout Europe, the term became shorthand for the perceived social dangers of welcoming economic migrants from other cultures.

Ten-Pound Poms

Australia tried to avoid the perceived problems brought about by multiculturalism in Europe by giving preference to Caucasian immigrants, particularly British and Irish citizens, or people of "British Isles stock". The White Australia Policy, as it was known, was in place in Australia from 1830 to 1973. Policies restricting non-white immigration suited the conservative majority of the Australian public, who did not want the perceived Anglo-Saxon character of the country to change. It was also a selling point for potential migrants from white, European countries. In the literature aimed at encouraging Brits to relocate to Australia, slogans such as "A

British Way of Life" were deemed as convincing as a "High Standard of Living" and "Australia's Famous Climate".

Such propaganda was often enough to persuade some Britons to opt to move to Australia, as opposed to Canada or New Zealand (many Britons who intended to emigrate considered all three options). But for many the deciding factor in favour of Australia was the "assisted passage scheme". In 1947, the Australian government undertook to pay most of the cost of transporting Britons to their new life abroad. Adult migrants had to pay just £10 towards the cost of their sea voyage, and children could travel for free. Most of the Britons who emigrated to Australia throughout the 1950s and 1960s were "ten-pound poms" who had leaped

Below: Australia was just one destination for people wanting to escape the gray austerity of postwar Britain. A legacy of empire was that there were plenty of warmer, more spacious, English-speaking countries around the globe – among them, Canada, New Zealand and South Africa.

at this offer. Assisted passage was not only a good deal: it was also interpreted as a pledge of a warm reception on arrival. Between 1945 and 1975, more than one million Britons sailed south to Australia.

The Rising Refugee Population

In the 1970s, the economic boom that had facilitated the immigration of the postwar years came to an end. In October 1973, the Organization of Arab Petroleum Exporting Countries announced that it would no longer supply petroleum to nations that had supported Israel in its conflict with Arab countries in the Middle East. This included the United States and its allies in Western Europe. As a result of the oil crisis, factories and entire industries withered and died, economies deflated and foreign workers were no longer required in such large numbers. In the late 1970s and 1980s, *gastarbeiter* and ten-pound poms became extinct. More than that, many governments throughout the developed world passed laws to restrict voluntary immigration. These legislative blockades were put in place not just to keep out economic migrants, but also to protect developed states from incoming refugees, the number of which had begun to rise in the last quarter of the 20th century.

Many of these refugees were fleeing war or repression. The Cold War was at its height, and the contradictory ideologies of the democratic and capitalist West and the communist East caused conflicts to erupt. In Vietnam, the victory of the communist North over the American-backed South produced a surge of emigration out of the region. From 1979 onwards, desperate people tried to escape political persecution or endemic poverty in Vietnam by taking to the open seas in small ships, hoping to make landfall in a more welcoming country. One-quarter of a million ethnic Chinese from Vietnam were resettled in China, and thousands of other "boat people", after being plucked from the water, found new homes in the United States, Australia, France and Canada. At the same time, more than 800,000 Cambodians fled across the border into Thailand to escape the regime of Pol Pot (r. 1975–1979), who was implementing radical reforms with a view to establishing a communist state. Another major war of the Cold War period occurred in Afghanistan. Soviet forces invaded the country in 1979 and installed a puppet communist regime. Their conflict with the *mujahedin* – Afghan guerrillas – generated six million refugees, most of whom crossed the Afghan border into Pakistan. In 1980 there were less than eight million refugees in the world, but by the close of the

1980s, as the Cold War came to an end, the number had risen to 15.2 million.

Although the collapse of communism in Europe brought freedom to many millions of people, in other areas the sudden removal of repressive government control made room for conflicts that had previously been contained. This was the case in Yugoslavia, which experienced successive episodes of war and population displacement in the 1990s. When the socialist ideology was abandoned in Yugoslavia, the formerly integrated communities within the country – the Serbs, Croats, Muslim Bosnians, Albanians and Montenegrins – began to split and separate. The war that resulted in Yugoslavia was the first in Europe since 1945. It was during this conflict that the euphemism "ethnic cleansing" was coined. The term is used to describe the process of using terror and mass murder, forced deportation and population exchange, concentration camps and military conquest to uncover armed opposition, force enemy civilians to leave a particular region and take possession of the territory once they are gone.

All sides in the Yugoslav war practised ethnic cleansing, and its techniques were also used by aggressors in other parts of the world. The most horrific example of ethnic

Above: This image of refugees, trudging away from their homes, comes from Rwanda in 1994. More or less identical scenarios have been played out around the globe for centuries. The displaced, like the poor, are always with us.

Opposite page:
Vietnamese boat people took terrifying risks to escape the brutal communist regime in their country. Adrift in the South China Sea, they were preyed on by pirates. And even those who made landfall suffered abuse and maltreatment in refugee camps.

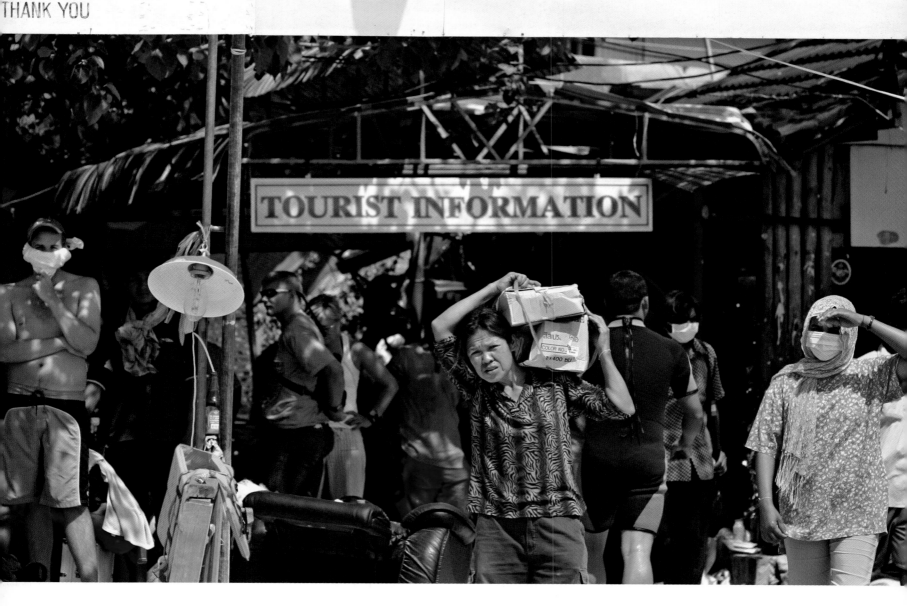

WELCOME TO PHI PHI ISLAND

TOURIST INFORMATION

Above: As climate change progresses, natural disasters are likely to become a more common cause of population displacement. After the tsunami that struck Indonesia, Sri Lanka, India and Thailand in 2004, thousands of people had to find new homes, and many were resettled in new countries.

cleansing occurred in Rwanda in the spring of 1994, when the Hutu militia systematically murdered more than one million members of the ethnically distinct Tutsi people. The horrifying conflict in Rwanda displaced more than two million Tutsi, of whom around 400,000 remain refugees in the Republic of Congo and elsewhere.

By the end of the 20th century, the global refugee crisis had somewhat abated. In 2005, the United Nations High Commissioner for Refugees estimated that the refugee population of the world was 9.2 million – the lowest level since 1980. The reduction had come about because fewer people around the world were experiencing the need to flee their homes, decreasing the flow of involuntary migrants. A second factor contributing to the decrease

was that existing refugees had been able to – or forced to – return to their homelands, or else had become integrated in the countries that offered them shelter.

Modern Migration

Despite the decrease in refugees recorded at the start of the new millennium, new currents of human migration are appearing all the time. Immigration, in all its varied forms, has in fact become one of the most troubled and contested political issues of the new century. Nations with long and noble traditions of accepting displaced and dispossessed persons have questioned whether they should continue to make room for "asylum seekers" – a politically loaded phrase that has become synonymous with "migrant" in public

discourse. In the developed world, it is commonly thought that an asylum seeker will abuse the hospitality of the receiving nation and become a social burden, and seeking asylum is often portrayed as a vaguely dishonest action. But modern-day asylum seekers, refugees from poverty and oppression, are essentially no different than the Irish who fled destitution in Ireland to go to the United States in the mid-19th century, or the Jews who fled persecution in Russia to settle in Britain in the 1880s. Patterns of European migration have also been influenced by the opening up of Western Europe's internal borders with the formation of the European Union in 1992. As the number of member countries of the EU continues to grow, migrants from the nations of Eastern Europe can move to their western neighbours. The perceived

number of Polish builders in Britain, for example, has led to their becoming a newspaper cliché, a migrational archetype such as the Pakistani shopkeeper of the 1970s or the Irish navvies of the 19th century.

At the extremes of discourse on the subject of human migration, there is talk of the potentially disastrous consequences of immigration – whereby native populations will be "inundated", "engulfed" or "overwhelmed" by immigrants. However, the surprising fact is that 97 per cent of the human population live and die in the country in which they were born. A mere 3 per cent are inclined or obliged to uproot themselves and adapt to life in a new nation. This book has been about the experiences and the achievements of that remarkable 1 in 30.

Above: Governmental attempts to restrict immigration do not always meet with popular approval. These demonstrators are protesting against a law that would make it harder for immigrants to bring their families into France.

CHRONOLOGY

1.9m B.C.E.	The first *Homo erectus* people leave Africa during a warm interlude in the planetary climate, and spread throughout Asia
400,000 B.C.E.	*Homo rhodesiensis*, the probable ancestor of modern humans, begins to evolve in Africa
250,000 B.C.E.	*Homo erectus* dies out everywhere
140–150,000 B.C.E.	"Mitochondrial Eve" walks the grassland of Africa
125,000 B.C.E.	First modern humans leave Africa and establish colony on eastern shores of the Mediterranean
85,000 B.C.E.	*Homo sapiens* begins a new coast-hugging migration out of Africa, reaching Java within 10,000 years
65,000 B.C.E.	Humans move from the Middle East northwards towards Europe
40,000 B.C.E.	Ancestors of Aborigines arrive on the Australian continent
20,000 B.C.E.	Humans may by now have found their way into North America
15,000 B.C.E.	*Homo sapiens* may have penetrated South America by boat
10,000 B.C.E.	Northern Europe is colonised as climate grows warmer and the ice recedes
c. 4000 B.C.E.	Speakers of Proto-Indo-European are living somewhere in the Black Sea region
c. 2000 B.C.E.	A separate Indo-European group moves south through Persia and into the Indian subcontinent. Around the same time, Asian people sail from mainland China and settle on Taiwan
c. 1700–1380 B.C.E.	The Minoan civilisation flourishes on Crete
c. 1500 B.C.E.	Taiwanese settlers begin to colonise the Pacific islands
1279–1213 B.C.E.	Reign of Ramses II, traditional time of the Exodus
c. 1050–750 B.C.E.	The "Dorian migrations": the northernmost Greeks, the Dorians, move south, displacing other Greek speakers and leading to the colonisation of Asia Minor by the Ionians and the Aeolians.
970 B.C.E.	King Solomon begins his reign in Jerusalem and starts the building of the First Temple
931 B.C.E.	Division of the Hebrew state into Israel in the north and Judah in the south
800 B.C.E.	There is by now an Iron Age settlement on the Palatine Hill – the future city of Rome
753 B.C.E.	According to Roman tradition, Rome is founded by Romulus and Remus
c. 750–550 B.C.E.	The rise of the Greek poleis. Greek-speaking people colonise Italy, western Mediterranean shores and the southern shores of the Black Sea
c. 600 B.C.E.	The rise of the two pre-eminent city-states, Sparta and Athens
587 B.C.E.	Nebuchadnezzar defeats Judah and deports part of the population to Babylon
334–323 B.C.E.	Alexander the Great invades the Persian Empire
320–198 B.C.E.	Jewish colonies are established in Damascus, Antioch, Ephesus and Alexandria
300 B.C.E.	Colonists from west Polynesia begin to explore and settle further east
202 B.C.E.–43 C.E.	Rome conquers northern Italy, then Greece, North Africa, Gaul, Germany and Britain
70 C.E.	Romans destroy the Second Temple. Many Jews flee into the established Jewish communities of the empire, and into Arabia, Georgia, Gaul and Spain
106	Dacia and Arabia become Roman provinces
376	Visigoths cross Danube and settle inside the Roman Empire
c. 400	Eastern Polynesian explorers reach Easter Island and Hawaii
406–410	Vandals and Visigoth penetrate deep into the Roman Empire; the Romans withdraw from Britain
c. 450	The Angles and Saxons begin their conquest of Britain
570	Muhammad is born in Mecca
615	The first Muslims emigrate to Abyssinia to escape persecution
633	The conquest of Persia by Arab Muslim armies begins
670	Arab armies advance across northwest Africa
711	Tariq ibn Ziyad invades Spain from North Africa
732	Arab armies are defeated by the Franks at Tours, marking the end of Muslim advance in Europe
793–9	Viking attacks are mounted against the island of Lindisfarne, then against the Scottish Isles, Ireland and the coast of Aquitaine
800–1000	Migrants from Tahiti begin the colonisation of New Zealand
c. 830	Viking settlement of Britain begins
c. 900	First recorded sighting of Greenland
1213	The Mongols invade northern China and destroy the Jin dynasty
1221	Central Asia, Transoxiana, Afghanistan and northern Persia are overrun by Mongols. The Khwarizm empire collapses
1237	The Mongol subjugation of Russia begins
1279	Qubilai (Kublai Khan) conquers southern China and puts an end to the Sung dynasty
1487	Bartolomeu Dias reaches the Cape of Good Hope, opening the way for an easterly sea-route to India
1492	The Genoese navigator Christopher Columbus discovers "West India", while sailing in the the opposite direction to Dias
1497	Italian navigator and explorer Giovanni Caboto, or John Cabot, encounters the North American continent
1494	Pope Alexander VI divides the New World into Spanish and Portuguese domains
1498	Vasco da Gama reaches India via the Cape of Good Hope
1499–1502	Amerigo Vespucci explores the coastline of the New World and realises it is a continent
1500	Pedro Cabral discovers eastern Brazil; Columbus, on his third voyage, lands on the mainland for the first time in Venezuela
1518	The first transport of slaves from Africa to the New World takes place
1531–34	Conquistador Francisco Pizarro destroys the Inca Empire in Peru
1606	120 English colonists go to Virginia
1612	Dutch traders begin to use Manhattan Island as a base for trading furs
1620	The Pilgrim Fathers sail from Plymouth in September, land at Cape Cod in November and found the Plymouth Colony

1630	1000 Puritans arrive in Massachussetts and found Boston; this is the beginning of a "great migration" that carries 20,000 Puritans to America in the next 13 years
mid 1600s	The American colonies begin to use slave labour to work on tobacco and rice plantations
1730s	Scotch-Irish and German immigrants colonise the American borderlands
1770	Captain Cook discovers Australia
1775	The American Revolution puts a stop to transportation to Virginia and Maryland
1788	Britain establishes a penal colony in Australia
1803	The Louisiana Purchase opens the American West to settlers
1815	The end of Napoleonic Wars ushers in a century of mass migration to the United States
1821	Inauguration of the Santa Fe Trail
1824	A colony for the "worst description" of convicts is founded on Norfolk Island in the South Pacific
1841	The first wagon train leaves on the six-month journey to California
1842	Settlement of the Oregon Territory via the Oregon Trail begins
1845	Potato blight strikes Ireland
1846	100,000 Irish peasants emigrate
1847	The Mormons leave Illinois en masse for the Great Salt Lake
1848	Mexico relinquishes its claims to land north of the Rio Grande
1849	The Gold Rush brings 80,000 prospectors to California, and hastens its incorporation as a US state
1852	20,000 Chinese migrants, almost all of them men, travel to California
1853	Transportation to Van Diemen's Land comes to an end
1863	Abraham Lincoln announces emancipation of all slaves in territory under Union control
1865	At the conclusion of the American Civil War, the Thirteenth Amendment to the constitution officially abolishes slavery
1868	The last convict ship, loaded with 60 Irish political prisoners, lands at Fremantle, western Australia
1879	The "Exodusters" leave for Kansas
1880s	The "Scramble for Africa": European powers rush to claim various territories on the African continent; mass migration from Italy to the United States begins: 4 million Italians will go to America in the next 40 years
1881	Assassination of Alexander II leads to anti-Jewish May Laws. Mass emigration from Russia begins
1882	The Exclusion Act prohibits Chinese labourers from entering the United States
1886	Slavery is finally abolished in Cuba
1888	Slavery is abolished in Brazil, by which time 3.5 million African slaves have been imported
1890	US Census announces that the frontier has closed
1892	Ellis Island in New York Harbour opens as a purpose-built centre for processing immigrants, replacing Castle Garden
1904	The volume of immigrants into the United States reaches 1 million a year and remains so until the outbreak of World War I
1905	Revolutionary unrest sweeps Russia; the following year, Jewish immigration to the United States reaches a new peak
1917	The October Revolution brings the Bolsheviks to power in Russia
1918	"Red Terror" is unleashed on enemies of the Bolshevik regime; the first labour camp is set up on Solovetsky Island
1924	The American Congress places quotas on immigrants according to nationality. The system remains in force until 1965
1930	The Gulag is officially established. Collectivisation of agriculture is accompanied by the liquidation or deportation of "kulaks"
1936–8	The height of the Great Terror, during which millions are shot or consigned to the Gulag
1939	Gulag population, including colonies, is more than 1.6 million
1940–45	Mass deportation of "enemy nationalities" inside the USSR
1943	Repeal of the US Chinese Exclusion Act
1945	World War II leaves the USSR in control of all Eastern Europe; Britain begins to dismantle its empire. There are millions of displaced persons (DPs) in Europe
1947	The first West Indians arrive in Britain; partition and "population exchange" take place in the Indian sub-continent
1948	The State of Israel is declared, and is immediately attacked by neighbouring Arab nations. In the course of the ensuing war, 75,000 Arabs are displaced
1948–1973	The population of Israel rises from 657,000 to more than 3 million as a result of continual immigration
1960s	623,000 Britons emigrate to Australia, mostly by means of assisted passage
1980s	The total global volume of migrants is about 30 million per year, of whom approximately 3.5 million are refugees
1989	33 of Africa's 52 countries are hosting refugees.
1990	Albanians migrate in large numbers to Greece and Italy; Liberians flee civil war to Ivory Coast and Sierra Leone
1990s	A million Russian Jews emigrate to Israel
1991	War breaks out in Yugoslavia, leading to the "ethnic cleansing" of the civilian population
1994	Genocide in Rwanda, in which more than one million Tutsi people are systematically murdered by Hutu militia, creates a massive refugee crisis
2004	The foreign-born population in the United States reaches 35.7 million, approximately 12 per cent of the total population. Of these, 29 per cent are unauthorised immigrants
2005	Europe begins to grapple with the problems of unintegrated second-generation immigrants, as riots break out in France and young Islamist militants commit terrorist acts in London

INDEX

Page numbers in *italic* refer to the illustrations

ACKNOWLEDGMENTS

Pages: 1c Bridgeman Art Library/Archives Charmet/ Bibliotheque Nationale, Paris; 2–3 Corbis/Michael Freeman; 5 Corbis/Bettmann Archive; 6 Corbis/Bettmann Archive; 8 Corbis/Paul A. Souders; 9t Corbis/Ed Kashi; 9b Bridgeman Art Library/American Antiquarian Society, Worcester, Mass; 11 Getty Images/Francis Miller/Time & Life Pictures; 12–13 Corbis/ Redlink; 14 Science Photo Library/John Reader; 16 The Art Archive Dagli Orti / Museo di Antropologia ed Etnografia Turin 18 Getty Images/Konrad Wothe/Minden Pictures; 22 Science Photo Library/John Reader; 23 Corbis/Ali Meyer; 24–25 Corbis/Pierre Vauthey/Sygma; 26 Corbis/Vittoriano Rastelli; 30 Lord Price Collection/Private Collection, courtesy of Sam Fogg (original map: *Sam Fogg London, 1996 catalogue no. 17*); 32 akg-images/Erich Lessing/Nationalmuseet, Copenhagen; 33 Corbis/Yann Arthus-Bertrand; 34 akg-images/ Erich Lessing/Musee du Louvre, Paris; 36 Corbis/Richard T. Nowitz; 37 Scala, Florence/Basilica of Santa Maria Maggiore, Rome; 38–39 Corbis/Sygma/Alain Keler; 41 Corbis/Richard T. Nowitz; 42 Corbis/Historical Picture Archive; 44 Bridgeman Art Library/Boltin Picture Library; 46–47 Corbis/Jim Zuckerman; 48 Corbis/Charles & Josette Lenars; 49 The Art Archive/Dagli Orti/Archaeological Museum, Naples; 50 Bridgeman Art Library/Museum of London; 52 Corbis/Christophe Boisvieux; 53 Corbis/Ric Ergenbright; 54 Corbis/Ramon Manent/Museum of Maritimo, Barcelona; 56 Bridgeman Art Library/Museo Arqueologico Nacional, Madrid/Giraudon; 58 Scala, Florence/ Church of San Vitale, Ravenna; 59 akg-images/Erich Lessing; 60 The Art Archive/British Museum; 61 Bridgeman Art Library/ Museo Arqueologico Nacional, Madrid/Giraudon; 64–65 Corbis/Kazuyoshi Nomachi; 66 Werner Forman Archive; 67 Alamy/eStock Photo; 70 akg-images/British Museum; 71 Corbis/Ted Spiegel; 72 Bridgeman Art Library/National Museum of Iceland, Reykjavik; 73 Courtesy of Yale Univeristy/ Beinecke Rare Book & Manuscript Library; 75t Bridgeman Art Library/National Palace Museum,Taipei; 76–77 akg- images/ VISIOARS/Bibliotheque Nationale, Paris; 78 Corbis/Liu Liqun; 79 The Art Archive/Eileen Tweedy/Victoria & Albert Museum, London; 80 akg-images; 82 akg-images/Museo Navale, Genoa; 84–85 The Art Archive/Museo Ciudad Mexico/Dagli Orti; 86 Werner Forman Archive/British Museum; 87 The Art

Archive/Stephanie Colasanti/National Museum, Lima; 88 Corbis/Bojan Brecelj; 90 The Art Archive; 92 Bridgeman Art Library/Private Collection, Peter Newark American Pictures; 93 akg-images; 94–95 Corbis/Bettmann Archive; 96 Bridgeman Art Library/Private Collection; 97 The Art Archive/Museum of the City of New York: Ms.29.100.2584; 98 The Art Archive/ British Museum, London/Eileen Tweedy; 100–104 National Library of Australia, Canberra; 105 Bridgeman Art Library/ National Library of Australia, Canberra; 106 Corbis/Bettmann Archive; 108cl Getty Images/Hulton Archive/Topical Press Agency; 111 Lord Price Collection; 114 Bridgeman Art Library/Victoria & Albert Museum 115 Lord Price Collection; 116Getty Images/ Hulton Archive/Yevgeny Khaldei; 119 Topham/Picturepoint; 120 Bridgeman Art Library/Private Collection, Peter Newark American Pictures; 123 Bridgeman Art Library/Private Collection, Peter Newark American Pictures; 124 Corbis; 126–127 Corbis/ Frederic Auguste Bartholdi; 128 Corbis/Bettmann Archive; 129 Rex Features; 130 Corbis/Christie's Images; 132 Corbis; 134 The Art Archive/Culver Pictures; 136 Scala, Florence/HIP/ Ann Ronan Collection; 137 Corbis/Bettmann Archive; 140 The Illustrated London News Picture Library; 141 Corbis/Bob Krist; 142 Getty Images/Hulton Archive/Imagno; 144 Getty Images/ Hulton Archive; 146 Getty Images/ Ewing Galloway/Hulton Archive; 147 Getty Images/Mario Tama; 149 Getty Images/ Jacob. A. Riis/Hulton Archive/Museum of the City of New York; 150 Ivo Marloh/Marshall Editions; 151 Getty Images/Jacob. A. Riis/Hulton Archive/Museum of the City of New York; 152 Corbis/ Bettmann Archive; 153 Corbis/Bob Krist; 156–157 Corbis; 159 Corbis/Underwood & Underwood; 160 Getty Images/ Hulton Archive/Haywood Magee/Picture Post; 162 Getty Images/Margaret Bourke-White/Time Life Pictures; 164 akg-images; 165 Rex Features/Sipa Press; 166 Getty Images/Hulton Archive/General Photographic Agency/Leo Kann; 169 Corbis/ Bettmann Archive; 170 Corbis/Les Stone/Sygma; 175 Topham/ Dinodia; 175 Getty Images/Hulton Archive; 176 Getty Images/ Margaret Bourke-White/Time Life Pictures; 180 Getty Images/ Thurston Hopkins/Hulton Archive; 181 Getty Images/Merlyn Severn/Hulton Archive; 182 Corbis/Jacques Pavlovsky/Sygma; 183 Rex Features/Markus Zeffler; 184 Getty Images/Paula Bronstein; 185 Getty Images/Gerard Julien/AFP